AF881496

2013-2014 Supplement

National Security Law
Fifth Edition

and

Counterterrorism Law
Second Edition

EDITORIAL ADVISORS

Vicki Been
Elihu Root Professor of Law
New York University School of Law

Erwin Chemerinsky
Dean and Distinguished Professor of Law
University of California, Irvine, School of Law

Richard A. Epstein
Laurence A. Tisch Professor of Law
New York University School of Law
Peter and Kirsten Bedford Senior Fellow
The Hoover Institution
Senior Lecturer in Law
The University of Chicago

Ronald J. Gilson
Charles J. Meyers Professor of Law and Business
Stanford University
Marc and Eva Stern Professor of Law and Business
Columbia Law School

James E. Krier
Earl Warren DeLano Professor of Law
The University of Michigan Law School

Richard K. Neumann, Jr.
Professor of Law
Maurice A. Deane School of Law at Hofstra University

Robert H. Sitkoff
John L. Gray Professor of Law
Harvard Law School

David Alan Sklansky
Yosef Osheawich Professor of Law
University of California at Berkeley School of Law

Kent D. Syverud
Dean and Ethan A. H. Shepley University Professor
Washington University School of Law

2013-2014 Supplement

National Security Law
Fifth Edition

and

Counterterrorism Law
Second Edition

Stephen Dycus
Professor of Law
Vermont Law School

William C. Banks
Board of Advisors Distinguished Professor
Syracuse University

Peter Raven-Hansen
Glen Earl Weston Research Professor of Law
George Washington University

Stephen I. Vladeck
Professor of Law and Associate Dean for Scholarship
American University Washington College of Law

Wolters Kluwer
Law & Business

Copyright © 2013 Stephen Dycus, William C. Banks, Peter Raven-Hansen, and Stephen I. Vladeck.

Published by Wolters Kluwer Law & Business in New York.

Wolters Kluwer Law & Business serves customers worldwide with CCH, Aspe Publishers, and Kluwer Law International products. (www.wolterskluwerlb.com)

No part of this publication may be reproduced or transmitted in any form or by any means electronic or mechanical, including photocopy, recording, or utilized by any informatio storage or retrieval system, without written permission from the publisher. For informatio about permissions or to request permissions online, visit us at www.wolterskluwerlb.com or a written request may be faxed to our permissions department at 212-771-0803.

To contact Customer Service, e-mail customer.service@wolterskluwer.com, call 1-800-234-1660, fax 1-800-901-9075, or mail correspondence to:

Wolters Kluwer Law & Business
Attn: Order Department
PO Box 990
Frederick, MD 21705

Printed in the United States of America.

1 2 3 4 5 6 7 8 9 0

ISBN 978-1-4548-4100-5

SFI Certified Chain of Custody
Product Line Contains At Least 20% Certified Forest Content
www.sfiprogram.org
SFI-00756

About Wolters Kluwer Law & Business

Wolters Kluwer Law & Business is a leading global provider of intelligent information and digital solutions for legal and business professionals in key specialty areas, and respected educational resources for professors and law students. Wolters Kluwer Law & Business connects legal and business professionals as well as those in the education market with timely, specialized authoritative content and information-enabled solutions to support success through productivity, accuracy and mobility.

Serving customers worldwide, Wolters Kluwer Law & Business products include those under the Aspen Publishers, CCH, Kluwer Law International, Loislaw, ftwilliam.com and MediRegs family of products.

CCH products have been a trusted resource since 1913, and are highly regarded resources for legal, securities, antitrust and trade regulation, government contracting, banking, pension, payroll, employment and labor, and healthcare reimbursement and compliance professionals.

Aspen Publishers products provide essential information to attorneys, business professionals and law students. Written by preeminent authorities, the product line offers analytical and practical information in a range of specialty practice areas from securities law and intellectual property to mergers and acquisitions and pension/benefits. Aspen's trusted legal education resources provide professors and students with high-quality, up-to-date and effective resources for successful instruction and study in all areas of the law.

Kluwer Law International products provide the global business community with reliable international legal information in English. Legal practitioners, corporate counsel and business executives around the world rely on Kluwer Law journals, looseleafs, books, and electronic products for comprehensive information in many areas of international legal practice.

Loislaw is a comprehensive online legal research product providing legal content to law firm practitioners of various specializations. Loislaw provides attorneys with the ability to quickly and efficiently find the necessary legal information they need, when and where they need it, by facilitating access to primary law as well as state-specific law, records, forms and treatises.

ftwilliam.com offers employee benefits professionals the highest quality plan documents (retirement, welfare and non-qualified) and government forms (5500/PBGC, 1099 and IRS) software at highly competitive prices.

MediRegs products provide integrated health care compliance content and software solutions for professionals in healthcare, higher education and life sciences, including professionals in accounting, law and consulting.

Wolters Kluwer Law & Business, a division of Wolters Kluwer, is headquartered in New York. Wolters Kluwer is a market-leading global information services company focused on professionals.

[illegible]

[illegible]

[illegible]

[illegible]

[illegible]

[illegible]

[illegible]

[illegible]

[illegible]

[illegible]

[illegible]

Contents

* * *

Preface

If we needed a reminder, the events of the last year confirm that the world remains a very complex and dangerous place. The ongoing war in Afghanistan, massive violence in Syria, escalating tensions with Iran and North Korea, the continuing debate about the use of drones for targeted killings, the Boston Marathon bombings, and new revelations about domestic electronic surveillance have dominated the headlines since the last *Supplement* was published.

These developments have important legal dimensions. They also reflect the currency and practical relevance of our study of national security law and counterterrorism law. Equally important, they provide special insights into the workings of law and government, and into the responsibility of lawyers to help keep us safe and free.

This year's *Supplement* includes a speech by President Obama about current U.S. counterterrorism efforts around the world; important new Supreme Court decisions on standing and the Alien Tort Statute; new materials on cyber warfare; official statements on drone policy; recent lower court decisions about Guantánamo detainees' right to counsel, the scope of offenses triable by military commissions, and public access to court martial records; and a variety of newly available information concerning domestic intelligence collection by the NSA.

This *Supplement* serves two closely related casebooks: *National Security Law (5th ed.)* and *Counterterrorism Law (2d ed.)*. This Preface is followed immediately by two Teacher's Guides, one for each book, which indicate the placement of supplemental materials in each casebook. Each document listed is accompanied by a reference to one or both casebooks. For example, the decision in *Al-Zahrani v. Rodriguez* appears with this instruction: **[NSL p. 810, CTL p. 424. Insert after the**

***Rasul* decision.]**. "NSL" refers to *National Security Law (5th ed.)*, "CTL" to *Counterterrorism Law (2d ed.)*.

Some of the materials included in this year's *Supplement* are U.S. government documents marked classified that were recently released by former NSA contractor employee Edward Snowden and published online, or they are based on such documents. As this is written, Mr. Snowden, now charged with various criminal offenses and on the run from the law, continues to release such documents. We will monitor future releases and make them available to adopters on a selective basis.

We wish to point out that at least one of our adopters, a U.S. government employee, has informed us that he is forbidden to read any leaked documents that have not been officially declassified. The same stricture may apply to some students. We also know that the Defense Department has blocked access from DOD computers to at least parts of the website for *The Guardian*, where some of the documents released by Snowden were initially published. With the documents now in the public domain and readily available to friends and enemies alike (and the subject of broad media analysis — much of it inaccurate), we believe that it would be pointless and irresponsible to ignore them here. Review of them in the classroom will help us understand what our government is doing in an area fraught with serious privacy and constitutional concerns, correct serious inaccuracies in the public discussion so far, and perhaps contribute indirectly to the development of better policy that is adopted and executed in accordance with the rule of law. Teachers and students will have to decide for themselves whether and how to use these materials.

As important new developments arise during the coming year, we will continue to document them by posting edited new materials on the websites for the two casebooks, from which they may be downloaded by teachers and shared with students. The website for *National Security Law (5th ed.)* is at http://www.aspenlawschool.com/books/dycus_nationalsecurity/; for *Counterterrorism Law (2d ed.)* at http://www.aspenlawschool.com/ books/ dycus_counterterrorism/.

As always, we are extremely grateful to our adopters, fellow members of the National Security Law Section of the Association of American Law Schools, fellow members of the Editorial Board of the *Journal of National Security Law & Policy*, fellow casebook authors (our collaborators in building the field), and our many friends in the national security community. We also want to thank George Washington University law student Kyle Jones for his assistance with research. Finally, we wish to express our gratitude to John Devins and Carol McGeehan of Wolters Kluwer Law & Business for their continued encouragement and support.

Stephen Dycus
William C. Banks
Peter Raven-Hansen
Stephen I. Vladeck

July 2013

* * *

Teacher's Guide for National Security Law (5th Edition)

Chapter 8. The Right to Wage War (jus ad bellum)

Chapter 14. Targeting Terrorists

Chapter 16. Organization and Authority of the Intelligence Community

Chapter 20. The Fourth Amendment and National Security

Chapter 21. Congressional Authority for Foreign Intelligence Surveillance

Chapter 22. Programmatic Electronic Surveillance for Foreign Intelligence

Chapter 23. Third-Party Records and Data Mining

Chapter 24. Screening for Security

Chapter 28. The Great Writ: Habeas Corpus After 9/11

Chapter 30. Military Detention After 9/11

Chapter 32. Case Study: Coercive Interrogation by U.S. Forces After 9/11

Chapter 33. Extraordinary Rendition

Chapter 35. Prosecuting Accused Terrorists and Their Supporters in Criminal Courts

Chapter 36. Trial by Military Commission

Chapter 41. Other Grounds for Access to National Security Information

Teacher's Guide for Counterterrorism Law (2d Edition)

Casebook Page		***Page in this Supplement***

Chapter 6. The Fourth Amendment and Counterterrorism

Chapter 7. Congressional Authority for Foreign Intelligence Surveillance

Chapter 8. Programmatic Electronic Surveillance for Foreign Intelligence

Chapter 9. Third-Party Records and Data Mining

Chapter 10. Screening for Security

Chapter 14. The Great Writ: Habeas Corpus After 9/11

Chapter 16. Military Detention After 9/11

Chapter 18. Case Study: Coercive Interrogation by U.S. Forces After 9/11

Chapter 19. Extraordinary Rendition

Chapter 21. Prosecuting Accused Terrorists and Their Supporters in Criminal Courts

Chapter 22. Trial by Military Commission

Chapter 26. Suing Terrorists and Their Supporters

* * *

Table of Cases

* * *

[NSL p. 4, insert at end of Chapter 1. CTL p. 1, insert at beginning of Chapter 1.]

Remarks of the President at the National Defense University

May 23, 2013

. . . With the collapse of the Berlin Wall, a new dawn of democracy took hold abroad, and a decade of peace and prosperity arrived here at home. And for a moment, it seemed the 21st century would be a tranquil time. And then, on September 11, 2001, we were shaken out of complacency. Thousands were taken from us, as clouds of fire and metal and ash descended upon a sun-filled morning. This was a different kind of war. No armies came to our shores, and our military was not the principal target. Instead, a group of terrorists came to kill as many civilians as they could.

And so our nation went to war. We have now been at war for well over a decade. I won't review the full history. What is clear is that we quickly drove al Qaeda out of Afghanistan, but then shifted our focus and began a new war in Iraq. . . .

Meanwhile, we strengthened our defenses — hardening targets, tightening transportation security, giving law enforcement new tools to prevent terror. Most of these changes were sound. Some caused inconvenience. But some, like expanded surveillance, raised difficult questions about the balance that we strike between our interests in security and our values of privacy. And in some cases, I believe we compromised our basic values — by using torture to interrogate our enemies, and detaining individuals in a way that ran counter to the rule of law.

So after I took office, we stepped up the war against al Qaeda but we also sought to change its course. We relentlessly targeted al Qaeda's leadership. We ended the war in Iraq, and brought nearly 150,000 troops home. We pursued a new strategy in Afghanistan, and increased our training of Afghan forces. We unequivocally banned torture, affirmed our commitment to civilian courts, worked to align our policies with the rule of law, and expanded our consultations with Congress.

Today, Osama bin Laden is dead, and so are most of his top lieutenants. There have been no large-scale attacks on the United States, and our homeland is more secure. Fewer of our troops are in harm's way, and over the next 19 months they will continue to come home. Our alliances are strong, and so is our standing in the world. In sum, we are safer because of our efforts.

Now, make no mistake, our nation is still threatened by terrorists. From Benghazi to Boston, we have been tragically reminded of that truth. But we have to recognize that the threat has shifted and evolved from the one that came to our shores on 9/11. With a decade of experience now to draw from, this is the moment to ask ourselves hard questions — about the nature of today's threats and how we should confront them. . . .

So America is at a crossroads. We must define the nature and scope of this struggle, or else it will define us. We have to be mindful of James Madison's warning that "No nation could preserve its freedom in the midst of continual warfare." Neither I, nor any President, can promise the total defeat of terror. We will never erase the evil that lies in the hearts of some human beings, nor stamp out every danger to our open society. But what we can do — what we must do — is dismantle networks that pose a direct danger to us, and make it less likely for new groups to gain a foothold, all the while maintaining the freedoms and ideals that we defend. And to define that strategy, we have to make decisions based not on fear, but on hard-earned wisdom. That begins with understanding the current threat that we face.

Today, the core of al Qaeda in Afghanistan and Pakistan is on a path to defeat. Their remaining operatives spend more time thinking about their own safety than plotting against us. They did not direct the attacks in Benghazi or Boston. They have not carried out a successful attack on our homeland since 9/11. Instead, what we've seen is the emergence of various al Qaeda affiliates. From Yemen to Iraq, from Somalia to North Africa, the threat today is more diffuse . . . .

Unrest in the Arab World has also allowed extremists to gain a foothold in countries like Libya and Syria. Here, too, there are differences from 9/11. In some cases, we confront state-sponsored networks like Hizbollah that engage in acts of terror to achieve political goals. Others are simply collections of local militias or extremists interested in seizing territory. While we are vigilant for signs that these groups may pose a transnational threat, most are focused on operating in the countries and regions where they are based. . . .

Finally, we face a real threat from radicalized individuals here in the United States. . . . Deranged or alienated individuals — often U.S. citizens or legal residents — can do enormous damage, particularly when inspired by larger notions of violent jihad. That pull towards extremism appears to have led to the shooting at Fort Hood, and the bombing of the Boston Marathon.

Lethal yet less capable al Qaeda affiliates. Threats to diplomatic facilities and businesses abroad. Homegrown extremists. This is the future of terrorism. We must take these threats seriously, and do all that we can to confront them. . . .

. . . [L]et me discuss the components of such a comprehensive counter-terrorism strategy.

First, we must finish the work of defeating al Qaeda and its associated forces.

In Afghanistan, we will complete our transition to Afghan responsibility for security. Our troops will come home. Our combat mission will come to an end. And we will work with the Afghan government to train security forces, and sustain a counter-terrorism force which ensures that al Qaeda can never again establish a safe-haven to launch attacks against us or our allies.

Beyond Afghanistan, we must define our effort not as a boundless "global war on terror" — but rather as a series of persistent, targeted efforts to dismantle specific networks of violent extremists that threaten America. In many cases, this will involve partnerships with other countries. . . .

Much of our best counter-terrorism cooperation results in the gathering and sharing of intelligence; the arrest and prosecution of terrorists. . . .

But despite our strong preference for the detention and prosecution of terrorists, sometimes this approach is foreclosed. . . .

[Here the President describes the ongoing U.S. campaign of targeting individual terrorists using armed drone aircraft. See *infra* p. 56 in this *Supplement*.]

I believe, however, that the use of force must be seen as part of a larger discussion about a comprehensive counter-terrorism strategy. Because for all the focus on the use of force, force alone cannot make us safe. We cannot use force everywhere that a radical ideology takes root; and in the absence of a strategy that reduces the well-spring of extremism, a perpetual war — through drones or Special Forces or troop deployments — will prove self-defeating, and alter our country in troubling ways.

So the next element of our strategy involves addressing the underlying grievances and conflicts that feed extremism, from North Africa to South Asia. . . .

This means patiently supporting transitions to democracy in places like Egypt, Tunisia and Libya — because the peaceful realization of individual aspirations will serve as a rebuke to violent extremists. We must strengthen the opposition in Syria, while isolating extremist elements — because the end of a tyrant must not give way to the tyranny of terrorism. We are working to promote peace between Israelis and Palestinians — because it is right, and because such a peace could help reshape attitudes in the region. And we must help countries modernize economies, upgrade education, and encourage entrepreneurship — because American leadership has always been elevated by our ability to connect with peoples' hopes, and not simply their fears.

Success on these fronts requires sustained engagement, but it will also require resources. I know that foreign aid is one of the least popular expenditures — even though it amounts to less than one percent of the federal budget. But foreign assistance cannot be viewed as charity. It is fundamental to our national security, and any sensible long-term strategy to battle extremism. . . .

Targeted action against terrorists. Effective partnerships. Diplomatic engagement and assistance. Through such a comprehensive strategy we can significantly reduce the chances of large scale attacks on the homeland and mitigate threats to Americans overseas. As we guard against dangers from abroad, however, we cannot neglect the daunting challenge of terrorism from within our borders.

As I said earlier, this threat is not new. But technology and the Internet increase its frequency and lethality. Today, a person can consume hateful propaganda, commit themselves to a violent agenda, and learn how to kill without leaving their home. To address this threat, two years ago my Administration did a comprehensive review, and engaged with law enforcement. The best way to prevent violent extremism is to work with the Muslim American community — which has consistently rejected terrorism — to identify signs of radicalization, and partner with law enforcement when an individual is drifting towards violence. . . .

Indeed, thwarting homegrown plots presents particular challenges in part because of our proud commitment to civil liberties for all who call America home. That's why, in the years to come, we will have to keep working hard to strike the appropriate balance between our need for security and preserving those freedoms that make us who we are. That means reviewing the authorities of law enforcement, so we can intercept new types of communication, and build in privacy protections to prevent abuse. That means that — even after Boston — we do not deport someone or throw someone in prison in the absence of evidence. That means putting careful constraints on the tools the government uses to protect sensitive information, such as the State Secrets doctrine. And that means finally having a strong Privacy and Civil Liberties Board to review those issues where our counter-terrorism efforts and our values may come into tension.

The Justice Department's investigation of national security leaks offers a recent example of the challenges involved in striking the right balance between our security and our open society. As Commander-in Chief, I believe we must keep information secret that protects our operations and our people in the field. To do so, we must enforce consequences for those who break the law and breach their commitment to protect classified information. But a free press is also essential for our democracy. I am troubled by the possibility that leak investigations may chill the investigative journalism that holds government accountable.

Journalists should not be at legal risk for doing their jobs. Our focus must be on those who break the law. That is why I have called on Congress to pass a media shield law to guard against government over-reach. I have raised these issues with the Attorney General, who shares my concern. So he has agreed to review existing Department of Justice guidelines governing investigations that involve reporters, and will convene a group of media organizations to hear their concerns as part of that review. . . .

All these issues remind us that the choices we make about war can impact — in sometimes unintended ways — the openness and freedom on which our way of life depends. And that is why I intend to engage Congress about the existing Authorization to Use Military Force, or AUMF, to determine how we can continue to fight terrorists without keeping America on a perpetual war-time footing.

The AUMF is now nearly twelve years old. The Afghan War is coming to an end. Core al Qaeda is a shell of its former self. Groups like AQAP must be dealt with, but in the years to come, not every collection of thugs that labels themselves al Qaeda will pose a credible threat to the United States. Unless we discipline our thinking and our actions, we may be drawn into more wars we don't need to fight, or continue to grant Presidents unbound[ed] powers more suited for traditional armed conflicts between nation states. So I look forward to engaging Congress and the American people in efforts to refine, and ultimately repeal, the AUMF's mandate. And I will not sign laws designed to expand this mandate further. Our systematic effort to dismantle terrorist organizations must continue. But this war, like all wars, must end. That's what history advises. That's what our democracy demands.

And that brings me to my final topic: the detention of terrorist suspects.

To repeat, as a matter of policy, the preference of the United States is to capture terrorist suspects. When we do detain a suspect, we interrogate them. And if the suspect can be prosecuted, we decide whether to try him in a civilian court or a Military Commission. During the past decade, the vast majority of those detained by our military were captured on the battlefield. In Iraq, we turned over thousands of prisoners as we ended the war. In Afghanistan, we have transitioned detention facilities to the Afghans, as part of the process of restoring Afghan sovereignty. So we bring law of war detention to an end, and we are committed to prosecuting terrorists whenever we can.

The glaring exception to this time-tested approach is the detention center at Guantanamo Bay. The original premise for opening GTMO — that detainees would not be able to challenge their detention – was found unconstitutional five years ago. In the meantime, GTMO has become a symbol around the world for an America that flouts the rule of law. . . .

As President, I have tried to close GTMO. I transferred 67 detainees to other countries before Congress imposed restrictions to effectively prevent us from either transferring detainees to other countries, or imprisoning them in the United States. These restrictions make no sense. . . .

Today, I once again call on Congress to lift the restrictions on detainee transfers from GTMO. I have asked the Department of Defense to designate a site in the United States where we can hold military commissions. . . . I am lifting the moratorium on detainee transfers to Yemen, so we can review them on a case by case basis. To the greatest extent possible, we will transfer detainees who have been cleared to go to other countries. Where appropriate, we will bring terrorists to justice in our courts and military justice system. And we will insist that judicial review be available for every detainee.

Even after we take these steps, one issue will remain: how to deal with those GTMO detainees who we know have participated in dangerous plots or attacks, but who cannot be prosecuted — for example because the evidence against them has been compromised or is inadmissible in a court of law. But once we commit to a process of closing GTMO, I am confident that this legacy problem can be resolved, consistent with our commitment to the rule of law. . . .

[NSL p. 137. Insert at the end of Note 2.]

Clapper v. Amnesty International USA

United States Supreme Court, Feb. 26, 2013
133 S. Ct. 1138

Justice ALITO delivered the opinion of the Court. Section 702 of the Foreign Intelligence Surveillance Act of 1978, 50 U.S.C. §1881a (2006 ed., Supp. V), allows the Attorney General and the Director of National Intelligence to acquire foreign intelligence information by jointly authorizing the surveillance of individuals who are not "United States persons"[1] and are reasonably believed to be located outside the United States. Before doing so, the Attorney General and the Director of National Intelligence normally must obtain the Foreign Intelligence Surveillance Court's approval. Respondents are United States persons whose work, they allege, requires them to engage in sensitive international communications with individuals who[m] they believe are likely targets of surveillance under §1881a. Respondents seek a declaration that §1881a is unconstitutional, as well as an injunction against §1881a-authorized surveillance. The question before us is whether respondents have Article III standing to seek this prospective relief.

Respondents assert that they can establish injury in fact because there is an objectively reasonable likelihood that their communications will be acquired under §1881a at some point in the future. But respondents' theory of *future* injury is too speculative to satisfy the well established requirement that threatened injury must be "certainly impending." *E.g., Whitmore v. Arkansas,* 495 U.S. 149, 158 (1990). And even if respondents could demonstrate that the threatened injury is certainly impending, they still would not be able to establish that this injury is fairly traceable to §1881a. As an alternative argument, respondents contend that they are suffering *present* injury because the risk of §1881a-authorized surveillance already has forced them to take costly and burdensome measures to protect the confidentiality of their international communications. But respondents cannot manufacture

---

1. The term "United States person" includes citizens of the United States, aliens admitted for permanent residence, and certain associations and corporations. 50 U.S.C. §1801(i); see §1881(a).

standing by choosing to make expenditures based on hypothetical future harm that is not certainly impending. We therefore hold that respondents lack Article III standing.

I

A

In 1978, after years of debate, Congress enacted the Foreign Intelligence Surveillance Act (FISA) to authorize and regulate certain governmental electronic surveillance of communications for foreign intelligence purposes. See 50 U.S.C. §1801 *et seq*. . . .

When Congress enacted the FISA Amendments Act of 2008 (FISA Amendments Act), 122 Stat. 2436, it left much of FISA intact, but it "established a new and independent source of intelligence collection authority, beyond that granted in traditional FISA." [1 D. Kris & J. Wilson, National Security Investigations & Prosecutions (2d ed.2012)] §9:11, at 349–350. As relevant here, §702 of FISA, 50 U.S.C. §1881a (2006 ed., Supp. V), which was enacted as part of the FISA Amendments Act, supplements pre-existing FISA authority by creating a new framework under which the Government may seek the FISC's authorization of certain foreign intelligence surveillance targeting the communications of non-U.S. persons located abroad. Unlike traditional FISA surveillance, §1881a does not require the Government to demonstrate probable cause that the target of the electronic surveillance is a foreign power or agent of a foreign power. And, unlike traditional FISA, §1881a does not require the Government to specify the nature and location of each of the particular facilities or places at which the electronic surveillance will occur. . . .

B

Respondents are attorneys and human rights, labor, legal, and media organizations whose work allegedly requires them to engage in sensitive and sometimes privileged telephone and e-mail communications with colleagues, clients, sources, and other individuals located abroad. Respondents believe that some of the people with whom they exchange foreign intelligence information are likely targets of surveillance under §1881a. Specifically, respondents claim that they communicate by telephone and e-mail with people the Government "believes or believed to be associated with terrorist organizations," "people located in geographic areas that are a special focus" of the Government's counterterrorism or diplomatic efforts, and activists who oppose governments that are supported by the United States Government.

Respondents claim that §1881a compromises their ability to locate witnesses, cultivate sources, obtain information, and communicate confidential information to their clients. Respondents also assert that they "have ceased engaging" in certain telephone and e-mail conversations. According to respondents, the threat of surveillance will compel them to travel abroad in order to have in-person conversations. In addition, respondents declare that they have undertaken "costly and burdensome measures" to protect the confidentiality of sensitive communications.

C

On the day when the FISA Amendments Act was enacted, respondents filed this action seeking (1) a declaration that §1881a, on its face, violates the Fourth Amendment, the First Amendment, Article III, and separation-of-powers principles and (2) a permanent injunction against the use of §1881a. . . .

II

Article III of the Constitution limits federal courts' jurisdiction to certain "Cases" and "Controversies." As we have explained, "[n]o principle is more fundamental to the judiciary's proper role in our system of government than the constitutional limitation of federal-court jurisdiction to actual cases or controversies." *DaimlerChrysler Corp. v. Cuno,* 547 U.S. 332, 341 (2006) (internal quotation marks omitted); *Raines v. Byrd,* 521 U.S. 811, 818 (1997); see, *e.g., Summers v. Earth Island Institute,* 555 U.S. 488, 492–493 (2009). "One element of the case-or-controversy requirement" is that plaintiffs "must establish that they have standing to sue." *Raines, supra,* at 818.

The law of Article III standing, which is built on separation-of-powers principles, serves to prevent the judicial process from being used to usurp the powers of the political branches. *Summers, supra,* at 492–493. In keeping with the purpose of this doctrine, "[o]ur standing inquiry has been especially rigorous when reaching the merits of the dispute would force us to decide whether an action taken by one of the other two branches of the Federal Government was unconstitutional." *Raines, supra,* at 819-820. "Relaxation of standing requirements is directly related to the expansion of judicial power," *United States v. Richardson,* 418 U.S. 166, 188 (1974) (Powell, J., concurring), and we have often found a lack of standing in cases in which the Judiciary has been requested to review actions of the political branches in the fields of intelligence gathering and foreign affairs, see, *e.g., Richardson, supra,* at 167–170 (plaintiff lacked standing to challenge the constitutionality of a statute permitting the Central Intelligence Agency to account for its expenditures solely on the certificate of the CIA Director); [*Schlesinger v. Reservists Comm. to Stop the War,* 418 U.S. 208 (1974)], at 209-211 (plaintiffs lacked standing to challenge the Armed Forces Reserve membership of Members of Congress); *Laird v. Tatum,* 408 U.S. 1, 11-16 (1972) (plaintiffs lacked standing to challenge an Army intelligence-gathering program).

To establish Article III standing, an injury must be "concrete, particularized, and actual or imminent; fairly traceable to the challenged action; and redressable by a favorable ruling." *Monsanto Co. v. Geertson Seed Farms,* 561 U.S. ——, —— (2010) (slip op., at 7). "Although imminence is concededly a somewhat elastic concept, it cannot be stretched beyond its purpose, which is to ensure that the alleged injury is not too speculative for Article III purposes — that the injury is *certainly* impending." *Id.,* at 565, n.2 (internal quotation marks omitted). Thus, we have repeatedly reiterated that "threatened injury must be *certainly impending* to constitute injury in fact," and that "[a]llegations of *possible* future injury" are not sufficient. *Whitmore,* 495 U.S., at 158 (emphasis added; internal quotation marks omitted).

III

A

Respondents assert that they can establish injury in fact that is fairly traceable to §1881a because there is an objectively reasonable likelihood that their communications with their foreign contacts will be intercepted under §1881a at some point in the future. This argument fails. As an initial matter, the . . . "objectively reasonable likelihood" standard is inconsistent with our requirement that "threatened injury must be certainly impending to constitute injury in fact." *Whitmore, supra,* at 158 (internal quotation marks omitted). Furthermore, respondents' argument rests on their highly speculative fear that: (1) the Government will decide to target the communications of non-U.S. persons with whom they communicate; (2) in doing so, the Government will choose to invoke its authority under §1881a rather than utilizing another method of surveillance; (3) the Article III judges who serve on the Foreign Intelligence Surveillance Court will conclude that the Government's proposed surveillance procedures satisfy §1881a's many safeguards and are consistent with the Fourth Amendment; (4) the Government will succeed in intercepting the communications of respondents' contacts; and (5) respondents will be parties to the particular communications that the Government intercepts. As discussed below, respondents' theory of standing, which relies on a highly attenuated chain of possibilities, does not satisfy the requirement that threatened injury must be certainly impending. Moreover, even if respondents could demonstrate injury in fact, the second link in the above-described chain of contingencies — which amounts to mere speculation about whether surveillance would be under §1881a or some other authority — shows that respondents cannot satisfy the requirement that any injury in fact must be fairly traceable to §1881a.

First, it is speculative whether the Government will imminently target communications to which respondents are parties. Section 1881a expressly provides that respondents, who are U.S. persons, cannot be targeted for surveillance under §1881a. Accordingly, it is no surprise that respondents fail to offer any evidence that their communications have been monitored under §1881a, a failure that substantially undermines their standing theory. Indeed, respondents do not even allege that the Government has sought the FISC's approval for surveillance of their communications. Accordingly, respondents' theory necessarily rests on their assertion that the Government will target *other individuals* — namely, their foreign contacts.

Yet respondents have no actual knowledge of the Government's §1881a targeting practices. Instead, respondents merely speculate and make assumptions about whether their communications with their foreign contacts will be acquired under §1881a. For example, journalist Christopher Hedges states: "I have no choice but to *assume* that any of my international communications *may* be subject to government surveillance, and I have to make decisions . . . in light of that *assumption*." . . . "The party invoking federal jurisdiction bears the burden of establishing" standing — and, at the summary judgment stage, such a party "can no longer rest on . . . 'mere allegations,' but must 'set forth' by affidavit or other evidence 'specific facts.'" [*Lujan v. Defenders of Wildlife,* 504 U.S. 555 (1992)], at 561. Respondents, however, have set forth no specific facts demonstrating that the communications of their foreign contacts will be targeted. Moreover, because §1881a at most *authorizes* — but does not *mandate* or *direct* — the surveillance that respondents fear, respondents' allegations are necessarily conjectural. Simply put, respondents can only speculate as to how the Attorney General and the Director of National Intelligence will exercise their discretion in determining which communications to target.[4]

Second, even if respondents could demonstrate that the targeting of their foreign contacts is imminent, respondents can only speculate as to whether the Government will seek to use §1881a authorized surveillance (rather than other methods) to do so. The Government has numerous other methods of conducting surveillance, none of which is challenged here. Even after the enactment of the FISA Amendments Act, for example, the Government may still conduct electronic surveillance of persons abroad under the older provisions of FISA so long as it satisfies the applicable requirements, including a demonstration of probable cause to believe that the person is a foreign power or agent of a foreign power. See §1805. The Government may also obtain information from the intelligence services of foreign nations. And, although we do not reach the question, the Government contends that it can conduct FISA-exempt human and technical surveillance programs that are governed by Executive Order 12333. See Exec. Order No. 12333, §§1.4,

---

4. It was suggested at oral argument that the Government could help resolve the standing inquiry by disclosing to a court, perhaps through an *in camera* proceeding, (1) whether it is intercepting respondents' communications and (2) what targeting or minimization procedures it is using. This suggestion is puzzling. As an initial matter, it is *respondents'* burden to prove their standing by pointing to specific facts, *Lujan v. Defenders of Wildlife,* 504 U.S. 555, 561 (1992), not the Government's burden to disprove standing by revealing details of its surveillance priorities. Moreover, this type of hypothetical disclosure proceeding would allow a terrorist (or his attorney) to determine whether he is currently under U.S. surveillance simply by filing a lawsuit challenging the Government's surveillance program. Even if the terrorist's attorney were to comply with a protective order prohibiting him from sharing the Government's disclosures with his client, the court's postdisclosure decision about whether to dismiss the suit for lack of standing would surely signal to the terrorist whether his name was on the list of surveillance targets.

2.1-2.5. Even if respondents could demonstrate that their foreign contacts will imminently be targeted — indeed, even if they could show that interception of their own communications will imminently occur — they would still need to show that their injury is fairly traceable to §1881a. But, because respondents can only speculate as to whether any (asserted) interception would be under §1881a or some other authority, they cannot satisfy the "fairly traceable" requirement.

Third, even if respondents could show that the Government will seek the Foreign Intelligence Surveillance Court's authorization to acquire the communications of respondents' foreign contacts under §1881a, respondents can only speculate as to whether that court will authorize such surveillance. In the past, we have been reluctant to endorse standing theories that require guesswork as to how independent decisionmakers will exercise their judgment. . . .

Fourth, even if the Government were to obtain the Foreign Intelligence Surveillance Court's approval to target respondents' foreign contacts under §1881a, it is unclear whether the Government would succeed in acquiring the communications of respondents' foreign contacts. And fifth, even if the Government were to conduct surveillance of respondents' foreign contacts, respondents can only speculate as to whether *their own communications* with their foreign contacts would be incidentally acquired.

In sum, respondents' speculative chain of possibilities does not establish that injury based on potential future surveillance is certainly impending or is fairly traceable to §1881a.[5]

---

5. Our cases do not uniformly require plaintiffs to demonstrate that it is literally certain that the harms they identify will come about. In some instances, we have found standing based on a "substantial risk" that the harm will occur, which may prompt plaintiffs to reasonably incur costs to mitigate or avoid that harm. *Monsanto Co. v. Geertson Seed Farms,* 561 U.S. ——, —— (2010) (slip op., at 11–12). But to the extent that the "substantial risk" standard is relevant and is distinct from the "clearly impending" requirement, respondents fall short of even that standard, in light of the attenuated chain of inferences necessary to find harm here. In addition, plaintiffs bear the burden of pleading and proving concrete facts showing that the defendant's actual action has caused the substantial risk of harm. Plaintiffs cannot rely on speculation about "'the unfettered choices made by independent actors not before the court.'" *Defenders of Wildlife,* 504 U.S., at 562.

B

Respondents' alternative argument — namely, that they can establish standing based on the measures that they have undertaken to avoid §1881a-authorized surveillance — fares no better. Respondents assert that they are suffering ongoing injuries that are fairly traceable to §1881a because the risk of surveillance under §1881a requires them to take costly and burdensome measures to protect the confidentiality of their communications. Respondents claim, for instance, that the threat of surveillance sometimes compels them to avoid certain e-mail and phone conversations, to "tal[k] in generalities rather than specifics," or to travel so that they can have in-person conversations. . . .

. . . Respondents' contention that they have standing because they incurred certain costs as a reasonable reaction to a risk of harm is unavailing — because the harm respondents seek to avoid is not certainly impending. In other words, respondents cannot manufacture standing merely by inflicting harm on themselves based on their fears of hypothetical future harm that is not certainly impending. See *Pennsylvania v. New Jersey,* 426 U.S. 660, 664 (1976) (*per curiam*). Any ongoing injuries that respondents are suffering are not fairly traceable to §1881a. . . .

Another reason that respondents' present injuries are not fairly traceable to §1881a is that [under FISA authority that predated §1881a], they had a similar incentive to engage in many of the countermeasures that they are now taking. . . .

Because respondents do not face a threat of certainly impending interception under §1881a, the costs that they have incurred to avoid surveillance are simply the product of their fear of surveillance, and our decision in *Laird* makes it clear that such a fear is insufficient to create standing. See 408 U.S., at 10–15. The plaintiffs in *Laird* argued that their exercise of First Amendment rights was being "chilled by the mere existence, without more, of [the Army's] investigative and data-gathering activity." *Id.,* at 10. While acknowledging that prior cases had held that constitutional violations may arise from the chilling effect of "regulations that fall short of a direct prohibition against the exercise of First Amendment rights," the Court declared that none of those cases involved a "chilling effect aris[ing] merely from the individual's knowledge that a governmental agency was engaged in certain activities or from the individual's concomitant fear that, armed with the fruits of those activities, the agency might in the future take some *other* and additional action detrimental to that individual." *Id.,* at 11. Because "[a]llegations of a subjective 'chill' are not an adequate substitute for a claim of specific present objective harm or a threat of specific future harm," *id.,* at 13–14, the plaintiffs in *Laird* [lacked] — and respondents here [lack —] standing.

For the reasons discussed above, respondents' self-inflicted injuries are not fairly traceable to the Government's purported activities under §1881a, and their subjective fear of surveillance does not give rise to standing.

IV . . .

B

Respondents also suggest that they should be held to have standing because otherwise the constitutionality of §1881a could not be challenged. It would be wrong, they maintain, to "insulate the government's surveillance activities from meaningful judicial review." Respondents' suggestion is both legally and factually incorrect. First, "'[t]he assumption that if respondents have no standing to sue, no one would have standing, is not a reason to find standing.'" [*Valley Forge Christian College v. Americans United for Separation of Church and State, Inc.,* 454 U.S. 464 (1982)], at 489.

Second, our holding today by no means insulates §1881a from judicial review. . . . Congress created a comprehensive scheme in which the Foreign Intelligence Surveillance Court evaluates the Government's certifications, targeting procedures, and minimization procedures — including assessing whether the targeting and minimization procedures comport with the Fourth Amendment. §§1881a(a), (c)(1), (i)(2), (i)(3). Any dissatisfaction that respondents may have about the Foreign Intelligence Surveillance Court's rulings — or the congressional delineation of that court's role — is irrelevant to our standing analysis.

Additionally, if the Government intends to use or disclose information obtained or derived from a §1881a acquisition in judicial or administrative proceedings, it must provide advance notice of its intent, and the affected person may challenge the lawfulness of the acquisition. §§1806(c), 1806(e), 1881e(a) (2006 ed. and Supp. V). Thus, if the Government were to prosecute one of respondent-attorney's foreign clients using §1881a-authorized surveillance, the Government would be required to make a disclosure. Although the foreign client might not have a viable Fourth Amendment claim, see, *e.g., United States v. Verdugo-Urquidez,* 494 U.S. 259, 261 (1990), it is possible that the monitoring of the target's conversations with his or her attorney would provide grounds for a claim of standing on the part of the attorney. Such an attorney would certainly have a stronger evidentiary basis for establishing standing than do respondents in the present case. In such a situation, unlike in the present case, it would at least be clear that the Government had acquired the foreign client's communications using §1881a-authorized surveillance.

Finally, any electronic communications service provider that the Government directs to assist in §1881a surveillance may challenge the lawfulness of that directive before the FISC. §1881a(h)(4), (6). Indeed, at the behest of a service provider, the Foreign Intelligence Surveillance Court of Review previously analyzed the constitutionality of electronic surveillance directives issued pursuant to a now-expired set of FISA amendments. See *In re Directives Pursuant to Section 105B of Foreign Intelligence Surveillance Act,* 551 F.3d 1004, 1006-1016 (2008) (holding that the provider had standing and that the directives were constitutional). . . .

We hold that respondents lack Article III standing because they cannot demonstrate that the future injury they purportedly fear is certainly impending and because they cannot manufacture standing by incurring costs in anticipation of non-imminent harm. . . .

Justice BREYER, with whom Justice GINSBURG, Justice SOTOMAYOR, and Justice KAGAN join, dissenting. The plaintiffs' standing depends upon the likelihood that the Government, acting under the authority of 50 U.S.C. §1881a (2006 ed., Supp. V), will harm them by intercepting at least some of their private, foreign, telephone, or e-mail conversations. In my view, this harm is not "speculative." Indeed it is as likely to take place as are most future events that commonsense inference and ordinary knowledge of human nature tell us will happen. This Court has often found the occurrence of similar future events sufficiently certain to support standing. I dissent from the Court's contrary conclusion. . . .

III

Several considerations, based upon the record along with commonsense inferences, convince me that there is a very high likelihood that Government, *acting under the authority of §1881a,* will intercept at least some of the communications just described. First, the plaintiffs have engaged, and continue to engage, in electronic communications of a kind that the 2008 amendment, but not the prior Act, authorizes the Government to intercept. These communications include discussions with family members of those detained at Guantanamo, friends and acquaintances of those persons, and investigators, experts and others with knowledge of circumstances related to terrorist activities. These persons are foreigners located outside the United States. They are not "foreign power[s]" or "agent[s] of . . . foreign power[s]." And the plaintiffs state that they exchange with these persons "foreign intelligence information," defined to include information that "relates to" "international terrorism" and "the national defense or the security of the United States." See 50 U.S.C. §1801 (2006 ed. and Supp. V).

Second, the plaintiffs have a strong *motive* to engage in, and the Government has a strong *motive* to listen to, conversations of the kind described. A lawyer representing a client normally seeks to learn the circumstances surrounding the crime (or the civil wrong) of which the client is accused. . . . Journalists and human rights workers have strong similar motives to conduct conversations of this kind.

At the same time, the Government has a strong motive to conduct surveillance of conversations that contain material of this kind. The Government, after all, seeks to learn as much as it can reasonably learn about suspected terrorists (such as those detained at Guantanamo), as well as about their contacts and activities, along with those of friends and family members. And the Government is motivated to do so, not simply by the desire to help convict those whom the Government believes guilty, but also by the critical, overriding need to protect America from terrorism.

Third, the Government's *past behavior* shows that it has sought, and hence will in all likelihood continue to seek, information about alleged terrorists and detainees through means that include surveillance of electronic communications. As just pointed out, plaintiff Scott McKay states that the Government (under the authority of the pre–2008 law) "intercepted some 10,000 telephone calls and 20,000 email communications involving [his client] Mr. Al–Hussayen."

Fourth, the Government has the *capacity* to conduct electronic surveillance of the kind at issue. . . .

Of course, to exercise this capacity the Government must have intelligence court authorization. But the Government rarely files requests that fail to meet the statutory criteria. . . .

The upshot is that (1) similarity of content, (2) strong motives, (3) prior behavior, and (4) capacity all point to a very strong likelihood that the Government will intercept at least some of the plaintiffs' communications, including some that the 2008 amendment, §1881a, but not the pre-2008 Act, authorizes the Government to intercept. . . .

Consequently, we need only assume that the Government is doing its job (to find out about, and combat, terrorism) in order to conclude that there is a high probability that the Government will intercept at least some electronic communication to which at least some of the plaintiffs are parties. The majority is wrong when it describes the harm threatened plaintiffs as "speculative."

IV

A

The majority more plausibly says that the plaintiffs have failed to show that the threatened harm is "*certainly impending.*" But, as the majority appears to concede, *certainty* is not, and never has been, the touchstone of standing. The future is inherently uncertain. Yet federal courts frequently entertain actions for injunctions and for declaratory relief aimed at preventing future activities that are reasonably likely or highly likely, but not absolutely certain, to take place. And that degree of certainty is all that is needed to support standing here. The Court's use of the term "certainly impending" is not to the contrary. Sometimes the Court has used the phrase "certainly impending" as if the phrase described a *sufficient,* rather than a *necessary,* condition for jurisdiction. See *Pennsylvania v. West Virginia,* 262 U.S. 553, 593 (1923) ("If the injury is certainly impending that is enough"). On other occasions, it has used the phrase as if it concerned *when,* not *whether,* an alleged injury would occur. Thus, in *Lujan,* 504 U.S., at 564, n.2, the Court considered a threatened future injury that consisted of harm that plaintiffs would suffer when they "soon" visited a government project area that (they claimed) would suffer environmental damage. . . .

On still other occasions, recognizing that "'imminence' is concededly a somewhat elastic concept," *Lujan, supra,* at 565, n. 2, the Court has referred to, or used (sometimes along with "certainly impending") other phrases such as "reasonable probability" that suggest less than absolute, or literal certainty. See *Babbitt, supra,* at 298 (plaintiff "must demonstrate a *realistic danger* of sustaining a direct injury" (emphasis added)). Taken together the case law uses the word "certainly" as if it emphasizes, rather than literally defines, the immediately following term "impending."

B . . .

3

The majority cannot find support in cases that use the words "certainly impending" to *deny* standing. . . .

4

In sum, as the Court concedes, the word "certainly" in the phrase "certainly impending" does not refer to absolute certainty. As our case law demonstrates, what the Constitution requires is something more akin to "reasonable probability" or "high probability." The use of some such standard is all that is necessary here to ensure the actual concrete injury that the Constitution demands. The . . . standard is readily met in this case. . . .

[NSL p. 195, insert after *Sosa v. Alvarez-Machain*. CTL p. 839, insert after Note 11.]

Kiobel v. Royal Dutch Petroleum Co.

Supreme Court of the United States, April 17, 2013
133 S. Ct. 1659

Chief Justice ROBERTS delivered the opinion of the Court. Petitioners, a group of Nigerian nationals residing in the United States, filed suit in federal court against certain Dutch, British, and Nigerian corporations. Petitioners sued under the Alien Tort Statute, 28 U.S.C. §1350, alleging that the corporations aided and abetted the Nigerian Government in committing violations of the law of nations in Nigeria. The question presented is whether and under what circumstances courts may recognize a cause of action under the Alien Tort Statute, for violations of the law of nations occurring within the territory of a sovereign other than the United States.

I

Petitioners were residents of Ogoniland, an area of 250 square miles located in the Niger delta area of Nigeria and populated by roughly half a million people. When the complaint was filed, respondents Royal Dutch Petroleum Company and Shell Transport and Trading Company, p.l.c., were holding companies incorporated in the Netherlands and England, respectively. Their joint subsidiary, respondent Shell Petroleum Development Company of Nigeria, Ltd. (SPDC), was incorporated in Nigeria, and engaged in oil exploration and production in Ogoniland. According to the complaint, after concerned residents of Ogoniland began protesting the environmental effects of SPDC's practices, respondents enlisted the Nigerian Government to violently suppress the burgeoning demonstrations. Throughout the early 1990's, the complaint alleges, Nigerian military and police forces attacked Ogoni villages, beating, raping, killing, and arresting residents and destroying or looting property. Petitioners further allege that respondents aided and abetted these atrocities by, among other things, providing the Nigerian forces with food, transportation, and compensation, as well as by allowing the Nigerian military to use respondents' property as a staging ground for attacks.

Following the alleged atrocities, petitioners moved to the United States where they have been granted political asylum and now reside as legal residents. They filed suit in the United States District Court for the Southern District of New York, alleging jurisdiction under the Alien Tort Statute and requesting relief under customary international law. The ATS provides, in full, that "[t]he district courts shall have original jurisdiction of any civil action by an alien for a tort only, committed in violation of the law of nations or a treaty of the United States." 28 U.S.C. §1350. According to petitioners, respondents violated the law of nations by aiding and abetting the Nigerian Government in committing (1) extrajudicial killings; (2) crimes against humanity; (3) torture and cruel treatment; (4) arbitrary arrest and detention; (5) violations of the rights to life, liberty, security, and association; (6) forced exile; and (7) property destruction. The District Court dismissed [portions of the complaint]. . . .

The Second Circuit dismissed the entire complaint, reasoning that the law of nations does not recognize corporate liability. 621 F.3d 111 (2010). We granted certiorari to consider that question. 565 U.S. —— (2011). After oral argument, we directed the parties to file supplemental briefs addressing an additional question: "Whether and under what circumstances the [ATS] allows courts to recognize a cause of action for violations of the law of nations occurring within the territory of a sovereign other than the United States." 565 U.S. —— (2012). We heard oral argument again and now affirm the judgment below, based on our answer to the second question.

II

Passed as part of the Judiciary Act of 1789, the ATS was invoked twice in the late 18th century, but then only once more over the next 167 years. Act of Sept. 24, 1789, §9, 1 Stat 77; see *Moxon v. The Fanny,* 17 F. Cas. 942 (No. 9,895) (DC Pa. 1793); *Bolchos v. Darrel,* 3 F. Cas. 810 (No. 1,607) (DC SC 1795); *O'Reilly de Camara v. Brooke,* 209 U.S. 45 (1908); *Khedivial Line, S.A.E. v. Seafarers' Int'l Union,* 278 F.2d 49, 51–52 (C.A.2 1960) (*per curiam*). The statute provides district courts with jurisdiction to hear certain claims, but does not expressly provide any causes of action. We held in *Sosa v. Alvarez-Machain,* 542 U.S. 692, 714 (2004), however, that the First Congress did not intend the provision to be "stillborn." The grant of jurisdiction is instead "best read as having been enacted on the understanding that the common law would provide a cause of action for [a] modest number of international law violations." *Id.,* at 724. We thus held that federal courts may "recognize private claims [for such violations] under federal common law." *Id.,* at 732. The Court in *Sosa* rejected the plaintiff's claim in that case for "arbitrary arrest and detention," on the ground that it failed to state a violation of the law of nations with the requisite "definite content and acceptance among civilized nations." *Id.,* at 699, 732.

The question here is not whether petitioners have stated a proper claim under the ATS, but whether a claim may reach conduct occurring in the territory of a foreign sovereign. Respondents contend that claims under the ATS do not, relying primarily on a canon of statutory interpretation known as the presumption against extraterritorial application. That canon provides that "[w]hen a statute gives no clear indication of an extraterritorial application, it has none," *Morrison v. National Australia Bank Ltd.,* 561 U.S. ——, —— (2010), and reflects the "presumption that United States law governs domestically but does not rule the world," *Microsoft Corp. v. AT & T Corp.,* 550 U.S. 437, 454 (2007).

This presumption "serves to protect against unintended clashes between our laws and those of other nations which could result in international discord." *EEOC v. Arabian American Oil Co.,* 499 U.S. 244, 248 (1991) (*Aramco*). As this Court has explained:

> "For us to run interference in . . . a delicate field of international relations there must be present the affirmative intention of the Congress clearly expressed. It alone has the facilities necessary to make fairly such an important policy decision where the possibilities of international discord are so evident and retaliative action so certain." *Benz v. Compania Naviera Hidalgo, S. A.,* 353 U.S. 138 (1957). The presumption against extraterritorial application helps ensure that the Judiciary does not erroneously adopt an interpretation of U.S. law that carries foreign policy consequences not clearly intended by the political branches.

We typically apply the presumption to discern whether an Act of Congress regulating conduct applies abroad. See, *e.g., Aramco, supra,* at 246 ("These cases present the issue whether Title VII applies extraterritorially to regulate the employment practices of United States employers who employ United States citizens abroad"); *Morrison, supra,* at —— (noting that the question of extraterritorial application was a "merits question," not a question of jurisdiction). The ATS, on the other hand, is "strictly jurisdictional." *Sosa,* 542 U.S., at 713. It does not directly regulate conduct or afford relief. It instead allows federal courts to recognize certain causes of action based on sufficiently definite norms of international law. But we think the principles underlying the canon of interpretation similarly constrain courts considering causes of action that may be brought under the ATS.

Indeed, the danger of unwarranted judicial interference in the conduct of foreign policy is magnified in the context of the ATS, because the question is not what Congress has done but instead what courts may do. This Court in *Sosa* repeatedly stressed the need for judicial caution in considering which claims could be brought under the ATS, in light of foreign policy concerns. As the Court explained, "the potential [foreign policy] implications . . . of recognizing . . . causes [under the ATS] should make courts particularly wary of impinging on the discretion of the Legislative and Executive Branches in managing foreign affairs." *Id.,* at 727; see also *id.,* at 727-728 ("Since many attempts by federal courts to craft remedies for the violation of new norms of international law would raise risks of adverse foreign policy consequences, they should be undertaken, if at all, with great caution"); *id.,* at 727 ("[T]he possible collateral consequences of making international rules privately actionable argue for judicial caution"). These concerns, which are implicated in any case arising under the ATS, are all the more pressing when the question is whether a cause of action under the ATS reaches conduct within the territory of another sovereign.

These concerns are not diminished by the fact that *Sosa* limited federal courts to recognizing causes of action only for alleged violations of international law norms that are "'specific, universal, and obligatory.'" *Id.*, at 732 (quoting *In re Estate of Marcos, Human Rights Litigation,* 25 F.3d 1467, 1475 (C.A.9 1994)). As demonstrated by Congress's enactment of the Torture Victim Protection Act of 1991, 106 Stat. 73, note following 28 U.S.C. §1350, identifying such a norm is only the beginning of defining a cause of action. See *id.,* §3 (providing detailed definitions for extrajudicial killing and torture); *id.,* §2 (specifying who may be liable, creating a rule of exhaustion, and establishing a statute of limitations). Each of these decisions carries with it significant foreign policy implications.

The principles underlying the presumption against extraterritoriality thus constrain courts exercising their power under the ATS.

III

Petitioners contend that even if the presumption applies, the text, history, and purposes of the ATS rebut it for causes of action brought under that statute. It is true that Congress, even in a jurisdictional provision, can indicate that it intends federal law to apply to conduct occurring abroad. See, *e.g.,* 18 U.S.C. §1091(e) (2006 ed., Supp. V) (providing jurisdiction over the offense of genocide "regardless of where the offense is committed" if the alleged offender is, among other things, "present in the United States"). But to rebut the presumption, the ATS would need to evince a "clear indication of extraterritoriality." *Morrison,* 561 U.S., at ——. It does not.

To begin, nothing in the text of the statute suggests that Congress intended causes of action recognized under it to have extraterritorial reach. The ATS covers actions by aliens for violations of the law of nations, but that does not imply extraterritorial reach — such violations affecting aliens can occur either within or outside the United States. Nor does the fact that the text reaches "*any* civil action" suggest application to torts committed abroad; it is well established that generic terms like "any" or "every" do not rebut the presumption against extraterritoriality.

Petitioners make much of the fact that the ATS provides jurisdiction over civil actions for "torts" in violation of the law of nations. They claim that in using that word, the First Congress "necessarily meant to provide for jurisdiction over extraterritorial transitory torts that could arise on foreign soil." For support, they cite the common-law doctrine that allowed courts to assume jurisdiction over such "transitory torts," including actions for personal injury, arising abroad. See *Mostyn v. Fabrigas,* 1 Cowp. 161, 177, 98 Eng. Rep. 1021, 1030 (1774) (Mansfield, L.) ("[A]ll actions of a transitory naturc that arise abroad may be laid as happening in an English county"); *Dennick v. Railroad Co.,* 103 U.S. 11, 18 (1881) ("Wherever, by either the common law or the statute law of a State, a right of action has become fixed and a legal liability incurred, that liability may be enforced and the right of action pursued in any court which has jurisdiction of such matters and can obtain jurisdiction of the parties").

Under the transitory torts doctrine, however, "the only justification for allowing a party to recover when the cause of action arose in another civilized jurisdiction is a well founded belief that it was a cause of action in that place." *Cuba R. Co. v. Crosby,* 222 U.S. 473, 479 (1912) (majority opinion of Holmes, J.). The question under *Sosa* is not whether a federal court has jurisdiction to entertain a cause of action provided by foreign or even international law. The question is instead whether the court has authority to recognize a cause of action under U.S. law to enforce a norm of international law. The reference to "tort" does not demonstrate that the First Congress "necessarily meant" for those causes of action to reach conduct in the territory of a foreign sovereign. In the end, nothing in the text of the ATS evinces the requisite clear indication of extraterritoriality.

Nor does the historical background against which the ATS was enacted overcome the presumption against application to conduct in the territory of another sovereign. See *Morrison, supra,* at —— (noting that "[a]ssuredly context can be consulted" in determining whether a cause of action applies abroad). We explained in *Sosa* that when Congress passed the ATS, "three principal offenses against the law of nations" had been identified by Blackstone: violation of safe conducts, infringement of the rights of ambassadors, and piracy. 542 U.S., at 723, 724; see 4 W. Blackstone, Commentaries on the Laws of England 68 (1769). The first two offenses have no necessary extraterritorial application. Indeed, Blackstone — in describing them — did so in terms of conduct occurring within the forum nation. See *ibid.* (describing the right of safe conducts for those "who are here"); 1 *id.,* at 251 (1765) (explaining that safe conducts grant a member of one society "a right to intrude into another"); *id.,* at 245-248 (recognizing the king's power to "receiv[e] ambassadors at home" and detailing their rights in the state "wherein they are appointed to reside").

Two notorious episodes involving violations of the law of nations occurred in the United States shortly before passage of the ATS. Each concerned the rights of ambassadors, and each involved conduct within the Union. In 1784, a French adventurer verbally and physically assaulted Francis Barbe Marbois — the Secretary of the French Legion — in Philadelphia. The assault led the French Minister Plenipotentiary to lodge a formal protest with the Continental Congress and threaten to leave the country unless an adequate remedy were provided. *Respublica v. De Longschamps,* 1 Dall. 111 (O.T. Phila.1784); *Sosa, supra,* at 716-717, and n.11. And in 1787, a New York constable entered the Dutch Ambassador's house and arrested one of his domestic servants. See Casto, The Federal Courts' Protective Jurisdiction over Torts Committed in Violation of the Law of Nations, 18 Conn. L. Rev. 467, 494 (1986). At the request of Secretary of Foreign Affairs John Jay, the Mayor of New York City arrested the constable in turn, but cautioned that because "'neither Congress nor our [State] Legislature have yet passed any act respecting a breach of the privileges of Ambassadors,'" the extent of any available relief would depend on the common law. See Bradley, The Alien Tort Statute and Article III, 42 Va. J. Int'l L. 587, 641-642 (2002) (quoting 3 Dept. of State, The Diplomatic Correspondence of the United States of America 447 (1837)). The two cases in which the ATS was invoked shortly after its passage also concerned conduct within the territory of the United States. See *Bolchos,* 3 F. Cas. 810 (wrongful seizure of slaves from a vessel while in port in the United States); *Moxon,* 17 F. Cas. 942 (wrongful seizure in United States territorial waters).

These prominent contemporary examples — immediately before and after passage of the ATS — provide no support for the proposition that Congress expected causes of action to be brought under the statute for violations of the law of nations occurring abroad.

The third example of a violation of the law of nations familiar to the Congress that enacted the ATS was piracy. Piracy typically occurs on the high seas, beyond the territorial jurisdiction of the United States or any other country. See 4 Blackstone, *supra,* at 72 ("The offence of piracy, by common law, consists of committing those acts of robbery and depredation upon the high seas, which, if committed upon land, would have amounted to felony there"). This Court has generally treated the high seas the same as foreign soil for purposes of the presumption against extraterritorial application. See, *e.g., Sale v. Haitian Centers Council, Inc.,* 509 U.S. 155, 173-174 (1993) (declining to apply a provision of the Immigration and Nationality Act to conduct occurring on the high seas); *Argentine Republic v. Amerada Hess Shipping Corp.,* 488 U.S. 428, 440 (1989) (declining to apply a provision of the Foreign Sovereign Immunities Act of 1976 to the high seas). Petitioners contend that because Congress surely intended the ATS to provide jurisdiction for actions against pirates, it necessarily anticipated the statute would apply to conduct occurring abroad.

Applying U.S. law to pirates, however, does not typically impose the sovereign will of the United States onto conduct occurring within the territorial jurisdiction of another sovereign, and therefore carries less direct foreign policy consequences. Pirates were fair game wherever found, by any nation, because they generally did not operate within any jurisdiction. See 4 Blackstone, *supra,* at 71. We do not think that the existence of a cause of action against them is a sufficient basis for concluding that other causes of action under the ATS reach conduct that does occur within the territory of another sovereign; pirates may well be a category unto themselves. See *Morrison,* 561 U.S., at —— ("[W]hen a statute provides for some extraterritorial application, the presumption against extraterritoriality operates to limit that provision to its terms"). . . .

Finally, there is no indication that the ATS was passed to make the United States a uniquely hospitable forum for the enforcement of international norms. As Justice Story put it, "No nation has ever yet pretended to be the custos morum of the whole world. . . ." *United States v. The La Jeune Eugenie,* 26 F. Cas. 832, 847 (No. 15,551) (CC. Mass.1822). It is implausible to suppose that the First Congress wanted their fledgling Republic — struggling to receive international recognition — to be the first. Indeed, the parties offer no evidence that any nation, meek or mighty, presumed to do such a thing.

The United States was, however, embarrassed by its potential inability to provide judicial relief to foreign officials injured in the United States. Bradley, 42 Va. J. Int'l L., at 641. Such offenses against ambassadors violated the law of nations, "and if not adequately redressed could rise to an issue of war." *Sosa,* 542 U.S., at 715. The ATS ensured that the United States could provide a forum for adjudicating such incidents. See *Sosa, supra,* at 715-718, and n.11. Nothing about this historical context suggests that Congress also intended federal common law under the ATS to provide a cause of action for conduct occurring in the territory of another sovereign.

Indeed, far from avoiding diplomatic strife, providing such a cause of action could have generated it. Recent experience bears this out. See *Doe v. Exxon Mobil Corp.,* 654 F.3d 11, 77-78 (C.A.D.C. 2011) (Kavanaugh, J., dissenting in part) (listing recent objections to extraterritorial applications of the ATS by Canada, Germany, Indonesia, Papua New Guinea, South Africa, Switzerland, and the United Kingdom). Moreover, accepting petitioners' view would imply that other nations, also applying the law of nations, could hale our citizens into their courts for alleged violations of the law of nations occurring in the United States, or anywhere else in the world. The presumption against extraterritoriality guards against our courts triggering such serious foreign policy consequences, and instead defers such decisions, quite appropriately, to the political branches.

We therefore conclude that the presumption against extraterritoriality applies to claims under the ATS, and that nothing in the statute rebuts that presumption. "[T]here is no clear indication of extraterritoriality here," *Morrison,* 561 U.S., at ——, and petitioners' case seeking relief for violations of the law of nations occurring outside the United States is barred.

IV

On these facts, all the relevant conduct took place outside the United States. And even where the claims touch and concern the territory of the United States, they must do so with sufficient force to displace the presumption against extraterritorial application. See *Morrison,* 561 U.S. ——. Corporations are often present in many countries, and it would reach too far to say that mere corporate presence suffices. If Congress were to determine otherwise, a statute more specific than the ATS would be required.

The judgment of the Court of Appeals is affirmed.

It is so ordered.

Justice KENNEDY, concurring. The opinion for the Court is careful to leave open a number of significant questions regarding the reach and interpretation of the Alien Tort Statute. In my view that is a proper disposition. Many serious concerns with respect to human rights abuses committed abroad have been addressed by Congress in statutes such as the Torture Victim Protection Act of 1991 (TVPA), 106 Stat. 73, note following 28 U.S.C. §1350, and that class of cases will be determined in the future according to the detailed statutory scheme Congress has enacted. Other cases may arise with allegations of serious violations of international law principles protecting persons, cases covered neither by the TVPA nor by the reasoning and holding of today's case; and in those disputes the proper implementation of the presumption against extraterritorial application may require some further elaboration and explanation.

Justice ALITO, with whom Justice THOMAS joins, concurring. I concur in the judgment and join the opinion of the Court as far as it goes. Specifically, I agree that when Alien Tort Statute (ATS) "claims touch and concern the territory of the United States, they must do so with sufficient force to displace the presumption against extraterritorial application." *Ante,* at 14. This formulation obviously leaves much unanswered, and perhaps there is wisdom in the Court's preference for this narrow approach. I write separately to set out the broader standard that leads me to the conclusion that this case falls within the scope of the presumption.

In *Morrison v. National Australia Bank Ltd.,* 561 U.S. —— (2010), we explained that "the presumption against extraterritorial application would be a craven watchdog indeed if it retreated to its kennel whenever *some* domestic activity is involved in the case." *Id.,* at ——. We also reiterated that a cause of action falls outside the scope of the presumption — and thus is not barred by the presumption — only if the event or relationship that was "the 'focus' of congressional concern" under the relevant statute takes place within the United States. *Ibid.* (quoting *EEOC v. Arabian American Oil Co.,* 499 U.S. 244, 255 (1991)). For example, because "the focus of the [Securities] Exchange Act [of 1934] is not upon the place where the deception originated, but upon purchases and sales of securities in the United States," we held in *Morrison* that §10(b) of the Exchange Act applies "only" to "transactions in securities listed on domestic exchanges, and domestic transactions in other securities." 561 U.S., at ——-——.

The Court's decision in *Sosa v. Alvarez–Machain,* 542 U.S. 692 (2004), makes clear that when the ATS was enacted, "congressional concern" was "'focus[ed],'" *Morrison, supra,* at ——, on the "three principal offenses against the law of nations" that had been identified by Blackstone: violation of safe conducts, infringement of the rights of ambassadors, and piracy, *Sosa,* 542 U.S., at 723-724. The Court therefore held that "federal courts should not recognize private claims under federal common law for violations of any international law norm with less definite content and acceptance among civilized nations than the historical paradigms familiar when [the ATS] was enacted." *Id.,* at 732. In other words, only conduct that satisfies *Sosa*'s requirements of definiteness and acceptance among civilized nations can be said to have been "the 'focus' of congressional concern," *Morrison, supra,* at ——, when Congress enacted the ATS. As a result, a putative ATS cause of action will fall within the scope of the presumption against extraterritoriality — and will therefore be barred — unless the domestic conduct is sufficient to violate an international law norm that satisfies *Sosa*'s requirements of definiteness and acceptance among civilized nations.

Justice BREYER, with whom Justice GINSBURG, Justice SOTOMAYOR and Justice KAGAN join, concurring in the judgment. I agree with the Court's conclusion but not with its reasoning. . . .

Unlike the Court, I would not invoke the presumption against extraterritoriality. Rather, guided in part by principles and practices of foreign relations law, I would find jurisdiction under this statute where (1) the alleged tort occurs on American soil, (2) the defendant is an American national, or (3) the defendant's conduct substantially and adversely affects an important American national interest, and that includes a distinct interest in preventing the United States from becoming a safe harbor (free of civil as well as criminal liability) for a torturer or other common enemy of mankind. See *Sosa v. Alvarez-Machain,* 542 U.S. 692, 732 (2004) ("'[F]or purposes of civil liability, the torturer has become — like the pirate and slave trader before him — *hostis humani generis,* an enemy of all mankind.'" (quoting *Filartiga v. Pena-Irala,* 630 F.2d 876, 890 (C.A.2 1980) (alteration in original))). See also 1 Restatement (Third) of Foreign Relations Law of the United States §§402, 403, 404 (1986). In this case, however, the parties and relevant conduct lack sufficient ties to the United States for the ATS to provide jurisdiction.

I

A

Our decision in *Sosa* frames the question. In *Sosa* the Court specified that the Alien Tort Statute (ATS), when enacted in 1789, "was intended as jurisdictional." 542 U.S., at 714. We added that the statute gives today's courts the power to apply certain "judge-made" damages law to victims of certain foreign affairs-related misconduct, including "three specific offenses" to which "Blackstone referred," namely "violation of safe conducts, infringement of the rights of ambassadors, and piracy." *Id.,* at 715. We held that the statute provides today's federal judges with the power to fashion "a cause of action" for a "modest number" of claims, "based on the present-day law of nations," and which "rest on a norm of international character accepted by the civilized world and defined with a specificity comparable to the features" of those three "18th-century paradigms." *Id.,* at 724-725.

. . . Adjudicating any such claim must, in my view, also be consistent with those notions of comity that lead each nation to respect the sovereign rights of other nations by limiting the reach of its own laws and their enforcement. *Id.,* at 761 (Breyer, J., concurring in part and concurring in judgment).

Recognizing that Congress enacted the ATS to permit recovery of damages from pirates and others who violated basic international law norms as understood in 1789, *Sosa* essentially leads today's judges to ask: Who are today's pirates? See 542 U.S., at 724-725 (majority opinion). We provided a framework for answering that question by setting down principles drawn from international norms and designed to limit ATS claims to those that are similar in character and specificity to piracy. *Id.,* at 725.

In this case we must decide the extent to which this jurisdictional statute opens a federal court's doors to those harmed by activities belonging to the limited class that *Sosa* set forth *when those activities take place abroad.* To help answer this question here, I would refer both to *Sosa* and, as in *Sosa,* to norms of international law.

B

In my view the majority's effort to answer the question by referring to the "presumption against extraterritoriality" does not work well. That presumption "rests on the perception that Congress ordinarily legislates with respect to domestic, not foreign matters." *Morrison v. National Australia Bank Ltd.*, 561 U.S. ——, —— (2010). The ATS, however, was enacted with "foreign matters" in mind. The statute's text refers explicitly to "alien[s]," "treat[ies]," and "the law of nations." 28 U.S.C. §1350. The statute's purpose was to address "violations of the law of nations, admitting of a judicial remedy and at the same time threatening serious consequences in international affairs." *Sosa,* 542 U.S., at 715. And at least one of the three kinds of activities that we found to fall within the statute's scope, namely piracy, *ibid.,* normally takes place abroad. See 4 W. Blackstone, Commentaries on the Law of England 72 (1769). The majority cannot wish this piracy example away by emphasizing that piracy takes place on the high seas. See *ante,* at 10. That is because the robbery and murder that make up piracy do not normally take place in the water; they take place on a ship. And a ship is like land, in that it falls within the jurisdiction of the nation whose flag it flies. See *McCulloch v. Sociedad Nacional de Marineros de Honduras,* 372 U.S. 10, 20-21 (1963); 2 Restatement §502, Comment *d* ("[F]lag state has jurisdiction to prescribe with respect to any activity aboard the ship"). Indeed, in the early 19th century Chief Justice Marshall described piracy as an "offenc[e] against the nation under whose flag the vessel sails, and within whose particular jurisdiction all on board the vessel are." *United States v. Palmer,* 3 Wheat. 610, 632 (1818). See *United States v. Furlong,* 5 Wheat. 184, 197, 5 L.Ed. 64 (1820) (a crime committed "within the jurisdiction" of a foreign state and a crime committed "in the vessel of another nation" are "the same thing").

The majority nonetheless tries to find a distinction between piracy at sea and similar cases on land. . . . But, as I have just pointed out, "[a]pplying U.S. law to pirates" *does* typically involve applying our law to acts taking place within the jurisdiction of another sovereign. Nor can the majority's words "territorial jurisdiction" sensibly distinguish land from sea for purposes of isolating adverse foreign policy risks, as the Barbary Pirates, the War of 1812, the sinking of the *Lusitania,* and the Lockerbie bombing make all too clear.

The majority also writes, "Pirates were fair game wherever found, by any nation, because they generally did not operate within any jurisdiction." *Ibid.* I very much agree that pirates were fair game "wherever found." Indeed, that is the point. That is why we asked, in *Sosa,* who are today's pirates? Certainly today's pirates include torturers and perpetrators of genocide. And today, like the pirates of old, they are "fair game" where they are found. Like those pirates, they are "common enemies of all mankind and all nations have an equal interest in their apprehension and punishment." 1 Restatement §404 Reporters' Note 1, p. 256 (quoting *In re Demjanjuk,* 612 F. Supp. 544, 556 (N.D. Ohio 1985) (internal quotation marks omitted)). See *Sosa, supra,* at 732. And just as a nation that harbored pirates provoked the concern of other nations in past centuries, so harboring "common enemies of all mankind" provokes similar concerns today.

Thus the Court's reasoning, as applied to the narrow class of cases that *Sosa* described, fails to provide significant support for the use of any presumption against extraterritoriality; rather, it suggests the contrary.

In any event, as the Court uses its "presumption against extraterritorial application," it offers only limited help in deciding the question presented, namely "'under what circumstances the Alien Tort Statute . . . allows courts to recognize a cause of action for violations of the law of nations occurring within the territory of a sovereign other than the United States.'" 565 U.S. —— (2012). The majority echoes in this jurisdictional context *Sosa*'s warning to use "caution" in shaping federal common-law causes of action. *Ante,* at 5. But it also makes clear that a statutory claim might sometimes "touch and concern the territory of the United States . . . with sufficient force to displace the presumption." *Ante,* at 14. It leaves for another day the determination of just when the presumption against extraterritoriality might be "overcome." *Ante,* at 8.

II

In applying the ATS to acts "occurring within the territory of a[nother] sovereign," I would assume that Congress intended the statute's jurisdictional reach to match the statute's underlying substantive grasp. That grasp, defined by the statute's purposes set forth in *Sosa,* includes compensation for those injured by piracy and its modern-day equivalents, at least where allowing such compensation avoids "serious" negative international "consequences" for the United States. 542 U.S., at 715. And just as we have looked to established international substantive norms to help determine the statute's substantive reach, *id.,* at 729, so we should look to international jurisdictional norms to help determine the statute's jurisdictional scope.

The Restatement (Third) of Foreign Relations Law is helpful. Section 402 recognizes that, subject to §403's "reasonableness" requirement, a nation may apply its law (for example, federal common law, see 542 U.S., at 729-730) not only (1) to "conduct" that "takes place [or to persons or things] within its territory" but also (2) to the "activities, interests, status, or relations of its nationals outside as well as within its territory," (3) to "conduct outside its territory that has or is intended to have substantial effect within its territory," and (4) to certain foreign "conduct outside its territory . . . that is directed against the security of the state or against a limited class of other state interests." In addition, §404 of the Restatement explains that a "state has jurisdiction to define and prescribe punishment for certain offenses recognized by the community of nations as of universal concern, such as piracy, slave trade," and analogous behavior.

Considering these jurisdictional norms in light of both the ATS's basic purpose (to provide compensation for those injured by today's pirates) and *Sosa*'s basic caution (to avoid international friction), I believe that the statute provides jurisdiction where (1) the alleged tort occurs on American soil, (2) the defendant is an American national, or (3) the defendant's conduct substantially and adversely affects an important American national interest, and that includes a distinct interest in preventing the United States from becoming a safe harbor (free of civil as well as criminal liability) for a torturer or other common enemy of mankind.

I would interpret the statute as providing jurisdiction only where distinct American interests are at issue. Doing so reflects the fact that Congress adopted the present statute at a time when, as Justice Story put it, "No nation ha[d] ever yet pretended to be the custos morum of the whole world." *United States v. La Jeune Eugenie,* 26 F. Cas. 832, 847 (No. 15,551) (CC Mass. 1822). That restriction also should help to minimize international friction. Further limiting principles such as exhaustion, *forum non conveniens,* and comity would do the same. So would a practice of courts giving weight to the views of the Executive Branch. See *Sosa,* 542 U.S., at 733, n.21; *id.,* at 761 (opinion of Breyer, J.).

As I have indicated, we should treat this Nation's interest in not becoming a safe harbor for violators of the most fundamental international norms as an important jurisdiction-related interest justifying application of the ATS in light of the statute's basic purposes — in particular that of compensating those who have suffered harm at the hands of, *e.g.,* torturers or other modern pirates. Nothing in the statute or its history suggests that our courts should turn a blind eye to the plight of victims in that "handful of heinous actions." *Tel-Oren v.*

Libyan Arab Republic, 726 F.2d 774, 781 (C.A.D.C. 1984) (Edwards, J., concurring). To the contrary, the statute's language, history, and purposes suggest that the statute was to be a weapon in the "war" against those modern pirates who, by their conduct, have "declar[ed] war against all mankind." 4 Blackstone 71.

International norms have long included a duty not to permit a nation to become a safe harbor for pirates (or their equivalent). . . .

More recently two lower American courts have, in effect, rested jurisdiction primarily upon that kind of concern. In *Filartiga,* 630 F.2d 876, an alien plaintiff brought a lawsuit against an alien defendant for damages suffered through acts of torture that the defendant allegedly inflicted in a foreign nation, Paraguay. Neither plaintiff nor defendant was an American national and the actions underlying the lawsuit took place abroad. The defendant, however, "had . . . resided in the United States for more than ninth months" before being sued, having overstayed his visitor's visa. *Id.,* at 878-879. Jurisdiction was deemed proper because the defendant's alleged conduct violated a well-established international law norm, and the suit vindicated our Nation's interest in not providing a safe harbor, free of damages claims, for those defendants who commit such conduct.

In *Marcos,* the plaintiffs were nationals of the Philippines, the defendant was a Philippine national, and the alleged wrongful act, death by torture, took place abroad. *In re Estate of Marcos, Human Rights Litigation,* 25 F.3d 1467, 1469, 1475 (C.A.9 1994); *In re Estate of Marcos Human Rights Litigation,* 978 F.2d 493, 495-496, 500 (C.A.9 1992). A month before being sued, the defendant, "his family, . . . and others loyal to [him] fled to Hawaii," where the ATS case was heard. *Marcos,* 25 F.3d, at 1469. As in *Filartiga,* the court found ATS jurisdiction.

And in *Sosa* we referred to both cases with approval, suggesting that the ATS allowed a claim for relief in such circumstances. 542 U.S., at 732. Not surprisingly, both before and after *Sosa,* courts have consistently rejected the notion that the ATS is categorically barred from extraterritorial application.

Application of the statute in the way I have suggested is consistent with international law and foreign practice. . . .

Many countries permit foreign plaintiffs to bring suits against their own nationals based on unlawful conduct that took place abroad.

Other countries permit some form of lawsuit brought by a foreign national against a foreign national, based upon conduct taking place abroad and seeking damages. Certain countries, which find "universal" criminal "jurisdiction" to try perpetrators of particularly heinous crimes such as piracy and genocide, see Restatement §404, also permit private persons injured by that conduct to pursue "*actions civiles,*" seeking civil damages in the criminal proceeding. . . .

At the same time Congress has ratified treaties obliging the United States to find and punish foreign perpetrators of serious crimes committed against foreign persons abroad. See Convention on the Prevention and Punishment of Crimes Against Internationally Protected Persons, Including Diplomatic Agents, Dec. 28, 1973, 28 U.S.T.1975, T.I.A.S. No. 8532; Convention for the Suppression of Unlawful Acts Against the Safety of Civil Aviation, Sept. 23, 1971, 24 U.S.T. 565, T.I.A.S. No. 7570; Convention for the Suppression of Unlawful Seizure of Aircraft, Dec. 16, 1970, 22 U.S.T. 1641, T.I.A.S. No. 7192.

And Congress has sometimes authorized civil damages in such cases. See generally note following 28 U.S.C. §1350 (Torture Victim Protection Act of 1991 (TVPA) (private damages action for torture or extrajudicial killing committed under authority of a foreign nation)); S. Rep. No. 102-249, p. 4 (1991) (ATS "should not be replaced" by TVPA); H.R. Rep. No. 102-367, pt. 1, p. 4 (TVPA intended to "enhance the remedy already available under" the ATS). But cf. *Mohamad v. Palestinian Authority,* 566 U.S. —— (2012) (TVPA allows suits against only natural persons). . . .

Thus, the jurisdictional approach that I would use is analogous to, and consistent with, the approaches of a number of other nations. It is consistent with the approaches set forth in the Restatement. Its insistence upon the presence of some distinct American interest, its reliance upon courts also invoking other related doctrines such as comity, exhaustion, and *forum non conveniens,* along with its dependence (for its workability) upon courts obtaining, and paying particular attention to, the views of the Executive Branch, all should obviate the majority's concern that our jurisdictional example would lead "other nations, also applying the law of nations," to "hale our citizens into their courts for alleged violations of the law of nations occurring in the United States, or anywhere else in the world." *Ante,* at 13.

Most importantly, this jurisdictional view is consistent with the substantive view of the statute that we took in *Sosa*. This approach would avoid placing the statute's jurisdictional scope at odds with its substantive objectives, holding out "the word of promise" of compensation for victims of the torturer, while "break[ing] it to the hope."

III

Applying these jurisdictional principles to this case, however, I agree with the Court that jurisdiction does not lie. The defendants are two foreign corporations. Their shares, like those of many foreign corporations, are traded on the New York Stock Exchange. Their only presence in the United States consists of an office in New York City (actually owned by a separate but affiliated company) that helps to explain their business to potential investors. The plaintiffs are not United States nationals but nationals of other nations. The conduct at issue took place abroad. And the plaintiffs allege, not that the defendants directly engaged in acts of torture, genocide, or the equivalent, but that they helped others (who are not American nationals) to do so.

Under these circumstances, even if the New York office were a sufficient basis for asserting general jurisdiction, it would be farfetched to believe, based solely upon the defendants' minimal and indirect American presence, that this legal action helps to vindicate a distinct American interest, such as in not providing a safe harbor for an "enemy of all mankind." Thus I agree with the Court that here it would "reach too far to say" that such "mere corporate presence suffices." *Ante,* at 14.

I consequently join the Court's judgment but not its opinion.

[NSL p. 209. Insert as new Note 1a.]

1a. *What Standard Is Congress Incorporating?* In 10 U.S.C. §821, Congress recognized the jurisdiction of military commissions "with respect to offenders or offenses that by statute or by the law of war may be tried by military commissions." *See Ex parte Quirin*, 317 U.S. 1, 27-28 (1942), NSL p. 823. In *Hamdan v. United States (Hamdan II)*, 696 F.3d 1238 (D.C. Cir. 2012), reproduced at p. 206 in this *Supplement*, a D.C. Circuit panel held, inter alia, that with this language Congress necessarily incorporated the *international* laws of war, and not the "U.S. common law of war." *See id.* at 1248 n.8.

The question in *Hamdan II* was how courts should assess *whether* a specific offense was recognized as part of that body of international law. Writing for the majority, and picking up on the themes of his *Al-Bihani* concurrence, Judge Kavanaugh stressed that "the imprecision of customary international law calls for significant caution by U.S. courts before permitting civil or criminal liability premised on violation of such a vague prohibition." *Id.* at 1250 n.10. He analogized to the Supreme Court's interpretation of the Alien Tort Statute in *Sosa v. Alvarez-Machain*, 542 U.S. 692 (2004), NSL p. 189, to hold that "imposing liability on the basis of a violation of 'international law' or the 'law of nations' or the 'law of war' generally must be based on norms firmly grounded in international law." 696 F.3d at 1250 n.10.

The *Sosa* Court ruled that "any claim based on the present-day law of nations [must] rest on a norm of international character accepted by the civilized world and defined with a specificity comparable to the features of the 18th-century paradigms we have recognized." 542 U.S. at 725. Is Judge Kavanaugh's analogy fair? Does it make sense to apply the "firmly grounded" standard to military commissions, thereby preventing, as *Hamdan II* does, military commission trials based upon the crimes of providing material support to terrorism and conspiracy, both well-established criminal offenses in the civilian sphere? For a pre-*Hamdan II* exchange anticipating this very issue, see Conference, *War, Terror, and the Federal Courts, Ten Years After 9/11*, 61 Am. U. L. Rev. 1253, 1280-1281 (2012).

[NSL p. 233, CTL p. 89. Insert at end of chapter.]

Leon Panetta, Secretary of Defense, Remarks to the Business Executives for National Security

New York City, Oct. 11, 2012
available at
http://www.defense.gov/transcripts/transcript.aspx?transcriptid=5136

. . . I'd like to discuss with you an issue at the very nexus of business and national security: the threats facing the United States in cyberspace, and the role the Defense Department must play in defending the nation from those threats. . . .

Cyberspace is the new frontier — full of possibilities to help advance security and prosperity in the 21st century. Yet with these possibilities also come new perils. The Internet is open and highly accessible — as it should be. But that also presents a new terrain for warfare where adversaries can seek to do harm to our country, our economy and our citizens.

When people think of cybersecurity today, they worry about criminals who prowl the Internet and steal people's identities, sensitive business information, or even national security secrets. Those threats are real and exist today.

But the even greater danger facing us in cyberspace goes beyond crime and harassment.

A cyber attack perpetrated by nation states or violent extremist groups could be as destructive as the terrorist attack of 9/11. Such a destructive cyber terrorist attack could paralyze the nation.

Let me give you some examples of the kinds of attacks that we have already experienced.

In recent weeks, as many of you know, some large U.S. financial institutions were hit by so-called "distributed denial of service" attacks. These attacks delayed or disrupted services on customer websites. While this kind of tactic isn't new, the scale and speed [were] unprecedented.

But even more alarming is an attack that happened two months ago, when a sophisticated virus called "Shamoon" infected computers at the Saudi Arabian state oil company, ARAMCO.

Shamoon included a routine called a "wiper," coded to self-execute. This routine replaced crucial system files with an image of a burning U.S. flag. It also put additional "garbage" data that overwrote all the real data on the machine. The more than 30,000 computers it infected were rendered useless, and had to be replaced.

Then just days after this incident, there was a similar attack on Ras Gas of Qatar — a major energy company in the region. All told, the Shamoon virus was probably the most destructive attack that the private sector has seen to date. . . .

These attacks mark a significant escalation of the cyber threat. And they have renewed concerns about still more destructive scenarios that could unfold. For example, we know that foreign cyber actors are probing America's critical infrastructure networks.

They are targeting the computer control systems that operate chemical, electricity and water plants, and those that guide transportation throughout the country.

We know of specific instances where intruders have successfully gained access to these control systems. We also know they are seeking to create advanced tools to attack these systems and cause panic, destruction, and even the loss of life. . . .

An aggressor nation or extremist group could gain control of critical switches and derail passenger trains, or trains loaded with lethal chemicals. They could contaminate the water supply in major cities, or shut down the power grid across large parts of the country.

The most destructive scenarios involve cyber actors launching several attacks on our critical infrastructure at once, in combination with a physical attack on our country. Attackers could also seek to disable or degrade critical military systems and communications networks.

The collective result of these kinds of attacks could be "cyber Pearl Harbor": an attack that would cause physical destruction and loss of life, paralyze and shock the nation, and create a profound new sense of vulnerability.

As director of CIA and now secretary of defense, I have understood that cyber threats are every bit as real as more well-known threats like terrorism, nuclear weapons proliferation, and the turmoil in the Middle East. And the cyber threats facing this country are growing. With dramatic advances in cyber technology, potential aggressors are exploiting vulnerabilities in our security.

But the good news is that we are aware of this potential; our eyes are wide open to these threats; and we are a nation at the cutting edge of this new technology.

The Department of Defense, in large part through the capabilities of the National Security Agency, has developed the world's most sophisticated system to detect cyber intruders or attackers. And we are acting aggressively to get ahead of this problem — putting in place measures to stop cyber attacks dead in their tracks.

We are doing this as part of a broad "whole of government" effort to confront cyber threats. The Department of Homeland Security has the lead for domestic cybersecurity. The FBI also has a key part to play investigating and preventing cyber attacks. And our intelligence agencies are focused on this potential threat. The State Department is forging an international consensus on the roles and responsibilities of nations to help secure cyberspace.

The Department of Defense also has a role. It is a supporting role. But it is an essential one. . . . I want to explain what that means.

But first, let me make clear what it does not mean. It does not mean the Defense Department will monitor citizens' personal computers, or provide for the day-to-day security of private and commercial networks. That is not our mission.

Our mission is to defend this nation. We defend. We deter. And if called upon, we take decisive action. In the past, we have done so through operations on land and at sea, in the skies and in space. In this new century, the United States military must help defend the nation in cyberspace as well.

If a foreign adversary attacked U.S. soil, the American people expect their national defense forces to respond. If a crippling cyber attack were launched against our nation, the American people must be protected. And if the Commander-in-Chief orders a response, the Defense Department must be ready to act.

To ensure we fulfill our role to defend the nation in cyberspace, the department is focusing on three main tracks: (1) developing new capabilities; (2) putting in place the policies and organizations we need to execute our mission, and; (3) building more effective cooperation with industry and international partners.

1. Develop new capabilities: DoD is investing more than $3 billion annually in cybersecurity to retain cutting-edge capabilities in this field. Following our new defense strategy, the department is continuing to increase many key investments in cybersecurity even in an era of fiscal restraint. . . .

. . . DoD is already in an intense daily struggle against thousands of cyber actors who probe the Defense Department's networks millions of times per day. Through the innovative efforts of our cyber operators, we are enhancing the department's cyber defense programs. These systems rely on sensors and software to hunt down malicious code before it harms our systems. We actively share our own experience defending our systems with those running the nation's critical private sector networks.

In addition to defending the department's networks, we also help deter attacks. Our cyber adversaries will be far less likely to hit us if they know we will be able to link them to the attack, or that their effort will fail against our strong defenses. The department has made significant advances in solving a problem that makes deterring cyber adversaries more complex: the difficulty of identifying the origins of an attack.

Over the last two years, the department has made significant investments in forensics to address this problem of attribution, and we are seeing returns on those investments. Potential aggressors should be aware that the United States has the capacity to locate them and hold them accountable for actions that harm America or its interests.

But we won't succeed in preventing a cyber attack through improved defenses alone. If we detect an imminent threat of attack that will cause significant physical destruction or kill American citizens, we need to have the option to take action to defend the nation when directed by the president.

For these kinds of scenarios, the department has developed the capability to conduct effective operations to counter threats to our national interests in cyberspace. . . .

. . . [W]e will only do so in a manner consistent with the policy principles and legal frameworks that the department follows for other domains, including the law of armed conflict. . . .

2. Policies and organizations: Responding to the cyber threat requires the right policies and organizations across the federal government. For the past year, the Department of Defense has been working closely with other agencies across the government to understand where the lines of responsibility in cyber defense will be drawn and how those responsibilities will be executed.

As part of that effort, the department is now finalizing the most comprehensive change to our rules of engagement in cyberspace in seven years. The new rules will make clear that the department has a responsibility not only to defend DoD's networks, but also to be prepared to defend the nation and our national interests against an attack in or through cyberspace. . . .

Three years ago, the department took a major step forward by establishing the United States Cyber Command.

Under the leadership of Gen. Keith Alexander, a four-star officer who also serves as the director of the National Security Agency, Cyber Command has matured into a world-class organization.

Cyber Command has the capacity to conduct a full range of missions in cyberspace. It is also working to develop a common, real-time understanding of the threats in cyberspace. That threat picture could be quickly shared with DoD's geographic and functional combatant commands, with DHS and FBI, and other agencies in government. After all, we need to see an attack coming in order to defend against it. . . .

3. Build stronger partnerships: As I've made clear, securing cyberspace is not the responsibility of the United States military, or even the sole responsibility of the United States government.

The private sector, government, military and our allies all share the same global infrastructure — and we all share the responsibility to protect it. Therefore, we are deepening cooperation with our closest allies with a goal of sharing threat information, maximizing shared capabilities and deterring malicious activities. . . .

Ultimately, no one has a greater interest in cybersecurity than the businesses that depend on a safe, secure and resilient global digital infrastructure — particularly those who operate the critical networks we must help defend.

To defend those networks more effectively, we must share information between the government and the private sector about threats in cyberspace.

We have made real progress in sharing information with the private sector, but we need Congress to act to ensure this sharing is timely and comprehensive. Companies should be able to share specific threat information with the government without the prospect of lawsuits hanging over their head. And a key principle must be to protect the fundamental liberties and privacy in cyberspace that we are all duty-bound to uphold. . . .

Working with the business community, we need to develop baseline standards for our most critical private-sector infrastructure — including power plants, water treatment facilities and gas pipelines. . . .

Although awareness is growing, the reality is that too few companies have invested in even basic cybersecurity. . . .

Congress must act, and it must act now on a comprehensive bill such as the bipartisan Cybersecurity Act of 2012 . . . . This legislation has bipartisan support, but it has fallen victim to legislative and political gridlock. . . .

While we wait for Congress to act, the administration is looking to enhance cybersecurity measures under existing authorities — by working with the private sector to promote cybersecurity best practices and increase information sharing. Issuing an executive order is one option under consideration.

There is no substitute for comprehensive legislation, but we need to move as far as we can in the meantime. We have no choice because the threat we face is already here. Congress has a responsibility to act. The president has a Constitutional responsibility to defend the country. . . .

This is a pre-9/11 moment. The attackers are plotting. . . .

[NSL p. 233, CTL p. 89. Insert at end of chapter.]

Harold Hongju Koh, Legal Adviser, U.S. Department of State, International Law in Cyberspace

Remarks at USCYBERCOM Inter-Agency Legal
Conference, Ft. Meade, MD, Sept. 18, 2012
transcript available at http://www.state.gov/s/l/releases/remarks/197924.htm

. . . [H]ow do we apply old laws of war to new cyber-circumstances, staying faithful to enduring principles, while accounting for changing times and technologies? . . .

I. International Law in Cyberspace: What We Know . . .

Question 1: Do established principles of international law apply to cyberspace?
Answer 1: Yes, international law principles do apply in cyberspace.

Everyone here knows how cyberspace opens up a host of novel and extremely difficult legal issues. But on this key question, this answer has been apparent, at least as far as the U.S. Government has been concerned.

Significantly, this view has not necessarily been universal in the international community. At least one country has questioned whether existing bodies of international law apply to the cutting edge issues presented by the internet. Some have also said that existing international law is not up to the task, and that we need entirely new treaties to impose a unique set of rules on cyberspace. But the United States has made clear our view that established principles of international law do apply in cyberspace.

Question 2: Is cyberspace a law-free zone, where anything goes?
Answer 2: Emphatically no.

Cyberspace is not a "law-free" zone where anyone can conduct hostile activities without rules or restraint. Think of it this way. This is not the first time that technology has changed and that international law has been asked to deal with those changes. In particular, because the tools of conflict are constantly evolving, one relevant body of law — international humanitarian law, or the law of armed conflict —

affirmatively anticipates technological innovation, and contemplates that its existing rules will apply to such innovation. To be sure, new technologies raise new issues and thus, new questions. Many of us in this room have struggled with such questions, and we will continue to do so over many years. But to those who say that established law is not up to the task, we must articulate and build consensus around how it applies and reassess from there whether and what additional understandings are needed.

Developing common understandings about how these rules apply in the context of cyberactivities in armed conflict will promote stability in this area.

That consensus-building work brings me to some questions and answers we have offered to our international partners to explain how both the law of going to war (*jus ad bellum*) and the laws that apply in conducting war (*jus in bello*) apply to cyberaction.

Question 3: Do cyber activities ever constitute a use of force?
Answer 3: Yes.

Cyber activities may in certain circumstances constitute uses of force within the meaning of Article 2(4) of the UN Charter and customary international law.

In analyzing whether a cyber operation would constitute a use of force, most commentators focus on whether the direct physical injury and property damage resulting from the cyber event looks like that which would be considered a use of force if produced by kinetic weapons. *Cyber activities that proximately result in death, injury, or significant destruction would likely be viewed as a use of force.* In assessing whether an event constituted a use of force in or through cyberspace, we must evaluate factors: including the context of the event, the actor perpetrating the action (recognizing challenging issues of attribution in cyberspace), the target and location, effects and intent, among other possible issues. Commonly cited examples of cyber activity that would constitute a use of force include, for example: (1) operations that trigger a nuclear plant meltdown; (2) operations that open a dam above a populated area causing destruction; or (3) operations that disable air traffic control resulting in airplane crashes. Only a moment's reflection makes you realize that this is common sense: if the physical consequences of a cyber attack work the kind of physical damage that dropping a bomb or firing a missile would, that cyber attack should equally be considered a use of force.

Question 4: May a State ever respond to a computer network attack by exercising a right of national self-defense?
Answer 4: Yes.

A State's national right of self-defense, recognized in Article 51 of the UN Charter, may be triggered by computer network activities that amount to an armed attack or imminent threat thereof. As the United States affirmed in its 2011 International Strategy for Cyberspace, "when warranted, the United States will respond to hostile acts in cyberspace as we would to any other threat to our country."

Question 5: Do *jus in bello* rules apply to computer network attacks?
Answer 5: Yes.

In the context of an armed conflict, the law of armed conflict applies to regulate the use of cyber tools in hostilities, just as it does other tools. The principles of necessity and proportionality limit uses of force in self-defense and would regulate what may constitute a lawful response under the circumstances.

There is no legal requirement that the response to a cyber armed attack take the form of a cyber action, as long as the response meets the requirements of necessity and proportionality.

Question 6: Must attacks distinguish between military and nonmilitary objectives?
Answer 6: Yes.

The *jus in bello* principle of *distinction* applies to computer network attacks undertaken in the context of an armed conflict. The principle of distinction applies to cyber activities that amount to an "attack" — as that term is understood in the law of war — in the context of an armed conflict. As in any form of armed conflict, the principle of distinction requires that the intended effect of the attack must be to harm a legitimate *military* target. We must distinguish military objectives — that is, objects that make an effective contribution to military action and whose destruction would offer a military advantage — from civilian objects, which under international law are generally protected from attack.

Question 7: Must attacks adhere to the principle of proportionality?
Answer 7: Yes.

The *jus in bello* principle of *proportionality* applies to computer network attacks undertaken in the context of an armed conflict. The principle of proportionality prohibits attacks that may be expected to cause incidental loss to civilian life, injury to civilians, or damage to civilian objects that would be excessive in relation to the concrete and direct military advantage anticipated. Parties to an armed conflict must assess what the expected harm to civilians is likely to be, and weigh the risk of such collateral damage against the importance of the expected military advantage to be gained. In the cyber context, this rule requires parties to a conflict to assess: (1) the effects of cyber weapons on both military and civilian infrastructure and users, including shared physical infrastructure (such as a dam or a power grid) that would affect civilians; (2) the potential physical damage that a cyber attack may cause, such as death or injury that may result from effects on critical infrastructure; and (3) the potential effects of a cyber attack on civilian objects that are not military objectives, such as private, civilian computers that hold no military significance, but may be networked to computers that are military objectives.

Question 8: How should States assess their cyber weapons?
Answer 8: States should undertake a legal review of weapons, including those that employ a cyber capability.

Such a review should entail an analysis, for example, of whether a particular capability would be *inherently indiscriminate*, i.e., that it could not be used consistent with the principles of distinction and proportionality. The U.S. Government undertakes at least two stages of legal review of the use of weapons in the context of armed conflict — first, an evaluation of new weapons to determine whether their use would be per se prohibited by the law of war; and second, specific operations employing weapons are always reviewed to ensure that each particular operation is also compliant with the law of war.

Question 9: In this analysis, what role does State sovereignty play?
Answer 9: States conducting activities in cyberspace must take into account the sovereignty of other States, including outside the context of armed conflict.

The physical infrastructure that supports the internet and cyber activities is generally located in sovereign territory and subject to the jurisdiction of the territorial State. Because of the interconnected, interoperable nature of cyberspace, operations targeting networked information infrastructures in one country may create effects in another country. Whenever a State contemplates conducting activities in cyberspace, the sovereignty of other States needs to be considered.

Question 10: Are States responsible when cyber acts are undertaken through proxies?
Answer 10: Yes.

States are legally responsible for activities undertaken through "proxy actors," who act on the State's instructions or under its direction or control. The ability to mask one's identity and geography in cyberspace and the resulting difficulties of timely, high-confidence attribution can create significant challenges for States in identifying, evaluating, and accurately responding to threats. But putting attribution problems aside for a moment, established international law does address the question of proxy actors. States are legally responsible for activities undertaken through putatively private actors, who act on the State's instructions or under its direction or control. If a State exercises a sufficient degree of control over an ostensibly private person or group of persons committing an internationally wrongful act, the State assumes responsibility for the act, just as if official agents of the State itself had committed it. These rules are designed to ensure that States cannot hide behind putatively private actors to engage in conduct that is internationally wrongful.

II. International Law in Cyberspace: Challenges and Uncertainties . . .

Unresolved Question 1: How can a use of force regime take into account all of the novel kinds of effects that States can produce through the click of a button?

. . . [T]here are [some] types of cyber actions that do not have a clear kinetic parallel, which raise profound questions about exactly what we mean by "force." At the same time, the difficulty of reaching a definitive legal conclusion or consensus among States on when and under what circumstances a hostile cyber action would constitute an armed attack does not automatically suggest that we need an entirely new legal framework specific to cyberspace. Outside of the cyber-context, such ambiguities and differences of view have long existed among States.

To cite just one example of this, the United States has for a long time taken the position that the inherent right of self-defense potentially applies against *any* illegal use of force. In our view, there is no threshold for a use of deadly force to qualify as an "armed attack" that may warrant a forcible response. But that is not to say that any illegal use of force triggers the right to use any and all force in response — such responses must still be *necessary* and of course *proportionate*. We recognize, on the other hand, that some other countries and commentators have drawn a distinction between the "use of force" and an "armed attack," and view "armed attack" — triggering the right to self-defense — as a subset of uses of force, which passes a higher threshold of gravity. . . .

Unresolved Question 2: What do we do about "*dual-use* infrastructure" in cyberspace?

As you all know, information and communications infrastructure is often shared between State militaries and private, civilian communities. The law of war requires that civilian infrastructure not be used to seek to immunize military objectives from attack, including in the cyber realm. But how, exactly, are the *jus in bello* rules to be implemented in cyberspace? Parties to an armed conflict will need to assess the potential effects of a cyber attack on computers that are *not* military objectives, such as private, civilian computers that hold no military significance, but may be networked to computers that are valid military objectives. Parties will also need to consider the harm to the civilian uses of such infrastructure in performing the necessary proportionality review. Any number of factual scenarios could arise, however, which will require a careful, fact-intensive legal analysis in each situation.

Unresolved Question 3: How do we address the problem of *attribution* in cyberspace?

As I mentioned earlier, cyberspace significantly increases an actor's ability to engage in attacks with "plausible deniability," by acting through proxies. I noted that legal tools exist to ensure that States are held accountable for those acts. What I want to highlight here is that many of these challenges — in particular, those concerning attribution — are as much questions of technical and policy nature rather than exclusively or even predominantly questions of law. Cyberspace remains a new and dynamic operating environment, and we cannot expect that all answers to the new and confounding questions we face will be *legal* ones. . . .

III. The Role of International Law in a "Smart Power" Approach to Cyberspace

This, in a nutshell, is where we are with regard to cyberconflict: We have begun work to build consensus on a number of answers, but questions continue to arise that must be answered in the months and years ahead. Beyond these questions and answers and unresolved questions, though, lies a much bigger picture, one that we are very focused on at the State Department. . . .

Final Question 1: Is international humanitarian law the only body of international law that applies in cyberspace?
Final Answer 1: No.

As important as international humanitarian law is, it is not the only international law that applies in cyberspace. Obviously, cyberspace has become pervasive in our lives, not just in the national defense arena, but also through social media, publishing and broadcasting, expressions of human rights, and expansion of international commerce, both through online markets and online commercial techniques. Many other bodies of international and national law address those activities, and how those different bodies of law overlap and apply with the laws of cyber conflict is something we will all have to work out over time.

Take human rights. At the same time that cyber activity can pose a threat, we all understand that cyber-communication is increasingly becoming a dominant mode of expression in the 21st century. More and more people express their views not by speaking on a soap box at Speakers' Corner, but by blogging, tweeting, commenting, or posting videos and commentaries. The 1948 Universal Declaration of Human Rights (UDHR) — adopted more than 70 years ago — was remarkably forward-looking in anticipating these trends. It says: "Everyone has the right to freedom of opinion and expression; this right includes freedom to hold opinions without interference and to seek, receive and impart information and ideas *through any media and regardless of frontiers*." (emphasis added) . . .

Final Question for this group: Why should U.S Government lawyers care about international law in cyberspace at all?

The Answer: Because compliance with international law *frees* us to do more, and do more legitimately, in cyberspace, in a way that more fully promotes our national interests. . . .

It is worth noting [that there] is a fundamental difference in philosophy about international law. One way to think about law, whether domestic or international, is as a straitjacket, a pure constraint. This approach posits that nations have serious, legitimate interests, and legal regimes restrict their ability to carry them out. One consequence of this view is that, since law is just something that constrains, it should be resisted whenever possible. Resisting so-called "extensions" of the law to new areas often seems attractive: because, after all, the old laws weren't built for these new challenges anyway, some say, so we should tackle those challenges without the legal straitjacket, while leaving the old laws behind.

But that is *not* the United States Government's view of the law, domestic or international. We see law not as a straitjacket, but as [what] one great university calls it when it confers its diplomas, a body of "wise restraints that make us free." International law is not purely constraint, it frees us and empowers us to do things we could never do without law's legitimacy. If we succeed in promoting a culture of compliance, we will reap the benefits. And if we earn a reputation for compliance, the actions we do take will earn enhanced legitimacy worldwide for their adherence to the rule of law. . . .

[NSL p. 233, CTL p. 89. Insert at end of chapter.]

Presidential Policy Directive/PPD-20 [1]

No date

MEMORANDUM FOR THE VICE PRESIDENT [ET AL.]

SUBJECT: U.S. Cyber Operations Policy (U)

I. Definitions (U) . . .

Cyberspace: The interdependent network of information technology infrastructures that includes the Internet, telecommunications networks, computers, information or communications systems, networks, and embedded processors and controllers. (U)

Network Defense: Programs, activities, and the use of tools necessary to facilitate them conducted on a computer, network, or information or communications system by the owner or with the consent of the owner and, as appropriate, the users for the primary purpose of protecting (1) that computer, network, or system; (2) data stored on, processed on, or transiting that computer, network, or system; or (3) physical and virtual infrastructure controlled by that computer, network, or system. . . . (U)

Cyber Effect: The manipulation, disruption, denial, degradation, or destruction of computers, information or communications systems, networks, physical or virtual infrastructure controlled by computers or information systems, or information resident thereon. (U)

Cyber Collection: Operations and related programs or activities conducted by or on behalf of the United States Government, in or

TOP SECRET/NOFORN
Reason: 1.4(a)(c)(e)(g)
Declassify on: 10/16/37

[1. Published by *The Guardian* on June 7, 2013, at http://www.guardian.co.uk/world/interactive/2013/jun/07/obama-cyber-directive-full-text.]

through cyberspace, for the primary purpose of collecting intelligence — including information that can be used for future operations — from computers, information or communications systems, or networks with the intent to remain undetected. . . . (C/NF)

Defensive Cyber Effects Operations (DCEO): Operations and related programs or activities — other than network defense or cyber collection — conducted by or on behalf of theUnited States Government, in or through cyberspace, that are intended to enable or produce cyber effects outside United States Government networks for the purpose of defending or protecting against imminent threats or ongoing attacks or malicious cyber activity against U.S. national interests from inside or outside cyberspace. (C/NF) . . .

Offensive Cyber Effects Operations (OCEO): Operations and related programs or activities — other than network defense, cyber collection, or DCEO — conducted by or on behalf of the United States Government, in or through cyberspace, that are intended to enable or produce cyber effects outside United States Government networks. (C/NF) . . .

Significant Consequences: Loss of life, significant responsive actions against the United States, significant damage to property, serious adverse U.S. foreign policy consequences, or serious economic impact on the United States. (U)

U.S. National Interests: Matters of vital interest to the United States to include national security, public safety, national economic security, the safe and reliable functioning of "critical infrastructure and the availability of "key resources." (U)

Emergency Cyber Action: A cyber operation undertaken at the direction of the head of a department or agency with appropriate authorities who has determined that such action is necessary, pursuant to the requirements of this directive, to mitigate an imminent threat or ongoing attack against U.S. national interests from inside or outside cyberspace and under circumstances that at the time do not permit obtaining prior Presidential approval to the extent that such approval would otherwise be required. (S/NF)

II. Purpose and Scope (U) . . .

The United States Government shall conduct all cyber operations consistent with the U.S. Constitution and other applicable laws and policies of the United States, including Presidential orders and directives. (C/NF)

The United States Government shall conduct DCEO and OCEO under this directive consistent with its obligations under international law, including with regard to matters of sovereignty and neutrality, and, as applicable, the law of armed conflict. (C/NF)

This directive pertains to cyber operations, including those that support or enable kinetic, information, or other types of operations. Most of this directive is directed exclusively to DCEO and OCEO. (S/NF) . . .

III. Guiding Principles for DCEO and OCEO (U)

DCEO and OCEO may raise unique national security and foreign policy concerns that require additional coordination and policy considerations because cyberspace is globally connected. DCEO and OCEO, even for subtle or clandestine operations, may generate cyber effects in locations other than the intended target, with potential unintended or collateral consequences that may affect U.S. national interests in many locations. (S/NF)

The United States Government shall conduct DCEO and OCEO in a manner consistent with applicable values, principles, and norms for state behavior that the United States Government promotes domestically and internationally as described in the 2011 "International Strategy for Cyberspace." (C/NF) . . .

The United States Government shall reserve the right to act in accordance with the United States' inherent right of self defense as recognized in international law, including through the conduct of DCEO. (C/NF)

The United States Government shall conduct neither DCEO nor OCEO that are intended or likely to produce cyber effects within the United States unless approved by the President. A department or agency, however, with appropriate authority may conduct a particular case of DCEO that is intended or likely to produce cyber effects within the United States if it qualifies as an Emergency Cyber Action as set forth in this directive and otherwise complies with applicable laws and policies, including Presidential orders and directives. (C/NF)

The United States Government shall obtain consent from countries in which cyber effects are expected to occur or those countries hosting U.S. computers and systems used to conduct DCEO or OCEO unless:

> Military actions approved by the President and ordered by the Secretary of Defense authorize nonconsensual DCEO or OCEO . . . ;
>
> DCEO is undertaken in accordance with the United States' inherent right of self defense as recognized in international law, and the United States Government provides notification afterwards in a manner consistent with the protection of U.S. military and intelligence capabilities and foreign policy considerations and in accordance with applicable law; or
>
> The President — on the recommendation of the Deputies Committee and, as appropriate, the Principals Committee — determines that an exception to obtaining consent is necessary, takes into account overall U.S. national interests and equities, and meets a high threshold of need and effective outcomes relative to the risks created by such an exception. (S/NF) . . .

The United States Government, to ensure appropriate application of these principles, shall make all reasonable efforts, under circumstances prevailing at the time, to identify the adversary and the ownership and geographic location of the targets and related infrastructure where DCEO or OCEO will be conducted or cyber effects are expected to occur, and to identify the people and entities, including U.S. persons, that could be affected by proposed DCEO or OCEO. (S/NF)

Additional Considerations for DCEO (U) . . .

The United States Government shall reserve use of DCEO to protect U.S. national interests in circumstances when network defense or law enforcement measures are insufficient or cannot be put in place in time to mitigate a threat, and when other previously approved measures would not be more appropriate, or if a Deputies or Principals Committee review determines that proposed DCEO provides an advantageous degree of effectiveness, timeliness, or efficiency compared to other methods commensurate with the risks;

The United States Government shall conduct DCEO with the least intrusive methods feasible to mitigate a threat;

The United States Government shall seek partnerships with industry, other levels of government as appropriate, and other nations and organizations to promote cooperative defensive capabilities, including, as appropriate, through the use of DCEO as governed by the provisions in this directive; and

Partnerships with industry and other levels of government for the protection of critical infrastructure shall be coordinated with the Department of Homeland Security (DHS), working with relevant sector-specific agencies and, as appropriate, the Department of Commerce (DOC). (S/NF) . . .

Offensive Cyber Effects Operations (U)

OCEO can offer unique and unconventional capabilities to advance U.S. national objectives around the world with little or no warning to the adversary or target and with potential effects ranging from subtle to severely damaging. The development and sustainment of OCEO capabilities, however, may require considerable time and effort if access and tools for a specific target do not already exist. (TS/NF)

The United States Government shall identify potential targets of national importance where OCEO can offer a favorable balance of effectiveness and risk as compared with other instruments of national power, establish and maintain OCEO capabilities integrated as appropriate with other U.S. offensive capabilities, and execute those capabilities in a manner consistent with the provisions of this directive. (TS/NF)

IV. Cyber Operations with Significant Consequences (U)

Specific Presidential approval is required for any cyber operations — including cyber collection, DCEO, and OCEO — determined by the head of a department or agency to conduct the operation to be reasonably likely to result in "significant consequences" as defined in this directive. . . . (S/NF)

V. Threat Response Operations (U) . . .

Emergency Cyber Actions (C/NF)

The Secretary of Defense is hereby authorized to conduct, or a department or agency head with appropriate authorities may conduct, under procedures approved by the President, Emergency Cyber Actions necessary to mitigate an imminent threat or ongoing attack using DCEO if circumstances at the time do not permit obtaining prior Presidential approval (to the extent that such approval would otherwise be required) and the department or agency head determines that:

> An emergency action is necessary in accordance with the United States inherent right of self-defense as recognized in international law to prevent imminent loss of life or significant damage with enduring national impact on the Primary Mission Essential Functions of the United States Government,[5] U.S. critical infrastructure and key resources, or the mission of U.S. military forces;
>
> Network defense or law enforcement would be insufficient or unavailable in the necessary timeframe, and other previously approved activities would not be more appropriate;
>
> The Emergency Cyber Actions are reasonably likely not to result in significant consequences;
>
> The Emergency Cyber Actions will be conducted in a manner intended to be nonlethal in purpose, action, and consequence;
>
> The Emergency Cyber Actions will be limited in magnitude, scope, and duration to that level of activity necessary to mitigate the threat or attack;
>
> The Emergency Cyber Actions, when practicable, have been coordinated with appropriate departments and agencies . . . ; and
>
> The Emergency Cyber Actions are consistent with the U.S. Constitution and other applicable laws and policies of the United States, including Presidential orders and directives. (S/NF) . . .

Department and agency heads shall report Emergency Cyber Actions to the President through the National Security Advisor as soon as feasible. . . . (S/NF) . . .

[NSL p. 403, CTL p. 117. Insert after Note 7.]

Remarks by the President at the National Defense University

May 23, 2013

. . . [D]espite our strong preference for the detention and prosecution of terrorists, sometimes this approach is foreclosed. Al Qaeda and its

---

5. As defined in NSPD-51/HSPD-20 on "National Continuity Policy" of May 9, 2007. (U)

affiliates try to gain a foothold in some of the most distant and unforgiving places on Earth. They take refuge in remote tribal regions. They hide in caves and walled compounds. They train in empty deserts and rugged mountains.

In some of these places — such as parts of Somalia and Yemen — the state has only the most tenuous reach into the territory. In other cases, the state lacks the capacity or will to take action. It is also not possible for America to simply deploy a team of Special Forces to capture every terrorist. And even when such an approach may be possible, there are places where it would pose profound risks to our troops and local civilians — where a terrorist compound cannot be breached without triggering a firefight with surrounding tribal communities that pose no threat to us, or when putting U.S. boots on the ground may trigger a major international crisis.

To put it another way, our operation in Pakistan against Osama bin Laden cannot be the norm. . . .

It is in this context that the United States has taken lethal, targeted action against al Qaeda and its associated forces, including with remotely piloted aircraft commonly referred to as drones. As was true in previous armed conflicts, this new technology raises profound questions — about who is targeted, and why; about civilian casualties, and the risk of creating new enemies; about the legality of such strikes under U.S. and international law; about accountability and morality.

Let me address these questions. To begin with, our actions are effective. Don't take my word for it. In the intelligence gathered at bin Laden's compound, we found that he wrote, "we could lose the reserves to the enemy's air strikes. We cannot fight air strikes with explosives." Other communications from al Qaeda operatives confirm this as well. Dozens of highly skilled al Qaeda commanders, trainers, bomb makers, and operatives have been taken off the battlefield. Plots have been disrupted that would have targeted international aviation, U.S. transit systems, European cities and our troops in Afghanistan. Simply put, these strikes have saved lives.

Moreover, America's actions are legal. We were attacked on 9/11. Within a week, Congress overwhelmingly authorized the use of force. Under domestic law, and international law, the United States is at war with al Qaeda, the Taliban, and their associated forces. We are at war with an organization that right now would kill as many Americans as they could if we did not stop them first. So this is a just war — a war waged proportionally, in last resort, and in self-defense.

And yet as our fight enters a new phase, America's legitimate claim of self-defense cannot be the end of the discussion. To say a military tactic is legal, or even effective, is not to say it is wise or moral in every instance. For the same human progress that gives us the technology to strike half a world away also demands the discipline to constrain that power — or risk abusing it. That's why, over the last four years, my Administration has worked vigorously to establish a framework that governs our use of force against terrorists – insisting upon clear guidelines, oversight and accountability that is now codified in Presidential Policy Guidancc that I signed yesterday. . . .

Beyond the Afghan theater, we only target al Qaeda and its associated forces. Even then, the use of drones is heavily constrained. America does not take strikes when we have the ability to capture individual terrorists — our preference is always to detain, interrogate, and prosecute them. America cannot take strikes wherever we choose — our actions are bound by consultations with partners, and respect for state sovereignty. America does not take strikes to punish individuals — we act against terrorists who pose a continuing and imminent threat to the American people, and when there are no other governments capable of effectively addressing the threat. And before any strike is taken, there must be near-certainty that no civilians will be killed or injured — the highest standard we can set. . . .

Where foreign governments cannot or will not effectively stop terrorism in their territory, the primary alternative to targeted, lethal action is the use of conventional military options. As I've said, even small Special Operations carry enormous risks. Conventional airpower or missiles are far less precise than drones, and likely to cause more civilian casualties and local outrage. And invasions of these territories lead us to be viewed as occupying armies; unleash a torrent of unintended consequences; are difficult to contain; and ultimately empower those who thrive on violent conflict. So it is false to assert that putting boots on the ground is less likely to result in civilian deaths, or to create enemies in the Muslim world. The result would be more U.S. deaths, more Blackhawks down, more confrontations with local populations, and an inevitable mission creep in support of such raids that could easily escalate into new wars. . . .

This is not to say that the risks [of drone strikes] are not real. Any U.S. military action in foreign lands risks creating more enemies, and impacts public opinion overseas. Our laws constrain the power of the President, even during wartime, and I have taken an oath to defend the

Constitution of the United States. The very precision of drones strikes, and the necessary secrecy involved in such actions can end up shielding our government from the public scrutiny that a troop deployment invites. It can also lead a President and his team to view drone strikes as a cure-all for terrorism.

For this reason, I've insisted on strong oversight of all lethal action. After I took office, my Administration began briefing all strikes outside of Iraq and Afghanistan to the appropriate committees of Congress. Let me repeat that — not only did Congress authorize the use of force, it is briefed on every strike that America takes. That includes the one instance when we targeted an American citizen: Anwar Awlaki, the chief of external operations for AQAP.

This week, I authorized the declassification of this action, and the deaths of three other Americans in drone strikes, to facilitate transparency and debate on this issue, and to dismiss some of the more outlandish claims. For the record, I do not believe it would be constitutional for the government to target and kill any U.S. citizen — with a drone, or a shotgun — without due process. Nor should any President deploy armed drones over U.S. soil.

But when a U.S. citizen goes abroad to wage war against America — and is actively plotting to kill U.S. citizens; and when neither the United States, nor our partners are in a position to capture him before he carries out a plot — his citizenship should no more serve as a shield than a sniper shooting down on an innocent crowd should be protected from a swat team. . . .

. . . I would have detained and prosecuted Awlaki if we captured him before he carried out a plot. But we couldn't. And as President, I would have been derelict in my duty had I not authorized the strike that took out Awlaki.

Of course, the targeting of any Americans raises constitutional issues that are not present in other strikes — which is why my Administration submitted information about Awlaki to the Department of Justice months before Awlaki was killed, and briefed the Congress before this strike as well. But the high threshold that we have set for taking lethal action applies to all potential terrorist targets, regardless of whether or not they are American citizens. This threshold respects the inherent dignity of every human life. . . .

Going forward, I have asked my Administration to review proposals to extend oversight of lethal actions outside of war zones that go beyond our reporting to Congress. Each option has virtues in theory, but poses difficulties in practice. For example, the establishment of a special court to evaluate and authorize lethal action has the benefit of bringing a third branch of government into the process, but raises serious constitutional issues about presidential and judicial authority. Another idea that's been suggested — the establishment of an independent oversight board in the executive branch — avoids those problems, but may introduce a layer of bureaucracy into national-security decision-making, without inspiring additional public confidence in the process. Despite these challenges, I look forward to actively engaging Congress to explore these — and other — options for increased oversight. . . .

[NSL p. 403, CTL p. 117. Insert after Note 7.]

U.S. Policy Standards and Procedures for the Use of Force in Counterterrorism Operations Outside the United States and Areas of Active Hostilities

May 22, 2013

available at http://www.whitehouse.gov/the-press-office/2013/05/23/fact-sheet-president-s-may-23-speech-counterterrorism

Since his first day in office, President Obama has been clear that the United States will use all available tools of national power to protect the American people from the terrorist threat posed by al-Qa'ida and its associated forces. The President has also made clear that, in carrying on this fight, we will uphold our laws and values and will share as much information as possible with the American people and the Congress, consistent with our national security needs and the proper functioning of the Executive Branch. To these ends, the President has approved, and senior members of the Executive Branch have briefed to the Congress, written policy standards and procedures that formalize and strengthen the Administration's rigorous process for reviewing and approving operations to capture or employ lethal force against terrorist targets outside the United States and outside areas of active hostilities. Additionally, the President has decided to share, in this document, certain key elements of these standards and procedures with the American people so that they can make informed judgments and hold the Executive Branch accountable. . . .

Preference for Capture

The policy of the United States is not to use lethal force when it is feasible to capture a terrorist suspect, because capturing a terrorist offers the best opportunity to gather meaningful intelligence and to mitigate and disrupt terrorist plots. Capture operations are conducted only against suspects who may lawfully be captured or otherwise taken into custody by the United States and only when the operation can be conducted in accordance with all applicable law and consistent with our obligations to other sovereign states.

Standards for the Use of Lethal Force

Any decision to use force abroad — even when our adversaries are terrorists dedicated to killing American citizens — is a significant one. Lethal force will not be proposed or pursued as punishment or as a substitute for prosecuting a terrorist suspect in a civilian court or a military commission. Lethal force will be used only to prevent or stop attacks against U.S. persons, and even then, only when capture is not feasible and no other reasonable alternatives exist to address the threat effectively. In particular, lethal force will be used outside areas of active hostilities only when the following preconditions are met:

First, there must be a legal basis for using lethal force, whether it is against a senior operational leader of a terrorist organization or the forces that organization is using or intends to use to conduct terrorist attacks.

Second, the United States will use lethal force only against a target that poses a continuing, imminent threat to U.S. persons. It is simply not the case that all terrorists pose a continuing, imminent threat to U.S. persons; if a terrorist does not pose such a threat, the United States will not use lethal force.

Third, the following criteria must be met before lethal action may be taken:

1) Near certainty that the terrorist target is present;

2) Near certainty that non-combatants[1] will not be injured or killed;

3) An assessment that capture is not feasible at the time of the operation;

4) An assessment that the relevant governmental authorities in the country where action is contemplated cannot or will not effectively address the threat to U.S. persons; and

5) An assessment that no other reasonable alternatives exist to effectively address the threat to U.S. persons.

Finally, whenever the United States uses force in foreign territories, international legal principles, including respect for sovereignty and the law of armed conflict, impose important constraints on the ability of the United States to act unilaterally — and on the way in which the United States can use force. The United States respects national sovereignty and international law.

U.S. Government Coordination and Review

Decisions to capture or otherwise use force against individual terrorists outside the United States and areas of active hostilities are made at the most senior levels of the U.S. Government, informed by departments and agencies with relevant expertise and institutional roles. Senior national security officials — including the deputies and heads of key departments and agencies — will consider proposals to make sure that our policy standards are met, and attorneys — including the senior lawyers of key departments and agencies — will review and determine the legality of proposals.

These decisions will be informed by a broad analysis of an intended target's current and past role in plots threatening U.S. persons; relevant

---

1. Non-combatants are individuals who may not be made the object of attack under applicable international law. The term "non-combatant" does not include an individual who is part of a belligerent party to an armed conflict, an individual who is taking a direct part in hostilities, or an individual who is targetable in the exercise of national self-defense. Males of military age may be non-combatants; it is not the case that all military-aged males in the vicinity of a target are deemed to be combatants.

intelligence information the individual could provide; and the potential impact of the operation on ongoing terrorism plotting, on the capabilities of terrorist organizations, on U.S. foreign relations, and on U.S. intelligence collection. Such analysis will inform consideration of whether the individual meets both the legal and policy standards for the operation.

Other Key Elements

U.S. Persons. If the United States considers an operation against a terrorist identified as a U.S. person, the Department of Justice will conduct an additional legal analysis to ensure that such action may be conducted against the individual consistent with the Constitution and laws of the United States.

Reservation of Authority. These new standards and procedures do not limit the President's authority to take action in extraordinary circumstances when doing so is both lawful and necessary to protect the United States or its allies.

Congressional Notification. Since entering office, the President has made certain that the appropriate Members of Congress have been kept fully informed about our counterterrorism operations. Consistent with this strong and continuing commitment to congressional oversight, appropriate Members of the Congress will be regularly provided with updates identifying any individuals against whom lethal force has been approved. In addition, the appropriate committees of Congress will be notified whenever a counterterrorism operation covered by these standards and procedures has been conducted.

[NSL p. 410, CTL p. 124. Insert at end of chapter.]

Department of Justice, White Paper: Lawfulness of a Lethal Operation Directed Against a U.S. Citizen Who Is a Senior Operational Leader of Al-Qa'ida or an Associated Force

Draft Nov. 8, 2011

available at www.fas.org/irp/eprint/doj-lethal.pdf

This white paper sets forth a legal framework for considering the circumstances in which the U.S. government could use lethal force in a foreign country outside the area of active hostilities against a U.S. citizen who is a senior operational leader of al-Qa'ida or an associated force[1] of al-Qa'ida — that is, an al-Qa'ida leader actively engaged in planning operations to kill Americans. The paper does not attempt to determine the minimum requirements necessary to render such an operation lawful; nor does it assess what might be required to render a lethal operation against a U.S. citizen lawful in other circumstances, including an operation against enemy forces on a traditional battlefield or an operation against a U.S. citizen who is not a senior operational leader of such forces. . . .

I.

The United States is in an armed conflict with al-Qa'ida and its associated forces, and Congress has authorized the President to use all necessary and appropriate force against those entities. *See* Authorization for Use of Military Force ("AUMF"), Pub. L. No. 107-40, §2(a), 115 Stat. 224, 224 (2001). In addition to the authority arising from the AUMF, the President's use of force against al-Qa'ida and associated forces is lawful under other principles of U.S. and international law, including the President's constitutional responsibility to protect the nation and the inherent right to national self-defense recognized in international law (*see, e.g.*, U.N. Charter art. 51). It was on these bases that the United States responded to the attacks of September 11, 2001, and "[t]hese domestic and international legal authorities continue to this

---

1. An associated force of al-Qa'ida includes a group that would qualify as a co-belligerent under the laws of war.

day." Harold Hongju Koh, Legal Adviser, U.S. Department of State, Address to the Annual Meeting of the American Society of International Law: The Obama Administration and International Law (Mar. 25, 2010) ("2010 Koh ASIL Speech").

Any operation of the sort discussed here would be conducted in a foreign country against a senior operational leader of al-Qa'ida or its associated forces who poses an imminent threat of violent attack against the United States. A use of force under such circumstances would be justified as an act of national self-defense. In addition, such a person would be within the core of individuals against whom Congress has authorized the use of necessary and appropriate force. The fact that such a person would also be a U.S. citizen would not alter this conclusion. The Supreme Court has held that the military may constitutionally use force against a U.S. citizen who is a part of enemy forces. See *Hamdi*, 542 U.S. 507, 518 (2004) (plurality opinion); *id.* at 587, 597 (Thomas, J., dissenting); *Ex Parte Quirin*, 317 U.S. at 37-38. Like the imposition of military detention, the use of lethal force against such enemy forces is an "important incident of war." *Hamdi*, 542 U.S. at 518 (plurality opinion) (quotation omitted). Accordingly, the Department does not believe that U.S. citizenship would immunize a senior operational leader of al-Qa'ida or its associated forces from a use of force abroad authorized by the AUMF or in national self-defense.

In addition, the United States retains its authority to use force against al-Qa'ida and associated forces outside the area of active hostilities when it targets a senior operational leader of the enemy forces who is actively engaged in planning operations to kill Americans. The United States is currently in a non-international armed conflict with al-Qa'ida and its associated forces. *See Hamdan v. Rumsfeld*, 548 U.S. 557, 628-31 (2006) (holding that a conflict between a nation and a transnational non-state actor, occurring outside the nation's territory, is an armed conflict "not of an international character" (quoting Common Article 3 of the Geneva Conventions) because it is not a "clash between nations"). Any U.S. operation would be part of this non-international armed conflict, even if it were to take place away from the zone of active hostilities. . . . None of the three branches of the U.S. Government has identified a strict geographical limit on the permissible scope of the AUMF's authorization.

Claiming that for purposes of international law, an armed conflict generally exists only when there is "protracted armed violence between governmental authorities and organized armed groups," *Prosecutor v.*

Tadic, Case No. IT-94-1AR72, Decision on the Defence Motion for Interlocutory Appeal on Jurisdiction, ¶70 (Int'l Crim. Trib. for the Former Yugoslavia, App. Chamber Oct. 2, 1995), some commenters have suggested that the conflict between the United States and al-Qa'ida cannot lawfully extend to nations outside Afghanistan in which the level of hostilities is less intense or prolonged than in Afghanistan itself. *See, e.g.*, Mary Ellen O'Connell, *Combatants and the Combat Zone*, 43 U. Rich. L. Rev. 845, 857-59 (2009). There is little judicial or other authoritative precedent that speaks directly to the question of the geographic scope of a non-international armed conflict in which one of the parties is a transnational, non-state actor and where the principal theater of operations is not within the territory of the nation that is a party to the conflict. Thus, in considering this potential issue, the Department looks to principles and statements from analogous contexts.

The Department has not found any authority for the proposition that when one of the parties to an armed conflict plans and executes operations from a base in a new nation, an operation to engage the enemy in that location cannot be part of the original armed conflict, and thus subject to the laws of war governing that conflict, unless the hostilities become sufficiently intense and protracted in the new location. That does not appear to be the rule of the historical practice, for instance, even in a traditional international conflict. *See* John R. Stevenson, Legal Adviser, Department of State, United States Military Action in Cambodia: Questions of International Law, Address before the Hammarskjold Forum of the Association of the Bar of the City of New York (May 28, 1970), *in* 3 *The Vietnam War and International Law: The Widening Context* 23, 28-30 (Richard A. Falk, ed. 1972) (arguing that in an international armed conflict, if a neutral state has been unable for any reason to prevent violations of its neutrality by the troops of one belligerent using its territory as a base of operations, the other belligerent has historically been justified in attacking those enemy forces in that state). Particularly in a non-international armed conflict, where terrorist organizations may move their base of operations from one country to another, the determination of whether a particular operation would be part of an ongoing armed conflict would require consideration of the particular facts and circumstances in each case, including the fact that transnational non-state organizations such as al-Qa'ida may have no single site serving as their base of operations. . . .

II.

The Department assumes that the rights afforded by Fifth Amendment's Due Process Clause, as well as the Fourth Amendment, attach to a U.S. citizen even while he is abroad. *See Reid v. Covert*, 354 U.S. 1, 5-6 (1957) (plurality opinion); *United States v. Verdugo-Urquidez*, 494 U.S. 259, 269-70 (1990); *see also In re Terrorist Bombings of U.S. Embassies in East Africa*, 552 F.3d 157, 170 n.7 (2d Cir. 2008). The U.S. citizenship of a leader of al-Qa'ida or its associated forces, however, does not give that person constitutional immunity from attack. . . .

A.

The Due Process Clause would not prohibit a lethal operation of the sort contemplated here. In *Hamdi*, a plurality of the Supreme Court used the *Mathews v. Eldridge* balancing test to analyze the Fifth Amendment due process rights of a U.S. citizen who had been captured on the battlefield in Afghanistan and detained in the United States, and who wished to challenge the government's assertion that he was part of enemy forces. The Court explained that the "process due in any given instance is determined by weighing 'the private interest that will be affected by the official action' against the Government's asserted interest, 'including the function involved' and the burdens the Government would face in providing greater process." *Hamdi*, 542 U.S. at 529 (plurality opinion) (quoting *Mathews v. Eldridge*, 424 U.S. 319, 335 (1976)). The due process balancing analysis applied to determine the Fifth Amendment rights of a U.S. citizen with respect to law-of-war detention supplies the framework for assessing the process due a U.S. citizen who is a senior operational leader of an enemy force planning violent attacks against Americans before he is subjected to lethal targeting.

In the circumstances considered here, the interests on both sides would be weighty. *See Hamdi*, 542 U.S. at 529 (plurality opinion) ("It is beyond question that substantial interests lie on both sides of the scale in this case."). An individual's interest in avoiding erroneous deprivation of his life is "uniquely compelling." *See Ake v. Oklahoma*, 470 U.S. 68, 178 (1985). No private interest is more substantial. At the same time, the government's interest in waging war, protecting its citizens, and removing the threat posed by members of enemy forces is also compelling. *Cf. Hamdi*, 542 U.S. at 531 (plurality opinion) ("On the other side of the scale are the weighty and sensitive governmental interests in ensuring that those who have in fact fought with the enemy during a war do not return to battle against the United States."). As the *Hamdi* plurality observed, in the "circumstances of war," "the risk of erroneous deprivation of a citizen's liberty in the absence of sufficient process . . . is very real," *id.* at 530 (plurality opinion), and, of course, the risk of an erroneous deprivation of a citizen's life is even more significant. But, "the realities of combat" render certain uses of force "necessary and appropriate," including force against U.S. citizens who have joined enemy forces in the armed conflict against the United States and whose activities pose an imminent threat of violent attack against the United States — and "due process analysis need not blink at those realities." *id.* at 531 (plurality opinion). These same realities must also be considered in assessing "the burdens the Government would face in providing greater process" to a member of enemy forces. *Id.* at 529, 531 (plurality opinion).

In view of these interests and practical considerations, the United States would be able to use lethal force against a U.S. citizen, who is located outside the United States and is an operational leader continually planning attacks against U.S. persons and interests, in at least the following circumstances: (1) where an informed, high-level official of the U.S. government has determined that the targeted individual poses an imminent threat of violent attack against the United States; (2) where a capture operation would be infeasible-and where those conducting the operation continue to monitor whether capture becomes feasible; and (3) where such an operation would be conducted consistent with applicable law of war principles. In these circumstances, the "realities" of the conflict and the weight of the government's interest in protecting its citizens from an · imminent attack are such that the Constitution would not require the government to provide further process to such a U.S. citizen before using lethal force. *Cf. Hamdi*, 542 U.S. at 535 (plurality opinion) (noting that the Court "accord[s] the greatest respect and consideration to the judgments of military authorities in matters relating to the actual prosecution of war, and . . . the scope of that discretion necessarily is wide").

Certain aspects of this legal framework require additional explication. *First*, the condition that an operational leader present an "imminent" threat of violent attack against the United States does not require the United States to have clear evidence that a specific attack on

U.S. persons and interests will take place in the immediate future. Given the nature of, for example, the terrorist attacks on September 11, in which civilian airliners were hijacked to strike the World Trade Center and the Pentagon, this definition of imminence, which would require the United States to refrain from action until preparations for an attack are concluded, would not allow the United States sufficient time to defend itself. The defensive options available to the United States may be reduced or eliminated if al-Qa'ida operatives disappear and cannot be found when the time of their attack approaches. Consequently, with respect to al-Qa'ida leaders who are continually planning attacks, the United States is likely to have only a limited window of opportunity within which to defend Americans in a manner that has both a high likelihood of success and sufficiently reduces the probabilities of civilian causalities. Furthermore, a "terrorist 'war' does not consist of a massive attack across an international border, nor does it consist of one isolated incident that occurs and is then past. It is a drawn out, patient, sporadic pattern of attacks. It is very difficult to know when or where the next incident will occur." Gregory M. Travalio, *Terrorism, International Law, and the Use of Military Force*, 18 Wis. Int'l L.J. 145, 173 (2000). Delaying action against individuals continually planning to kill Americans until some theoretical end stage of the planning for a particular plot would create an unacceptably high risk that the action would fail and that American casualties would result.

By its nature, therefore, the threat posed by al-Qa'ida and its associated forces demands a broader concept of imminence in judging when a person continually planning terror attacks presents an imminent threat, making the use of force appropriate. In this context, imminence must incorporate considerations of the relevant window of opportunity, the possibility of reducing collateral damage to civilians, and the likelihood of heading off future disastrous attacks on Americans. Thus, a decision maker determining whether an al-Qa'ida operational leader presents an imminent threat of violent attack against the United States must take into account that certain members of al-Qa'ida (including any potential target of lethal force) are continually plotting attacks against the United States; that al-Qa'ida would engage in such attacks regularly to the extent it were able to do so; that the U.S. government may not be aware of all al-Qa'ida plots as they are developing and thus cannot be confident that none is about to occur; and that, in light of these predicates, the nation may have a limited window of opportunity within which to strike in a manner that both has a high likelihood of success and reduces the probability of American casualties.

With this understanding, a high-level official could conclude, for example, that an individual poses an "imminent threat" of violent attack against the United States where he is an operational leader of al-Qa'ida or an associated force and is personally and continually involved in planning terrorist attacks against the United States. Moreover, where the al-Qa'ida member in question has recently been involved in activities posing an imminent threat of violent attack against the United States, and there is no evidence suggesting that he has renounced or abandoned such activities, that member's involvement in al-Qa'ida's continuing terrorist campaign against the United States would support the conclusion that the member poses an imminent threat.

Second, regarding the feasibility of capture, capture would not be feasible if it could not be physically effectuated during the relevant window of opportunity or if the relevant country were to decline to consent to a capture operation. Other factors such as undue risk to U.S. personnel conducting a potential capture operation also could be relevant. Feasibility would be a highly fact-specific and potentially time-sensitive inquiry.

Third, it is a premise here that any such lethal operation by the United States would comply with the four fundamental law-of-war principles governing the use of force: necessity, distinction, proportionality, and humanity (the avoidance of unnecessary suffering). For example, it would not be consistent with those principles to continue an operation if anticipated civilian casualties would be excessive in relation to the anticipated military advantage. An operation consistent with the laws of war could not violate the prohibitions against treachery and perfidy, which address a breach of confidence by the assailant. These prohibitions do not, however, categorically forbid the use of stealth or surprise, nor forbid attacks on identified individual soldiers or officers. And the Department is not aware of any other law-of-war grounds precluding use of such tactics. Relatedly, "there is no prohibition under the laws of war on the use of technologically advanced weapons systems in armed conflict — such as pilotless aircraft or so-called smart bombs — as long as they are employed in conformity with applicable laws of war." 2010 Koh ASIL Speech. Further, under this framework, the United States would also be required to accept a surrender if it were feasible to do so. . . .

B.

Similarly, assuming that a lethal operation targeting a U.S. citizen abroad who is planning attacks against the United States would result in a "seizure" under the Fourth Amendment, such an operation would not violate that Amendment in the circumstances posited here. The Supreme Court has made clear that the constitutionality of a seizure is determined by "balanc[ing] the nature and quality of the intrusion on the individual's Fourth Amendment interests against the importance of the governmental interests alleged to justify the intrusion." *Tennessee v. Garner*, 471 U.S. 1, 8 (1985) (internal quotation marks omitted). Even in domestic law enforcement operations, the Court has noted that "[w]here the officer has probable cause to believe that the suspect poses a threat of serious physical harm, either to the officer or to others, it is not constitutionally unreasonable to prevent escape by using deadly force." *Garner*, 471 U.S. at 11. . . .

The Fourth Amendment "reasonableness" test is situation-dependent. What would constitute a reasonable use of lethal force for purposes of domestic law enforcement operations differs substantially from what would be reasonable in the situation and circumstances discussed in this white paper. But at least in circumstances where the targeted person is an operational leader of an enemy force and an informed, high-level government official has determined that he poses an imminent threat of violent attack against the United States, and those conducting the operation would carry out the operation only if capture were infeasible, the use of lethal force would not violate the Fourth Amendment. Under such circumstances, the intrusion on any Fourth Amendment interests would be outweighed by the "importance of the governmental interests [that] justify the intrusion," *Garner*, 471 U.S. at 8 — the interests in protecting the lives of Americans.

C.

Finally, the Department notes that under the circumstances described in this paper, there exists no appropriate judicial forum to evaluate these constitutional considerations. It is well-established that "[m]atters intimately related to foreign policy and national security are rarely proper subjects for judicial intervention," *Haig v. Agee*, 453 U.S. 280, 292 (1981), because such matters "frequently turn on standards that defy judicial application," or "involve the exercise of a discretion demonstrably committed to the executive or legislature," *Baker v. Carr*, 369 U.S. 186, 211 (1962). Were a court to intervene here, it might be required inappropriately to issue an ex ante command to the President and officials responsible for operations with respect to their specific tactical judgment to mount a potential lethal operation against a senior operational leader of al-Qa'ida or its associated forces. And judicial enforcement of such orders would require the Court to supervise inherently predictive judgments by the President and his national security advisors as to when and how to use force against a member of an enemy force against which Congress has authorized the use of force.

III.

Section 1119(b) of title 18 provides that a "person who, being a national of the United States, kills or attempts to kill a national of the United States while such national is outside the United States but within the jurisdiction of another country shall be punished as provided under sections 1111, 1112, and 1113." 18 U.S.C. §1119(b) (2006). Because the person who would be the target of the kind of operation discussed here would be a U.S. citizen, it might be suggested that section 1119(b) would prohibit such an operation. Section 1119, however, incorporates the federal murder and manslaughter statutes, and thus its prohibition extends only to "unlawful killing[s]," 18 U.S.C. §§1111(a), 1112(a) (2006). Section 1119 is best construed to incorporate the "public authority" justification, which renders lethal action carried out by a government official lawful in some circumstances. . . .

A. . . .

Guidance as to the meaning of the phrase "unlawful killing" in sections 1111 and 1112 — and thus for purposes of section 1119(b) — can be found in the historical understandings of murder and manslaughter. That history shows that states have long recognized justifications and excuses to statutes criminalizing "unlawful" killings. . . . Accordingly, section 1119 does not proscribe killings covered by a justification traditionally recognized under the common law or state and federal murder statutes. . . .

B.

The public authority justification is well-accepted, and it may be available even in cases where the particular criminal statute at issue does not expressly refer to a public authority justification. Prosecutions where such a "public authority" justification is invoked are understandably rare, and thus there is little case law in which courts have analyzed the scope of the justification with respect to the conduct of government officials. Nonetheless, discussions in the leading treatises and in the Model Penal Code demonstrate its legitimacy. *See* 2 Wayne R. LaFave, *Substantive Criminal Law* §10.2(b), at 135 (2d ed. 2003). . . .

The public authority justification would not excuse all conduct of public officials from all criminal prohibitions. The legislature may design some criminal prohibitions to place bounds on the kinds of governmental conduct that can be authorized by the Executive. Or the legislature may enact a criminal prohibition in order to limit the scope of the conduct that the legislature has otherwise authorized the Executive to undertake pursuant to another statute. But the generally recognized public authority justification reflects that it would not make sense to attribute to Congress the intent to criminalize all covered activities undertaken by public officials in the legitimate exercise of their otherwise lawful authorities, even if Congress clearly intends to make those same actions a crime when committed by persons not acting pursuant to public authority. In some instances, therefore, the best interpretation of a criminal prohibition is that Congress intended to distinguish persons who are acting pursuant to public authority from those who are not, even if the statute does not make that distinction express.

The touchstone for the analysis whether section 1119 incorporates not only justifications generally, but also the public authority justification in particular, is the legislative intent underlying this statute. Here, the statute should be read to exclude from its prohibitory scope killings that are encompassed by traditional justifications, which include the public authority justification. The statutory incorporation of two other criminal statutes expressly referencing "unlawful" killings is one indication. Moreover, there are no indications that Congress had a contrary intention. Nothing in the text or legislative history of sections 1111-1113 of title 18 suggests that Congress intended to exclude the established public authority justification from those justifications that Congress otherwise must be understood to have imported through the use of the modifier "unlawful" in those statutes. Nor is there anything in the text or legislative history of section 1119 itself to suggest that Congress intended to abrogate or otherwise affect the availability of this traditional justification for killings. . . .

The Department thus concludes that section 1119 incorporates the public authority justification. . . .

C. . . .

The United States is currently in the midst of a congressionally authorized armed conflict with al-Qa'ida and associated forces, and may act in national self-defense to protect U.S. persons and interests who are under continual threat of violent attack by certain al-Q'aida operatives planning operations against them. The public authority justification would apply to a lethal operation of the kind discussed in this paper if it were conducted in accord with applicable law of war principles. As one legal commentator has explained, "if a soldier intentionally kills an enemy combatant in time of war and within the rules of warfare, he is not guilty of murder," whereas, for example, if that soldier intentionally kills a prisoner of war — a violation of the laws of war — "then he commits murder." 2 LaFave, *Substantive Criminal Law* §10.2(c), at 136. . . .

The fact that an operation may target a U.S. citizen does not alter this conclusion. . . .

. . . [T]he Department believes that the use of lethal force addressed in this white paper would constitute a lawful killing under the public authority doctrine if conducted in a manner consistent with the fundamental law of war principles governing the use of force in a non-international armed conflict. Such an operation would not violate the assassination ban in Executive Order No. 12333. Section 2.11 of Executive Order No. 12333 provides that "[n]o person employed by or acting on behalf of the United States Government shall engage in, or conspire to engage in, assassination." 46 Fed. Reg. 59,941, 59, 952 (Dec. 4, 1981). A lawful killing in self-defense is not an assassination. In the Department's view, a lethal operation conducted against a U.S. citizen whose conduct poses an imminent threat of violent attack against the United States would be a legitimate act of national self-defense that would not violate the assassination ban. Similarly, the use of lethal force, consistent with the laws of war, against an individual who is a legitimate military target would be lawful and would not violate the assassination ban.

IV.

The War Crimes Act, 18 U.S.C. §2441 (2006) makes it a federal crime for a member of the Armed Forces or a national of the United States to "commit[] a war crime." *Id.* §2441(a). The only potentially applicable provision of section 2441 to operations of the type discussed herein makes it a war crime to commit a "grave breach" of Common Article 3 of the Geneva Conventions when that breach is committed "in the context of and in association with an armed conflict not of an international character." *Id.* §2441(c)(3). As defined by the statute, a "grave breach" of Common Article 3 includes "[m]urder," described in pertinent part as "[t]he act of a person who intentionally kills, or conspires or attempts to kill . . . one or more persons taking no active part in the hostilities, including those placed out of combat by sickness, wounds, detention, or any other cause." *Id.* §2441(d)(1)(D).

Whatever might be the outer bounds of this category of covered persons, Common Article 3 does not alter the fundamental law of war principle concerning a belligerent party's right in an armed conflict to target individuals who are part of an enemy's armed forces or eliminate a nation's authority to take legitimate action in national self-defense. The language of Common Article 3 "makes clear that members of such armed forces [of both the state and non-state parties to the conflict] . . . are considered as 'taking no active part in the hostilities' only once they have disengaged from their fighting function ('have laid down their arms') or are placed *hors de combat*; mere suspension of combat is insufficient." International Committee of the Red Cross, *Interpretive Guidance on the Notion of Direct Participation in Hostilities Under International Humanitarian Law* 28 (2009). An operation against a senior operational leader of al-Qa'ida or its associated forces who poses an imminent threat of violent attack against the United States would target a person who is taking "an active part in hostilities" and therefore would not constitute a "grave breach" of Common Article 3. . . .

[NSL p. 464. Insert at the end of Note 2.]

Over time, an informal system of congressional oversight has developed regarding certain particularly sensitive *non-covert action intelligence* (mostly collection) activities. So-called "Gang of Four" notifications of such activities are given to the chairs and ranking

Members of the two congressional intelligence committees, when "the intelligence community believes a particular intelligence activity to be of such sensitivity that a restricted notification is warranted in order to reduce the risk of disclosure, inadvertent or otherwise." John Rollins & Rebecca S. Lange, *"Gang of Four" Congressional Intelligence Notifications* (Cong. Res. Serv. R40698), Nov. 19, 2012. Other non-covert action activities are generally briefed to the full committees.

[NSL p. 464. Insert after Note 2.]

In November 2011, Director of National Intelligence James Clapper issued an Intelligence Community Directive that elaborates on reporting required by statute to keep the congressional intelligence committees "fully and currently informed of the intelligence activities of the United States" (see p. 504). The Directive adds to statutory obligations by requiring agencies of the Intelligence Community to report in writing, to report on intelligence failures, and to resolve any doubts in favor of reporting. But it does not apply to separately prescribed reporting of covert actions (see p. 505).

Office of the Director of National Intelligence, Intelligence Community Directive Number 112: Congressional Notification

Nov. 16, 2011

http://www.dni.gov/electronic_reading_room/ICD_112.pdf

C. APPLICABILITY . . .

3. This Directive does not apply to reporting of covert actions to the Congressional intelligence committees, to statutory reporting requirements for IC Inspectors General, or to routine informational briefings.

D. POLICY . . .

2. The provisions of this Directive shall be interpreted with a presumption of notification in fulfillment of the statutory requirement to keep the Congressional intelligence committees fully and currently informed of all intelligence activities.

3. It is IC policy that IC elements shall, in a timely manner, keep the Congressional intelligence committees fully informed, in writing, of all significant anticipated intelligence activities, significant intelligence failures, significant intelligence activities, and illegal activities. . . .

5. Determining whether written notification should be provided of a particular intelligence activity is a judgment based on all the facts and circumstances known to the IC element, and on the nature and extent of previous notifications or briefings to Congress on the same matter. Not every intelligence activity warrants written notification. Facts and circumstances of intelligence activities change over time; therefore, IC elements must continually assess whether there is an obligation to report a matter pursuant to the National Security Act and this Directive.

6. As required by the National Security Act, Congress must receive written notification of significant anticipated intelligence activities and significant intelligence failures. General guidelines for determining the types of intelligence activities that warrant written notification follow:

a. Significant anticipated intelligence activities include:

(1) intelligence activities that entail, with reasonable foreseeability, significant risk of exposure, compromise, and loss of human life;

(2) intelligence activities that are expected to have a major impact on important foreign policy or national security interests;

(3) an IC element's transfer, to a recipient outside that IC element, of defense articles, personnel services, or "controlled equipment" valued in excess of $1 million as provided in Section 505 of the National Security Act;

(4) extensive organizational changes in an IC element;

(5) deployment of new collection techniques that represent a significant departure from previous operations or activities or that result from evidence of significant foreign developments;

(6) significant activities undertaken pursuant to specific direction of the President or the National Security Council (this is not applicable to covert action, which is covered by Section 503 of the National Security Act); or

(7) significant acquisition, reprogramming, or non-routine budgetary actions that are of Congressional concern and that are not otherwise reportable under the National Intelligence Program Procedures for Reprogramming and Transfers.

b. Significant intelligence failures are failures that are extensive in scope, continuing in nature, or likely to have a serious impact on United States (US) national security interests and include:

(l) the loss or compromise of classified information on such a scale or over such an extended period as to indicate a systemic loss or compromise of classified intelligence information that may pose a substantial risk to US national security interests;

(2) a significant unauthorized disclosure of classified intelligence infonnation that may pose a substantial risk to US national security interests;

(3) a potentially pervasive failure, interruption, or compromise of a collection capability or collection system; or

(4) a conclusion that an intelligence product is the result of foreign deception or denial activity, or otherwise contains major errors in analysis, with a significant impact on US national security policies, programs, or activities.

7. As a matter of policy, IC elements shall provide Congress written notification of other significant intelligence activities and illegal activities. General guidelines for determining these types of intelligence activities warranting notification follow.

a. Significant intelligence activities include:

(1) substantial changes in the capabilities or known vulnerabilities of US intelligence operations or intelligence systems or resources;

(2) programmatic developments likely to be of Congressional interest, such as major cost overruns, a major modification of, or the termination of a significant contract;

(3) developments that affect intelligence programs, projects, or activities that are likely to be of Congressional concern because of their substantial impact on national security or foreign policy;

(4) the loss of life in the performance of an intelligence activity; or

(5) significant developments in, or the resolution of, a matter previously reported under these procedures.

b. Illegal activities include:

(1) An intelligence activity believed to be in violation of US law, including any corrective action taken or planned in

connection with such activity;

(2) Significant misconduct by an employee of an IC element or asset that is likely to seriously affect intelligence activities or otherwise is of congressional concern, including human rights violations; or

(3) Other serious violations of US criminal law by an employee of an IC element or asset, which in the discretion of the head of an IC element warrants congressional notification.

8. Criteria described in Sections D.6 and D.7 above are not exhaustive. The absence of any of these criteria shall not be seen as determinative. Each potential determination shall be addressed on its particular merits. If it is unclear whether a notification is appropriate, IC elements should decide in favor of notification. . . .

[NSL p. 554, CTL p. 167. Substitute for paragraph at top of each page.]

In 1978, Congress codified a foreign intelligence collection authority in the Foreign Intelligence Surveillance Act (FISA). In NSL Chapter 21/CTL Chapter 7, we turn to this statutory authority for electronic surveillance and, eventually, "black bag jobs" (surreptitious entry). We see that FISA originally authorized court orders for individually targeted surveillance based on probable cause to believe that the target was a foreign power or its agent.

Beginning in 2005, media stories, first about the so-called Terrorist Surveillance Program and later about an NSA program called "PRISM," awakened many Americans to the fact that our government was conducting some kind of surveillance in the United States of the contents of Internet and telephone traffic to or from foreign targets. NSL Chapter 22/CTL Chapter 8 examines the 2008 extension of FISA procedures to permit this kind of "programmatic surveillance" without individualized targeting, or what one might call wholesale instead of retail electronic surveillance.

When we mail a letter through the U.S. postal system, we have no reasonable expectation that the addresses on the outside of the envelope will be private, because we know that postal workers can see them (and must see the destination address to deliver the letter). But we do reasonably expect that no one other than the addressee will open our letter and read the contents. In a pair of early cases, the Supreme Court recognized this distinction between what could be called "envelope" information and "content" information. The Court denied traditional Fourth Amendment protection to dialed telephone numbers and certain bank records that customers necessarily disclose to their phone companies and banks. In NSL Chapter 23/CTL Chapter 9, we take up statutory authority for government collection of what we call "third-party records" — tangible and electronic transactional data held by private third parties, including "telephony" (telephone metadata like calling and called numbers, as well as time and duration of calls), telephone customer transactional data (including billing records, names, and addresses), and a broad range of other data (including credit card records), using court orders under USA Patriot Act §215, national security letters pursuant to several statutes, and subpoenas. We consider whether the original envelope-contents distinction still makes sense for contemporary digital data, such as stored Internet search requests, and whether expectations of privacy are different for searchable data sets in the aggregate than they are for individual items of information.

In NSL Chapter 24/CTL Chapter 10, we shift our focus from collecting the data "dots" to connecting them. Dots are connected for the purpose of profiling and "watchlisting" terrorist suspects and for screening access to transportation systems, critical infrastructure, and other possible targets for terrorism.

Finally, in NSL Chapter 25/CTL Chapter 11, we again shift our focus, this time from domestic intelligence collection to the U.S. law governing national security surveillance abroad. U.S. persons and even aliens with a substantial connection to the United States have constitutionally protected expectations of privacy when they travel abroad, but not necessarily the same expectations they have at home. The Fourth Amendment has never been interpreted to protect expectations of privacy by aliens abroad who have no connection to the United States, however. For this reason, traditional "spying" abroad on such aliens has not been subject to constitutional regulation, although it may, of course, be illegal in the foreign country where it occurs. This chapter explores the implications of these differences.

[NSL p. 579, CTL p. 192. Insert at the end of Note 6.]

The GPS issue was confronted by the Court in *United States v. Jones*, 132 S. Ct. 945 (2012), where the Justices unanimously concluded that Jones was searched when police attached a GPS device to the undercarriage of his car and tracked his movements for four weeks. Yet none of the three opinions expressly required that police obtain a warrant for GPS tracking, and the opinions yielded no clear indication of the nature or degree of suspicion that is required to attach a GPS device and monitor the target's movements.

The opinion of the Court by Justice Scalia ruled that the government's installation of the GPS device was a trespass, a physical intrusion of private property that would have constituted a "search" when the Fourth Amendment was ratified in 1791. Eschewing the *Katz* "reasonable expectation of privacy" formula, Justice Scalia wrote that Fourth Amendment rights are based on the privacy that existed when the Fourth Amendment was adopted. According to Justice Scalia, to constitute a Fourth Amendment violation, in addition to the trespass, the government must have "attempt[ed] to find something or to obtain information." 132 S. Ct. at 951 n.5.

As the concurring Justices noted, the property-based approach of the majority did nothing to guide law enforcement or intelligence officials or the lower courts in determining the permissible uses of new surveillance technologies. Concurring in the judgment for himself and Justices Ginsburg, Breyer, and Kagan, Justice Alito would have applied *Katz* to decide *Jones*. *Id.* at 957-964. For Justice Alito, the long-term monitoring of Jones' movements, not the installation of the device on his car, violated his privacy. Justice Alito asked whether "GPS tracking in a particular case involve[s] a degree of instrusion that a reasonable person would not have anticipated." *Id.* at 964. Separately, Justice Sotomayor approved Justice Scalia's opinion, but also supported Justice Alito's *Katz*-based approach. She argued that the courts should take into account that "GPS monitoring generates a precise, comprehensive record of a person's public movements that reflects a wealth of detail about her familial, political, professional, religious, and sexual associations." *Id.* at 955.

Is an intrusiveness assessment any different from one based on a reasonable expectation of privacy? As Justice Alito noted, if an auto manufacturer installed a GPS in the cars it produces, the Court's theory would not protect the owner. What should be the Fourth Amendment rule for pre-installed GPS tracking? For the same tracking when GPS is pre-installed on cell phones? Or when some form of ID card, such as drivers' licenses or passports, is embedded with GPS capabilities, allowing the government to track every citizen's movements?

In *Knotts*, police discovered the location of a secluded drug lab by enclosing a beeper in a can of chloroform sold to one of the defendants. The can carrying the chloroform transmitted signals that enabled the police to track the defendant's car after earlier efforts to find the lab failed. *Knotts*, 460 U.S. at 278. Why isn't the GPS device used by the police in *Jones* simply an advanced beeper? The *Knotts* Court was careful to note that the beeper provided only location information, and that a car driving down the road is subject to scrutiny in that public space. The Court found no constitutional difference between traditional visual surveillance and this then-new form of electronic surveillance. *Id.* 460 U.S. at 281. Why should *Jones* be decided differently than *Knotts*?

[NSL p. 607, CTL p. 220. Insert after the first paragraph of C. FISA Trends.]

Of 1,856 applications submitted to the FISC in calendar year 2012 for authority to conduct electronic surveillance and/or physical searches for foreign intelligence purposes, none was denied, although unspecified modifications were made to 40 proposed orders. *See* Letter from Peter J. Kadzik, Assistant Attorney General, to Honorable Joseph R. Biden, Jr. (April 30, 2013), *available at* http://www.fas.org/irp/agency/doj/fisa/2012rept.pdf.

[NSL p. 613, CTL p. 226, add to Note 1.]

A somewhat different and more detailed description of the TSP was provided in a 2009 draft NSA Inspector General report disclosed in June 2013 by the London *Guardian* newspaper and *The Washington Post* in the wave of disclosures of classified documents by former NSA contractor Edward Snowden. What was later called the TSP was created as the President's Surveillance Program (PSP) on October 4, 2001, without FISC orders, on the basis of the President's putative constitutional powers. PSP included four components under the code name STELLARWIND — collection of contents and metadata from telephone calls and emails. Robert O'Harrow Jr. & Ellen Nakashima, *President's Surveillance Program Worked with Private Sector to Collect Data after September 11, 2001*, Wash. Post, June 27, 2013.

According to the following excerpt from the 57-page draft report,

NSA began collecting data from U.S. telephone numbers on communications links to some foreign countries a few days after 9/11.

TOP SECRET//STLW//COMINT/ORCON/NOFORN

Office of the Inspector General, National Security Agency/Central Security Service, 1109-0002 Working Draft [1]

Mar. 24, 2009

available at http://www.guardian.co.uk/world/interactive/2013/jun/27/nsa-inspector general-report-document-data-collection

. . . **Actions Taken After 9/11**

On 14 September 2001, three days after terrorist attacks in the United States, [the NSA Director, General Michael] Hayden approved the targeting of terrorist-associated foreign telephone numbers on communication links between the United States and foreign countries where terrorists were known to be operating. Only specified, pre-approved numbers were allowed to be tasked for collection against U.S.-originating links. He authorized this collection at Special Collection Service and Foreign Satellite sites with access to links between the United States and countries of interest, including Afghanistan. According to the Deputy General Counsel, General Hayden determined by 26 September that any Afghan telephone number in contact with a U.S. telephone number on or after 26 September was presumed to be of foreign intelligence value and could be disseminated to the FBI.

NSA OGC said General Hayden's action was a lawful exercise of his power under Executive Order (E.O.) 12333, United States Intelligence Activities, as amended. The targeting of communication links with one end in the United States was a more aggressive use of E.O. 12333 authority than that exercised by former Directors. General Hayden was operating in a unique environment in which it was a widely

---

[1. This document was published online in Glenn Greenwald & Spencer Ackerman, *NSA Collected US Email Records in Bulk for More than Two Years under Obama*, The Guardian, June 27, 13, 2013, http://www.guardian.co.uk/world/2013/jun/27/nsa-data-mining-authorised-obama.]

held belief that additional terrorist attacks on U.S. soil were imminent. General Hayden said this was a "tactical decision."

On 2 October 2001, General Hayden briefed the House Permanent Select Committee on Intelligence (HPSCI) on this decision and later informed members of the Senate Select Committee on Intelligence (SSCI) by telephone. He had also informed DCI George Tenet.

At the same time NSA was assessing collection gaps and increasing efforts against terrorist targets immediately after the 11 September attacks, it was responding to Department of Defense (DOD), Director of Central Intelligence Community Management Staff questions about its ability to counter the new threat.

Need to Expand NSA Authority

General Hayden said that soon after he told Mr. Tenet about NSA actions to counter the threat, Mr. Tenet shared the information with the "Oval Office." Mr. Tenet relayed that the Vice President wanted to know if NSA could be doing more. General Hayden replied that nothing else could be done within existing NSA authorities. In a follow-up telephone conversation, Mr. Tenet asked General Hayden what could be done if he had additional authorities. General Hayden said that these discussions were not documented.

NSA Identifies SIGINT Collection Gaps

To respond to the Vice President, General Hayden met with NSA personnel who were already working to identify and fill SIGINT collection gaps in light of the recent terrorist attacks. General Hayden stated that he met with personnel to identify which additional authorities would be operationally useful and technically feasible. In particular, discussions focused on how NSA might bridge the "international gap." An NSA Technical Director described that gap in these terms:

> "Here is NSA standing at the U.S. border looking outward for foreign threats. There is the FBI looking within the United States for domestic threats. But no one was looking at the foreign threats coming into the United States. That was a huge gap that NSA wanted to cover."

Possible Solutions. Among other things, NSA considered how to tweak transit collection — the collection of communications transiting through but not originating or terminating in the United States. NSA personnel also resurfaced a concept proposed in 1999 to address the Millennium Threat. NSA proposed that it would perform contact chaining on metadata it had collected. Analysts would chain through masked U.S. telephone numbers to discover foreign connections to those numbers, without specifying, even for analysts, the U.S. number involved. In December 1999, the Department of Justice Office of Intelligence Policy Review (OIPR) told NSA that the proposal fell within one of the FISA definitions of electronic surveillance and, therefore, was not permissible when applied to metadata associated with presumed U.S. persons (i.e., U.S. telephone numbers not approved for targeting by the FISC).

Collection gaps not adequately filled by FISA authorized intercept. NSA determined that FISA authorization did not allow sufficient flexibility to counter the new terrorist threat. First, it believed that because of technological advances, the jurisdiction of the FISC went beyond the original intent of the statute. For example, most communications signals no longer flowed through radio or via phone systems as they did in 1978 when the FISA was written. By 2001, Internet communications were used worldwide, undersea cables carried huge volumes of communications, and a large amount of the world's communications passed through the United States. Because of language used in the Act in 1978, NSA was required to obtain court orders to target email accounts used by non-U.S. persons outside the United States if it intended to intercept the communications at a webmail service within the United States. Large numbers of terrorists were using such accounts in 2001.

Second, NSA believed that the FISA process was unable to accommodate the number of terrorist targets or the speed with which they changed their communications. From the time NSA sent FISA requests to the OIPR until the time data arrived at NSA, the average wait was between four and six weeks. Terrorists could have changed their telephone numbers or internet addresses before NSA received FISC approval to target them. NSA believed the large number of terrorist targets and their frequently changing communications would have overwhelmed the existing FISA process.

Emergency FISA provision not an option. NSA determined that even using emergency FISA court orders would not provide the speed and flexibility needed to counter the terrorist threat. First, although the emergency authorization provision permitted 72 hours of surveillance without obtaining a court order, it did not — as many believed — allow the Government to undertake surveillance immediately. Rather, the Attorney General had to ensure that emergency surveillance would ultimately be acceptable to the FISC. He had to be certain the court would grant a warrant before initiating emergency surveillance. Additionally, before NSA surveillance requests were submitted to the Attorney General, they had to be reviewed by NSA intelligence officers, NSA attorneys, and Department of Justice attorneys. Each reviewer had to be satisfied that standards had been met before the request proceeded to the next review group, and each request was certified by a senior official in the DoD, usually the Secretary or Deputy Secretary. From the time NSA sent a request to Justice's OIPR until the time data arrived at NSA, the average wait was between a day and a day and a half. In the existing threat environment with U.S. interests at risk, NSA deemed the wait too long.

Early Efforts to Amend FISA

Given the limitations of FISA, there were early efforts to amend the statute. For example, shortly after 11 September, the HPSCI asked NSA for technical assistance in drafting a proposal to amend Section of FISA that would give the President the authority to conduct electronic surveillances without a court order for the purpose of obtaining foreign intelligence information. On 20 September 2001, the NSA General Counsel wrote to Judge Alberto Gonzales, Counsel to the President, asking whether the proposal had merit. We found no record of a response.

We could not determine why early efforts to amend FISA were abandoned. Anecdotal evidence suggests that government officials feared the public debate surrounding any changes to FISA would compromise intelligence sources and methods.

NSA identifies SIGINT collection gaps to Vice President's Office.

Because early discussions about expanding NSA's authority were not documented, we do not have records of specific topics discussed or people who attended General Hayden's meetings with White House representatives. General Hayden stated that after consulting with NSA personnel, he described to the White House how NSA collection of communications on a wire inside the United States was constrained by the FISA statute. Specifically, NSA could not collect from a wire in the United States, without a court order, either content or metadata from communications links with either one or both ends in the United States. Furthermore, General Hayden pointed out that communications metadata did not have the same level of constitutional protection as content and that access to metadata of communications with one end in the United States would significantly enhance NSA's analytic capabilities. General Hayden suggested that the ability to collect communications with one end in the United States without a court order would increase NSA's speed and agility. General Hayden stated that after two additional meetings with the Vice President, the Vice President asked him to work with his Counsel, David Addington.

Presidential Authorization Drafted and Signed

According to General Hayden, the Vice President's Counsel, David Addington, drafted the first Authorization. General Hayden described himself as the "subject matter expert" but stated that no other NSA personnel participated in the drafting process, including the General Counsel. He also said that Department of Justice (DOJ) representatives were not involved in any of the discussions that he attended and he did not otherwise inform them.

General Hayden said he was "surprised with a small 's'" when the Authorization was signed on 4 October 2001, and that it only changed the location from which NSA could collect communications. Rules for minimizing U.S. person information still had to be followed.

SIGINT Activity Authorized by the President

On 4 October 2001, the President delegated authority through the Secretary of Defense to the Director of NSA to conduct specified electronic surveillance on targets related to Afghanistan and international terrorism for 30 days. Because the surveillance included wire and cable communications carried into or out of the United States, it would otherwise have required FISC authority.

The Authorization allowed NSA to conduct four types of collection activity:

- Telephony content
- Internet content
- Telephony metadata
- Internet metadata

NSA could collect the content and associated metadata of telephony and Internet communications for which there was probable cause to believe that one of the communicants was in Afghanistan or that one communicant was engaged in or preparing for acts of international terrorism. In addition, NSA was authorized to acquire telephony and Internet metadata for communications with at least one communicant outside the United States or for which no communicant was known to be a citizen of the United States. NSA was also allowed to retain, process, analyze and disseminate intelligence from the communications acquired under the authority.

Subsequent Changes to the Authorization

After the first Presidential authorization, the specific terms, wording, or interpretation of the renewals periodically changed. . . .

The report goes on to state that 3,018 people inside the United States had the contents of their phone or emails targeted between October 2001 and January 17, 2007, while 34,646 targets, or 92 percent of the total, were outside the United States. The Vice President's Counsel, David Addington, apparently prepared the PSP authorization for the President and obtained Attorney General and OLC approval. When the NSA General Counsel asked Addington if he could see the legal opinion authorizing PSP, he was turned down. NSA Director Hayden did not ask to see or read it. During the period when the leadership at OLC changed hands in 2003, and OLC head Jack Goldsmith joined senior DOJ officials in refusing to approve a reauthorization of the TSP in 2004 (*see infra*, Note 10), NSA lawyers were briefed on the PSP and provided comments on revised OLC opinions concerning the legality of PSP. *Id.* at 21-22. As early as June 2002, more than 500 people were cleared into PSP, including select members of Congress and two FISC judges. *Id.* at 24.

After the *New York Times* story broke in December 2005, the new

NSA Director, Gen. Keith B. Alexander, briefed all FISC judges on PSP in January 2006. *Id.* at 37. When FISC judges then took over responsibility for reviewing PSP (*see infra*, Note 3), the metadata components of STELLARWIND were authorized under pen register/trap and trace and business records orders, *id.* at 39-40, and the contents collection components were authorized under foreign and domestic content orders, on the theory that the U.S. gateway or cable head that foreign targets used for communications were "facilit[ies]" under traditional FISA definitions. *Id.* at 41.

[NSL p. 629, CTL p. 242. Insert at the end of Note 3.]

Congress acted to extend the FAA on December 28, 2012, three days before it was set to expire. It was extended for five years, until December 31, 2017. FISA Amendments Act Reauthorization Act of 2012, Pub. L. No. 112-238, 126 Stat. 1631. Although the Senate debated several amendments that would have addressed instances of inadvertent over-collection of U.S. persons communications under the FAA, all were defeated.

[NSL p. 632, CTL p. 245. Insert at end of chapter.]

c. The Snowden Leaks

In June 2013, former NSA contractor Edward Snowden disclosed to *The Guardian* and *The Washington Post* a series of classified documents that shed light on many details of some foreign intelligence collection programs implemented by NSA and other agencies after the 9/11 attacks. Some of these are excerpted elsewhere in this *Supplement*, *supra* p. 83 and *infra* pp. 91, 100.

One of the NSA programs first reported by *The Washington Post* is code-named PRISM. PRISM was launched as a result of agreements between the government and several U.S.-based Internet companies that permit NSA to monitor the contents of online communications of non-U.S. persons believed to by physically located outside the United States. Barton Gellman & Laura Poitras, *Documents: U.S. Mining Data from 9 Leading Internet Firms; Companies Deny Knowledge*, Wash. Post, June 6, 2013. According to briefing slides obtained by *The Post* and intended for senior NSA analysts, PRISM has become one of the most important sources of intelligence, including those that contribute to the President's Daily Brief. *Id.*

The leaked slides list the U.S. companies that have cooperated in PRISM operations: Microsoft, Yahoo, Google, Facebook, PalTalk, AOL, Skype, YouTube, and Apple. *Id.* Although NSA could conceivably extract anything at will from a company's data stream, following FAA §702 (50 U.S.C. §1881a) requirements and the resulting directives, NSA analysts apparently employ search terms inside a company's data set that purports to produce at least 51 percent confidence in a target's "foreignness." *Id.* Through contact chaining — building a list or network by modeling the communication patterns of targeted entities and their associates from communications sent or received by the targets — NSA would typically search two "hops," or degrees of separation from the target. *See* Office of the Inspector General, National Security Agency/Central Security Service, *1109-0002 Working Draft*, Mar. 24, 2009, at 13, *available at* http://www.guardian.co.uk/world/interactive/2013/jun/27/nsa- inspector-general-report-document-data-collection.

A release by DNI James Clapper declared that "PRISM is not an undisclosed collection or data mining program. It is an internal government computer system used to facilitate the government's statutorily authorized collection of foreign intelligence information from electronic communication service providers under court supervision. . . . The Government cannot target anyone under the court-approved procedures [prescribed by the FAA] unless there is an appropriate, and documented, foreign intelligence purpose for the acquisition. . . ." Director Of National Intelligence, *Facts on the Collection of Intelligence Pursuant to Section 702 of the Foreign Intelligence Surveillance Act*, June 8, 2013, http://www.dni.gov/index.php/newsroom/press-releases/191-press-releases-2013/871-facts-on-the-collection-of-intelligence-pursuant-to-section-702-of-the-foreign-intelligence-surveillance-act. Director Clapper also stated that PRISM enabled the government to acquire "information on a terrorist organization's strategic planning efforts . . . intelligence regarding proliferation networks . . . [and] significant and unique intelligence regarding potential cyber threats to the United States." *Id.*

Within days of the initial disclosures, *The Guardian* released additional classified documents provided by Snowden. Two of them set out procedures for implementing FAA Section 702 programmatic surveillance.

TOP SECRET//COMINT//NOFORN//20320108

EXHIBIT A[2]

Procedures Used by the National Security Agency for Targeting Non-United States Persons Reasonably Believed to Be Located Outside the United States to Acquire Foreign Intelligence Information Pursuant to Section 702 of the Foreign Intelligence Surveillance Act of 1978, as Amended . . .

I. DETERMINATION OF WHETHER THE ACQUISITION TARGETS NON-UNITED STATES PERSONS REASONABLY BELIEVED TO BE LOCATED OUTSIDE THE UNITED STATES

NSA determines whether a person is a non-United States person reasonably believed to be outside the United States in light of the totality of the circumstances based on the information available with respect to that person, including information concerning the communications facility or facilities used by that person.

NSA analysts examine the following three categories of information, as appropriate under the circumstances, to make the above determination: (1) they examine the lead information they have received regarding the potential target or the facility that has generated interest in conducting surveillance to determine what that lead information discloses about the person's location; (2) they conduct research in NSA databases, available reports and collateral information (i.e., information to which NSA has access but did not originate, such as reports from other agencies and publicly available information) to determine whether NSA knows the location of the person, or knows information that would provide evidence concerning that location; and (3) they conduct technical analyses of the facility or facilities to determine or verify

Derived From: NSA/CSSM 1-52
Dated: 20070108
Declassify On: 20320108

[2. This document was reportedly filed with the FISC in 2009. It was published online in Glenn Greenwald & James Ball, *The Top Secret Rules That Allow NSA to Use US Data Without a Warrant*, The Guardian, June 20, 2013.]

information about the person's location. NSA may use information from any one or a combination of these categories of information in evaluating the totality of the circumstances to determine that the potential target is located outside the United States.

In addition, in those cases where NSA seeks to acquire communications about the target that are not to or from the target, NSA will either employ an Internet Protocol filter to ensure that the person from whom it seeks to obtain foreign intelligence information is located overseas, or it will target Internet links that terminate in a foreign country. In either event, NSA will direct surveillance at a party to the communication reasonably believed to be outside the United States.

Lead Information

When NSA proposes to direct surveillance at a target, it does so because NSA has already learned something about the target or the facility or facilities the target uses to communicate. Accordingly, NSA will examine the lead information to determine what it reveals about the physical location of the target, including the location of the facility or facilities being used by the potential target.

The following are examples of the types of lead information that NSA may examine:

(a) Has the target stated that he is located outside the United States? For example, has NSA or another intelligence agency collected a statement or statements made by the target indicating that he is located outside the United States?

(b) Has a human intelligence source or other source of lead information indicated that the target is located outside the United States?

(c) Does the lead information provided by an intelligence or law enforcement agency of
the United States government or an intelligence or law enforcement service of a foreign government indicate that the target is located outside the United States?

(d) Was the lead information about the target found on a hard drive or other medium that
was seized in a foreign country?

(e) With whom has the target had direct contact, and what do we know about the location of such persons? For example, if lead information indicates the target is in direct contact with several members of a foreign-based terrorist organization or foreign-based political organization who themselves are located overseas, that may suggest, depending on the totality of the circumstances, that the target is also located overseas.

Information NSA Has About the Target's Location and/or Facility or Facilities Used by the Target

NSA may also review information in its databases, including repositories of information collected by NSA and by other intelligence agencies, as well as publicly available information, to determine if the person's location, or information providing evidence about the person's location, is already known. The NSA databases that would be used for this purpose contain information culled from signals intelligence, human intelligence, law enforcement information, and other sources. For example, NSA databases may include a report produced by the Central Intelligence Agency (CIA) with the fact that a known terrorist is using a telephone with a particular number, or detailed information on worldwide telephony numbering plans for wire and wireless telephone systems.

NSA Technical Analysis of the Facility

NSA may also apply technical analysis concerning the facility from which it intends to acquire foreign intelligence information to assist it in making determinations concerning the location of the person at whom NSA intends to direct surveillance. . . . [Examples include the country code of the telephone number, numbering databases for indications of the type of telephone being used that may provide an understanding of the location of the target, data repositories for previous Internet activity (which may contain network layer (e.g., Internet Protocol addresses) or machine identifier (e.g., Media Access Control addresses) information).]

Assessment of the Non-United States Person Status of the Target

In many cases, the information that NSA examines in order to determine whether a target is reasonably believed to be located outside the United States may also bear upon the non-United States person status of that target. For example, lead information provided by an intelligence or law enforcement service of a foreign government may indicate not only that the target is located in a foreign country, but that the target is a citizen of that or another foreign country. Similarly, information contained in NSA databases, including repositories of information collected by NSA and by other intelligence agencies, may indicate that the target is a non-United States person.

Furthermore, in order to prevent the inadvertent targeting of a United States person, NSA maintains records of telephone numbers and electronic communications accounts/addresses/ identifiers that NSA has reason to believe are being used by United States persons. Prior to targeting, a particular telephone number or electronic communications account/address/identifier will be compared against those records in order to ascertain whether NSA has reason to believe that telephone number or electronic communications account/address/identifier is being used by a United States person.

In the absence of specific information regarding whether a target is a United States person, a person reasonably believed to be located outside the United States or whose location is not known will be presumed to be a non-United States person unless such person can be positively identified as a United States person, or the nature or circumstances of the person's communications give rise to a reasonable belief that such person is a United States person.

Assessment of the Foreign Intelligence Purpose of the Targeting

In assessing whether the target possesses and/or is likely to communicate foreign intelligence information concerning a foreign power or foreign territory, NSA considers, among other things, the following factors:

a. With respect to telephone communications:
   - Information indicates that the telephone number has been used to communicate directly with another telephone number reasonably believed by the U.S. Intelligence Community to be used by an individual associated with a foreign power or foreign territory;
   - Information indicates that a user of the telephone number has communicated directly with an individual reasonably believed by the U.S. Intelligence Community to be associated with a foreign power or foreign territory;
   - Information indicates that the telephone number is listed in the telephone directory of a telephone used by an individual associated with a foreign power or foreign territory;

- Information indicates that the telephone number has been transmitted during a telephone call or other communication with an individual reasonably believed by the U.S. Intelligence Community to be associated with a foreign power or foreign territory;
- Publicly available sources of information (e.g., telephone listings) match the telephone number to an individual reasonably believed by the U.S. Intelligence Community to be associated with a foreign power or foreign territory;
- Information contained in various NSA-maintained knowledge databases containing foreign intelligence information acquired by any lawful means, such as electronic surveillance, physical search, or the use of a pen register and trap or trace device, or other information, reveals that the telephone number has been previously used by an individual associated with a foreign power or foreign territory; or
- Information made available to NSA analysts as a result of processing telephony metadata records acquired by any lawful means, such as electronic surveillance, physical search, or the use of a pen register or trap and trace device, or other information, reveals that the telephone number is used by an individual associated with a foreign power or foreign territory.

b. With respect to Internet communications: [a similar list of factors follows] . . . .

II. POST-TARGETING ANALYSIS BY NSA

After a person has been targeted for acquisition by NSA, NSA will conduct post-targeting analysis. Such analysis is designed to detect those occasions when a person who when targeted was reasonably believed to be located outside the United States has since entered the United States, and will enable NSA to take steps to prevent the intentional acquisition of any communication as to which the sender and all intended recipients are known at the time of acquisition to be located in the United States, or the intentional targeting of a person who is inside the United States. Such analysis may include:

For telephone numbers:

- Routinely comparing telephone numbers tasked pursuant to

these procedures against information that has been incidentally collected from the Global System for Mobiles (GSM) Home Location Registers (HLR). These registers receive updates whenever a GSM phone moves into a new service area. Analysis of this HLR information provides a primary indicator of a foreign user of a mobile telephone entering the United States.

- NSA analysts may analyze content for indications that a foreign target has entered or intends to enter the United States. Such content analysis will be conducted according to analytic and intelligence requirements and priorities.

For electronic communications accounts/addresses/identifiers:

- Routinely checking all electronic communications accounts/addresses/identifiers tasked pursuant to these procedures against available databases that contain Internet communications data (including metadata) to determine if an electronic communications account/address/identifier was accessed from overseas. Such databases contain communications contact information and summaries of communications activity from NSA signals intelligence collection. The foreign access determination is made based on comparing the Internet Protocol address associated with the account activity to other information NSA possesses about geographical area(s) serviced by particular Internet Protocol addresses. If the IP address associated with the target activity is identified as a U.S.-based network gateway (e.g., a Hotmail server) or a private Internet Protocol address, then NSA analysts will be required to perform additional research to determine if the access was in a foreign country using additional criteria such as machine identifier or case notation (NSA circuit identifier) of a communications link known to be foreign. Such databases normally maintain information about such activity for a 12-month period. This data will be used in an attempt to rule out false positives from U.S.-based network gateways. If the account access is determined to be from a U.S.-based machine, further analytic checks will be performed using content collection to determine if the target has moved into the United States.
- Routinely comparing electronic communications accounts/addresses/identifiers tasked pursuant to these procedures against a list of electronic communications accounts/addresses/identifiers already identified by NSA as being

accessed from inside the United States. This will help ensure that no target has been recognized to be located in the United States.

- NSA analysts may analyze content for indications that a target has entered or intends to enter the United States. Such content analysis will be conducted according to analytic and intelligence requirements and priorities.

If NSA determines that a target has entered the United States, it will follow the procedures set forth in section IV of this document, including the termination of the acquisition from the target without delay. In cases where NSA cannot resolve an apparent conflict between information indicating that the target has entered the United States and information indicating that the target remains located outside the United States, NSA will presume that the target has entered the United States and will terminate the acquisition from that target. If at a later time NSA determines that the target is in fact located outside the United States, NSA may re-initiate the acquisition in accordance with these procedures.

If NSA determines that a target who at the time of targeting was believed to be a non-United States person was in fact a United States person, it will follow the procedures set forth in section IV of this document, including the termination of the acquisition from the target without delay.

III. DOCUMENTATION

Analysts who request tasking will document in the tasking database a citation or citations to the information that led them to reasonably believe that a targeted person is located outside the United States. Before tasking is approved, the database entry for that tasking will be reviewed in order to verify that the database entry contains the necessary citations.

A citation is a reference that identifies the source of the information, such as a report number or communications intercept identifier, which NSA will maintain. The citation will enable those responsible for conducting oversight to locate and review the information that led NSA analysts to conclude that a target is reasonably believed to be located outside the United States.

Analysts also will identify the foreign power or foreign territory about which they expect to obtain foreign intelligence information pursuant to the proposed targeting.

IV. OVERSIGHT AND COMPLIANCE

NSA's Signals Intelligence Directorate (SID) Oversight and Compliance, with NSA's Office of General Counsel (OGC), will develop and deliver training regarding the applicable procedures to ensure intelligence personnel responsible for approving the targeting of persons under these procedures, as well as analysts with access to the acquired foreign intelligence information understand their responsibilities and the procedures that apply to this acquisition. SID Oversight and Compliance has established processes for ensuring that raw traffic is labeled and stored only in authorized repositories, and is accessible only to those who have had the proper training. SID Oversight and Compliance will conduct ongoing oversight activities and will make any necessary reports, including those relating to incidents of noncompliance, to the NSA Inspector General and OGC, in accordance with its NSA charter. SD Oversight and Compliance will also ensure that necessary corrective actions are taken to address any identified deficiencies. To that end, SID Oversight and Compliance will conduct periodic spot checks of targeting decisions and intelligence disseminations to ensure compliance with established procedures, and conduct periodic spot checks of queries in data repositories,

The Department of Justice (DOI) and the Office of the Director of National Intelligence (ODNI) will conduct oversight of NSA's exercise of the authority under section 702 of the Act, which will include periodic reviews by DOJ and ODNI personnel to evaluate the implementation of the procedures. Such reviews will occur at least once every sixty days.

NSA will report to DOJ, to the ODNI Office of General Counsel, and to the ODNI Civil Liberties Protection Officer any incidents of noncompliance with these procedures by NSA personnel that result in the intentional targeting of a person reasonably believed to be located in the United States, the intentional targeting of a United States person, or the intentional acquisition of any communication in which the sender and all intended recipients are known at the time of acquisition to be located within the United States. NSA will provide such reports within five business days of learning of the incident. Any information acquired by intentionally targeting a United States person or a person not reasonably believed to be outside the United States at the time of such targeting will be purged from NSA databases.

NSA will report to DOJ through the Deputy Assistant Attorney General in the National Security Division with responsibility for intelligence operations and oversight, to the ODNI Office of General Counsel, and to the ODNI Civil Liberties Protection Officer, any incidents of noncompliance (including overcollection) by any electronic communication service provider to whom the Attorney General and Director of National Intelligence issued a directive under section 702. Such report will be made within five business days after determining that the electronic communication service provider has not complied or does not intend to comply with a directive.

In the event that NSA concludes that a person is reasonably believed to be located outside the United States and after targeting this person learns that the person is inside the United States, or if NSA concludes that a person who at the time of targeting was believed to be a non-United States person was in fact a United States person, it will take the following steps:

1) Terminate the acquisition without delay and determine whether to seek a Court order under another section of the Act. If NSA inadvertently acquires a communication sent to or from the target while the target is or was located inside the United States, including any communication where the sender and all intended recipients are reasonably believed to be located inside the United States at the time of acquisition, such communication will be treated in accordance with the applicable minimization procedures.

2) Report the incident to DOJ through the Deputy Assistant Attorney General in the National Security Division with responsibility for intelligence operations and oversight, to the ODNI Office of General Counsel, and to the ODNI Civil Liberties Protection Officer within five business days.

V. DEPARTURE FROM PROCEDURES

If, in order to protect against an immediate threat to the national security, NSA determines that it must take action, on a temporary basis, in apparent departure from these procedures and that it is not feasible to obtain a timely modification of these procedures from the Attorney General and Director of National Intelligence, NSA may take such action and will report that activity promptly to DOJ through the Deputy Assistant Attorney General in the National Security Division with responsibility for intelligence operations and oversight, to the ODNI Office of General Counsel, and to the ODNI Civil Liberties Protection Officer. Under such circumstances, the Government will continue to adhere to all of the statutory limitations set forth in subsection 702(b) of the Act.

7-28-09 *Eric H. Holder, Jr.*
Date Attorney General of the United States

SECRET//COMINT//NOFORN//20320108

EXHIBIT B[3]

Minimization Procedures Used by the National Security Agency in Connection with Acquisitions of Foreign Intelligence Information Pursuant to Section 702 of the Foreign Intelligence Surveillance Act of 1978, as Amended

Section 1 — Applicability and Scope

These National Security Agency (NSA) minimization procedures apply to the acquisition, retention, use, and dissemination of non-publicly available information concerning unconsenting United States persons that is acquired by targeting non-United States persons reasonably believed to be located outside the United States in accordance with section 702 of the Foreign Intelligence Surveillance Act of 1978, as amended ("the Act").

If NSA determines that it must take action in apparent departure from these minimization procedures to protect against an immediate threat to human life (e.g., force protection or hostage situations) and that it is not feasible to obtain a timely modification of these procedures, NSA may take such action immediately. NSA will report the action taken to the Office of the Director of National Intelligence and to the National Security Division of the Department of Justice, which will promptly notify the Foreign Intelligence Surveillance Court of such activity.

[3. This document was reportedly filed with the FISC in 2009. It was published online in Glenn Greenwald & James Ball, *The Top Secret Rules That Allow NSA to Use US Data Without a Warrant*, The Guardian, June 20, 2013.]

Section 2 — Definitions

In addition to the definitions in sections 101 and 701 of the Act, the following definitions will apply to these procedures: . . .

(b) Communications concerning a United States person include all communications in which
a United States person is discussed or mentioned, except where such communications reveal only publicly-available information about the person. . . .

(f) Identification of a United States person means the name, unique title, address, or other personal identifier of a United States person in the context of activities conducted by that person or activities conducted by others that are related to that person. A reference to a product by brand name, or manufacturer's name or the use of a name in a descriptive sense, e.g., "Monroe Doctrine," is not an identification of a United States person. . . .

(j) United States person means a United States person as defined in the Act. The following guidelines apply in determining whether a person whose status is unknown is a United States person:

(1) A person known to be currently in the United States will be treated as a United States person unless positively identified as an alien who has not been admitted for permanent residence, or unless the nature or circumstances of the person's communications give rise to a reasonable belief that such person is not a United States person.

(2) A person known to be currently outside the United States, or whose location is unknown, will not be treated as a United States person unless such person can be positively identified as such, or the nature or circumstances of the person's communications give rise to a reasonable belief that such person is a United States person.

(3) A person known to be an alien admitted for permanent residence loses status as a United States person if the person leaves the United States and is not in compliance with 8 U.S.C. §1203 enabling re-entry into the United States. Failure to follow the statutory procedures provides a reasonable basis to conclude that the alien has abandoned any intention of maintaining his status as a permanent resident alien.

(4) An unincorporated association whose headquarters or primary office is located outside the United States is presumed not to be a United States person unless there is information indicating that

a substantial number of its members are citizens of the United States or aliens lawfully admitted for permanent residence.

Section 3 — Acquisition and Processing — General . . .

(b) Monitoring, Recording, and Processing

(1) Personnel will exercise reasonable judgment in determining whether information acquired must be minimized and will destroy inadvertently acquired communications of or concerning a United States person at the earliest practicable point in the processing cycle at which such communication can be identified either: as clearly not relevant to the authorized purpose of the acquisition (e.g., the communication does not contain foreign intelligence information); or, as not containing evidence of a crime which may be disseminated under these procedures. Such inadvertently acquired communications of or concerning a United States person may be retained no longer than five years in any event. The communications that may be retained include electronic communications acquired because of limitations on NSA's ability to filter communications.

(2) Communications of or concerning United States persons that may be related to the authorized purpose of the acquisition may be forwarded to analytic personnel responsible for producing intelligence information from the collected data. Such communications or information may be retained and disseminated only in accordance with Sections 4, 5, 6, and 8 of these procedures.

(3) Magnetic tapes or other storage media that contain acquired communications may be processed.

(4) As a communication is reviewed, NSA analyst(s) will determine whether it is a domestic or foreign communication to, from, or about a target and is reasonably believed to contain foreign intelligence information or evidence of a crime. Only such communications may be processed. All other communications may be retained or disseminated only in accordance with Sections 5, 6, and 8 of these procedures.

(5) Magnetic tapes or other storage media containing communications acquired pursuant to section 702 may be scanned by computer to identify and select communications for analysis. Computer selection terms used for scanning, such as telephone numbers, key words or phrases, or other discriminators, will not include United States person names or identifiers and will be limited

to those selection terms reasonably likely to return information about foreign intelligence targets.

(6) Further processing, retention and dissemination of foreign communications will be made in accordance with Sections 4, 6, 7, and 8 as applicable, below. Further processing, storage and dissemination of inadvertently acquired domestic communications will be made in accordance with Sections 4, 5, and 8 below.

(c) Destruction of Raw Data

Communications and other information, including that reduced to graphic or "hard copy" form such as facsimile, telex, computer data, or equipment emanations, will be reviewed for retention in accordance with the standards set forth in these procedures. Communications and other information, in any form, that do not meet such retention standards and that are known to contain communications of or concerning United States persons will be destroyed upon recognition, and may be retained no longer than five years in any event. The communications that may be retained include electronic communications acquired because of limitations on NSA's ability to filter communications.

(d) Change in Target's Location or Status

(1) In the event that NSA determines that a person is reasonably believed to be located outside the United States and after targeting this person learns that the person is inside the United States, or if NSA concludes that a person who at the time of targeting was believed to be a non-United States person is in fact a United States person, the acquisition from that person will be terminated without delay.

(2) Any communications acquired through the targeting of a person who at the time of targeting was reasonably believed to be located outside the United States but is in fact located inside the United States at the time such communications were acquired, and any communications acquired by targeting a person who at the time of targeting was believed to be a non-United States person but was in fact a United States person, will be treated as domestic communications under these procedures.

Section 4 — Acquisition and Processing — Attorney-Client Communications

As soon as it becomes apparent that a communication is between a person who is known to be under criminal indictment in the United

States and an attorney who represents that individual in the matter under indictment (or someone acting on behalf of the attorney), monitoring of that communication will cease and the communication will be identified as an attorney-client communication in a log maintained for that purpose. The relevant portion of the communication containing that conversation will be segregated and the National Security Division of the Department of Justice will be notified so that appropriate procedures may be established to protect such communications from review or use in any criminal prosecution, while preserving foreign intelligence information contained therein. Additionally, all proposed disseminations of information constituting United States person attorney-client privileged communications must be reviewed by the NSA Office of General Counsel prior to dissemination.

Section 5 — Domestic Communications

A communication identified as a domestic communication will be promptly destroyed upon recognition unless the Director (or Acting Director) of NSA specifically determines, in writing, that:

(1) the communication is reasonably believed to contain significant foreign intelligence information. Such communication may be provided to the Federal Bureau of Investigation (FBI) (including United States person identities) for possible dissemination by the FBI in accordance with its minimization procedures;

(2) the communication does not contain foreign intelligence information but is reasonably believed to contain evidence of a crime that has been, is being, or is about to be committed. Such communication may be disseminated (including United States person identities) to appropriate Federal law enforcement authorities, in accordance with 50 U.S.C. §§1806(b) and 1825(c), Executive Order No. 12333. . . . Such communications may be retained by NSA for a reasonable period of time, not to exceed six months unless extended in writing by the Attorney General, to permit law enforcement agencies to determine whether access to original recordings of such communications is required for law enforcement purposes;

(3) the communication is reasonably believed to contain technical data base information, as defined in Section 2(i), or information necessary to understand or assess a communications

security vulnerability. Such communication may be provided to the FBI and/or disseminated to other elements of the United States Government. . . .

Notwithstanding the above, if a domestic communication indicates that a target has entered the United States, NSA may advise the FBI of that fact. Moreover, technical data regarding domestic communications may be retained and provided to the FBI and CIA for collection avoidance purposes.

Section 6 — Foreign Communications of or Concerning United States Persons

(a) Retention

Foreign communications of or concerning United States persons collected in the course of an acquisition authorized under section 702 of the Act may be retained only:

(1) if necessary for the maintenance of technical data bases. Retention for this purpose is permitted for a period sufficient to allow a thorough exploitation and to permit access to data that are, or are reasonably believed likely to become, relevant to a current or future foreign intelligence requirement. Sufficient duration may vary with the nature of the exploitation. . . .

(2) if dissemination of such communications with reference to such United States persons would be permitted under subsection (b) below; or

(3) if the information is evidence of a crime that has been, is being, or is about to be committed and is provided to appropriate federal law enforcement authorities.

(b) Dissemination

A report based on communications of or concerning a United States person may be disseminated in accordance with Section 7 or 8 if the identity of the United States person is deleted and a generic term or symbol is substituted so that the information cannot reasonably be connected with an identifiable United States person. Otherwise, dissemination of intelligence reports based on communications of or concerning a United States person may only be made to a recipient requiring the identity of such person for the performance of official duties but only if at least one of the following criteria is also met:

(1) the United States person has consented to dissemination or the information of or concerning the United States person is

available publicly;

(2) the identity of the United States person is necessary to understand foreign intelligence information or assess its importance, e.g., the identity of a senior official in the Executive Branch;

(3) the communication or information indicates that the United States person may be:

a. an agent of a foreign power;

b. a foreign power as defined in Section 101(a) of the Act;

c. residing outside the United States and holding an official position in the government or military forces of a foreign power;

d. a corporation or other entity that is owned or controlled directly or indirectly by a foreign power; or

e. acting in collaboration with an intelligence or security service of a foreign power and the United States person has, or has had, access to classified national security information or material;

(4) the communication or information indicates that the United States person may be the target of intelligence activities of a foreign power;

(5) the communication or information indicates that the United States person is engaged in the unauthorized disclosure of classified national security information or the United States person's identity is necessary to understand or assess a communications security vulnerability, but only after the agency that originated the information certifies that it is properly classified;

(6) the communication or information indicates that the United States person may be engaging in international terrorist activities;

(7) the acquisition of the United States person's communication was authorized by a court order issued pursuant to the Act and the communication may relate to the foreign intelligence purpose of the surveillance; or

(8) the communication or information is reasonably believed to contain evidence that a crime has been, is being, or is about to be committed, provided that dissemination is for law enforcement purposes and is made in accordance with 50 U.S.C. §§1806(b) and 1825(c), Executive Order No. 12333 . . . .

(c) Provision of Unminimized Communications to CIA and FBI

(1) NSA may provide to the Central Intelligence Agency (CIA) unminimized communications acquired pursuant to section 702 of the Act. CIA will identify to NSA targets for which NSA may

provide unminimized communications to CIA. CIA will process any such unminimized communications received from NSA in accordance with CIA minimization procedures adopted by the Attorney General, in consultation with the Director of National Intelligence, pursuant to subsection 702(e) of the Act.

(2) NSA may provide to the FBI unminimized communications acquired pursuant to section 702 of the Act. . . .

Section 7 — Other Foreign Communications

Foreign communications of or concerning a non-United States person may be retained, used, and disseminated in any form in accordance with other applicable law, regulation, and policy.

Section 8 — Collaboration with Foreign Governments . . . .

7-28-09	*Eric H. Holder, Jr.*
Date	Attorney General of the United States

---

1. *What's the Big Deal?* Is PRISM focused on just what the FAA authorized — realtime collection against non-U.S. persons outside the United States? If so, why would the government object to its disclosure? Who would benefit from knowing the identities of U.S. companies cooperating with NSA under Section 702 agreements?

2. *The Value of PRISM*. In June 18, 2013 testimony before the House Intelligence Committee the NSA Director, General Keith Alexander, stated that PRISM and a metadata collection program described in this *Supplement*, *infra* p. 113, have helped "prevent . . . potential terrorist events over 50 times since 9/11." Sean Sullivan, *NSA Head: Surveillance Helped Thwart More than 50 Terror Plots*, Wash. Post, June 18, 2013. Publicly disclosed examples included the cases of Najibullah Zazi, who pleaded guilty to planning suicide attacks in New York City, and David Headley, a co-conspirator in the 2008 terrorist attacks by Pakistani operatives in Mumbai, India. *Id*. If General Alexander's claims are accurate, do you see any downsides to PRISM?

3. *Just What Does PRISM Collect?* Can you tell from the descriptions of PRISM and the targeting procedures in *Exhibit A* what

data are or may be collected by NSA? Does PRISM include email messages, Facebook posts, instant messages? Audio and video chats, or photographs? Facebook reported that in the last six months of 2012 the company provided law enforcement (federal, state, and local, including NSA) the private data of between 18,000 and 19,000 user accounts. Ted Ullyot, *Facebook Releases Data, Including All National Security Requests*, facebook Newsroom, June 14, 2013, http://newsroom.fb.com/News/636/Facebook-Releases-Data-Including-All-National-Security-Requests. Do you suppose that the extent and nature of the collection varies from company to company? In what ways?

4. *The Targeting Procedures*. The NSA targeting and minimization procedures are dated January 8, 2007 (the date appears on the bottom of the first pages of Exhibits A and B, respectively), during the period when the FISC was providing periodic review and approval of TSP and a few months before Congress approved the Protect America Act. Attorney General Eric Holder signed both sets of procedures on July 28, 2009. Although we cannot be sure that these procedures remain in effect, the mechanisms described are consistent with details provided by NSA Director Keith Alexander and others following the Snowden leaks.

As reported in the 2009 NSA Inspector General report, *supra*, NSA apparently relies on Section 702 collection and PRISM to provide the basis for a form of link analysis, known as contact chaining, in which an analyst begins with a phone number, e-mail address, or Internet identifier, and then uses algorithms to find other communications linked to the original source.

Do these procedures for wholesale data collection occurs satisfy FISA and the Constitution? Consider the following issues:

a. *Avoiding U.S. Persons?* Does the list of questions posed in deriving lead information sufficiently protect U.S. persons? What guidance would you add? How about the location and facility guidance? If NSA believes that the data it has collected pertain to a U.S. person, is the agency obligated to destroy the data? Under what circumstances may the data be retained? For how long?

b. *Foreign Intelligence Redux and Post-Targeting Analysis*. Do the lists of factors considered by NSA in assessing whether a potential target possesses or is likely to communicate foreign intelligence information provide adequate guidance to agency personnel? Is the post-targeting analysis likely to prevent over-collection when a target has traveled to the United States? The phrase "foreign intelligence" is pervasive in describing authorized collection activities, including those authorized by FISA and its programmatic title.

Significantly, the term is still defined by geography: targeting is permitted against those reasonably believed to be outside the United States. Through PRISM, massive quantities of the contents of emails and other electronic communications are collected on the basis of presumed location. Given the imperfections of presuming location through Internet or phone use, does the "foreign intelligence" objective of programmatic collection lead inevitably to collection on Americans?

c. *Collection against U.S. Persons*. PRISM collection also inevitably acquires information from U.S. persons as a byproduct of contact chaining and the "hops" from the initial non-U.S.-person targets believed to be abroad. Given that U.S.-person communications are intermingled with foreign communications collected from U.S. companies' fiber optic cables in the United States, PRISM collection has no way of ensuring that only non-U.S.-person communications are scooped up. NSA has reportedly interpreted the FAA to require that in keying in its search terms it need only ensure 51 percent confidence in the target's "foreignness." Gellman, *supra*. In theory, then, nearly half of the time NSA could mistakenly target U.S. persons.

For now, a U.S. person is more likely to have her communications collected if she communicates with someone abroad, given the authorized targeting. However, the NSA slides leaked by Snowden and reported by *The Washington Post* promised that PRISM would soon expand to include cloud computing companies. If so, then two U.S. persons communicating domestically could have their communications intercepted, too. Gellman, *supra*.

NSA is increasingly able to store and process massive amounts of data available at any time to its analysts. Open source software like Hadoop lets NSA preserve aggregated data on agency computers until an analyst needs the information. The analyst can look at what was collected and make the non-U.S.-person/U.S.-person distinctions later. Shane Harris, *The NSA Can't Tell the Difference Between an American and a Foreigner*, Foreign Policy, June 28, 2013, http://www.foreignpolicy.com/articles/2013/06/27/the_nsa_cant_tell_the_difference_between_an_american_and_a_foreigner. Implicitly, then, the combination of big data and sophisticated software makes it more likely that U.S.-

persons communications will be reviewed by NSA analysts.

Does the incidental collection of U.S. person information under PRISM violate the FAA? The Constitution? If the initial search of the PRISM database is conducted entirely by computer, can a computer by itself violate your privacy? *See* Richard A. Posner, *Privacy, Surveillance, and Law*, 75 U. Chi. L. Rev. 245, 254 (2008) ("Computer searches do not invade privacy because computers are not sentient beings.").

Within days of the Snowden leaks, NSA Director Alexander ordered removed from the NSA website a fact sheet that asserted that the program "allows only the targeting . . . of communications of foreign persons who are located abroad." Letter from General Keith B. Alexander to Senators Ron Wyden & Mark Udall, June 25, 2013, http://images.politico.com/global/2013/06/25/nsawydenudallltr.html. How would you revise the NSA fact sheet, based on what you know about PRISM? Can you think of ways to limit this form of over-collection without compromising the utility of PRISM?

d. *Oversight and Compliance*. Do you believe that the guidelines and training contemplated by the targeting procedures will effectively ensure against over-collection against U.S. persons? If not, how would you modify the requirements? Are you comfortable with the procedures for reporting departures from the targeting procedures?

5. *Section 702 Minimization*. Recall that the statutory minimization requirements for programmatic surveillance in the FAA parrot the language of traditional FISA minimization. Should legal standards for minimization associated with individualized and programmatic electronic collection be the same? Consider the following issues:

a. *Culling the U.S. Person Data*. Reviewing the classified Section 702 minimization procedures, would you say that minimization fairly protects U.S. persons whose private information is inadvertently collected? Are the definitional guidelines and identifiers sufficiently clear? Are the presumptions set as they should be, consistent with FISA and the Constitution?

b. *Acquisition and Processing*. The threshold "reasonable judgment" made by NSA personnel is critical in determining whether what is collected is minimized or destroyed. Would you say that the analysts have sufficient guidance from these procedures to make these decisions, including the domestic vs. foreign determination? What exactly can NSA do with the realtime intelligence it collects? How does NSA decide what to do when a question arises about a communicant's nationality or location, or about attorney-client communications?

c. *Domestic Communications*. Once identified as domestic communication, data will normally be promptly destroyed. Are you satisfied that the conditions that permit senior NSA officials to retain U.S. person communications are sufficiently attentive to the needs for both foreign intelligence and the privacy of innocent persons? What is the justification for retaining data that may contain U.S. person information for up to five years? What do you suppose is the measure of a "threat of harm" as a justification for retaining inadvertently collected U.S. person information? Should NSA keep information on criminal activity unrelated to terrorism?

d. *Foreign Communications of or Concerning U.S. Persons*. Under what circumstances may NSA personnel overcome the presumption against retention and dissemination of U.S. persons data? Can you imagine circumstances in which knowledge of the identity of a U.S. person is necessary to understand or assess the importance of foreign intelligence? For unminimized communications provided to the CIA or FBI, can you predict what minimization standards will guide those agencies' use of the shared information?

6. *The Role of the FISC*. What legal standards were applied by the FISC in approving the PRISM directives? The targeting and minimization procedures? Does the FISC have a role in monitoring the PRISM directives? In October 2011, the FISC ruled that NSA minimization violated the Fourth Amendment in some undisclosed way. Spencer Ackerman, *U.S. Admits Surveillance Violated Constitution At Least Once*, Danger Room, July 20, 2012, http://www.wired.com/dangerroom/2012/07/surveillance-spirit-law/. Can you piece together how the FISC would have had an opportunity to make such a determination?

If the FISC's only role is periodic re-approval of the procedures, as opposed to individualized approval of their application, is that role properly characterized as adjudicative? Or is it more administrative (or, perhaps, legislative)? *Should* an Article III court be engaged in such rule approval?

[NSL p. 649, CTL p. 262. Insert after Note 5.]

6. *Requiem for Smith and Miller?* The assumptions underlying *Smith* and *Miller* may be eroding even in the Supreme Court. In a recent case in which the Court unanimously sustained a Fourth Amendment challenge to the use of a hidden GPS tracking device on a suspect's vehicle, Justice Sotomayor wrote in a concurring opinion:

> [I]t may be necessary to reconsider the premise that an individual has no reasonable expectation of privacy in information voluntarily disclosed to third parties. *E.g., Smith* [*v. Maryland*, 442 U.S. 735 (1979)], at 742; *United States v. Miller*, 425 U.S. 435 (1976). This approach is ill suited to the digital age, in which people reveal a great deal of information about themselves to third parties in the course of carrying out mundane tasks. People disclose the phone numbers that they dial or text to their cellular providers; the URLs that they visit and the e-mail addresses with which they correspond to their Internet service providers; and the books, groceries, and medications they purchase to online retailers. Perhaps, as Justice Alito notes, some people may find the "tradeoff" of privacy for convenience "worthwhile," or come to accept this "diminution of privacy" as "inevitable," *post*, at 962, and perhaps not. I for one doubt that people would accept without complaint the warrantless disclosure to the Government of a list of every Web site they had visited in the last week, or month, or year. But whatever the societal expectations, they can attain constitutionally protected status only if our Fourth Amendment jurisprudence ceases to treat secrecy as a prerequisite for privacy. I would not assume that all information voluntarily disclosed to some member of the public for a limited purpose is, for that reason alone, disentitled to Fourth Amendment protection. See *Smith*, at 749 (Marshall, J., dissenting) ("Privacy is not a discrete commodity, possessed absolutely or not at all. Those who disclose certain facts to a bank or phone company for a limited business purpose need not assume that this information will be released to other persons for other purposes"); see also *Katz* [*v. United States*, 389 U.S. 347], at 351–352 ("[W]hat [a person] seeks to preserve as private, even in an area accessible to the public, may be constitutionally protected"). [*United States v. Jones*, 132 S. Ct. 945, 957 (2012).]

[NSL p. 668, CTL p. 281. Add to end of Note 4.]

Before the 2013 Snowden document dump (see *supra* this *Supplement* pp. 82, 89), many thought that Section 215 orders were used only case-by-case for individually targeted collection of transactional data. However, the documents included an April 25, 2013 order from the FISC to Verizon for production

> on an ongoing daily basis thereafter for the duration of this Order [ninety days] . . . [of] an electronic copy of the following tangible things: all call detail records or "telephony metadata" created by Verizon for communications (i) between the United States and abroad; or (ii) wholly within the United States, including local telephone calls. . . . Telephony metadata includes comprehensive communications routing information, including but not limited to session identifying information (*e.g.*, originating and terminating telephone number, International Mobile Subscriber Identity (IMSI) number, International Mobile station Equipment Identity (IMEI) number, etc.), trunk identifier, telephone calling card numbers, and time and duration of call. Telephony metadata does not include the substantive content of any communication, as identified by 18 U.S.C. §2510(8), or the name, address, or financial information of a subscriber or customer.

In re Application of the Federal Bureau of Investigation for an Order Requiring the Production of Tangible Things from Verizon Business Network Services, Inc. on Behalf of MCI Communication Services, Inc. d/b/a Verizon Business Services, Foreign Intell. Surv. Ct., No. BR 13-80, April 25, 2013. (This order, marked "Top Secret," was published online in Glenn Greenwald, *NSA Collecting Phone Records of Millions of Verizon Customers Daily*, The Guardian, June 5, 2013, http://www.guardian.co.uk/world/2013/jun/06/nsa-phone-records-verizon-court-order.)[1]

---

1. A Congressional Research Service report suggests how Section 215 data have been used in conjunction with Section 702 programmatic intercepts:

> NSA, using 702 authorities, intercepted an email between an extremist in Pakistan and an individual in the United States. NSA provided this email to the FBI, which identified and began to surveil Colorado-based Najibulla Zazi. NSA then received Zazi's phone number from the FBI, checked it against phone records procured using 215 authorities, and identified one of Zazi's accomplices, an individual named Adis Medunjanin. Zazi and Medunjanin were both subsequently arrested and convicted of planning to

The use of Section 215 to collect telephone information was not a surprise. But the leaked order showed, for the first time, that the government was using it not just to access "specific items about specific persons on a case-by-case basis, but also as a means to create giant databases of telephony metadata that might later be queried on a case-by-case basis." Robert Chesney & Benjamin Wittes, *A Tale of Two NSA Leaks*, June10, 2013, www.newrepublic.com/article/ 113427/nsa-spying-scandal-one-leak-more-damaging-other#.

How is the bulk pre-collection of telephony data relevant to an authorized investigation to protect against terrorism? If your answer is that it *might* be relevant to a future more individualized investigation, because there could be a needle somewhere in the haystack, then what data set *isn't* relevant in the same sense? Do you suppose that this kind of potential usefulness is what Congress had in mind when it amended the relevancy standard?

> When dealing with a physical object, we naturally treat relevance on an object-by-object basis. Sets of records are different. If Verizon has a database containing billions of phone calls made by millions of customers, is that database a single thing, millions of things, or billions of things? Is relevance measured by each record, each customer, or the relevance of the entire database as a whole? If the entire massive database has a single record that is relevant, does that make the entire database relevant, too?

Id. (quoting Orin Kerr at the *Volokh Conspiracy*).

If the government's aggressive view of relevancy concerns you, would back-end controls (minimization), including durational limits on maintenance of the database, tighter relevancy restrictions on secondary access requests, and limits on distribution compensate? Verizon and other telecommunications companies that presumably received similar access orders apparently do not keep telephony data sets for any significant period of time. Does that make a difference in judging the need for the bulk collection? In judging its legality?

---

bomb the New York City subway.

Marshall Curtis Erwin & Edward C. Liu, *NSA Surveillance Leaks: Background and Issues for Congress* 10 (Cong. Res. Serv. R43134), July 2, 2013.

Even before the bulk Section 215 orders, certain "Internet metadata" were collected without any court order or any apparent statutory authority, according to a 2009 report of the Inspector General of the National Security Agency. *See* Office of the Inspector General, National Security Agency/Central Security Service, *1109-0002 Working Draft,* Mar. 24, 2009, *available at* http://www.guardian.co.uk/world/interactive/2013/jun/27/nsa-inspector-general-report-document-data-collection. This collection was temporarily halted by a "palace revolt" by Department of Justice officials, who resisted White House efforts to have the then seriously ill Attorney General John Ashcroft sign an order authorizing the program's continuation. *Id.* See NSL p. 618, n.10; CTL p. 231, n.10, erroneously connecting this controversy to the TSP. The collection effort was then resumed after an order was obtained from the FISC. This effort was reportedly discontinued in 2011 as a result of an interagency review. Office of the Inspector General, *supra.*

[NSL p. 671; CTL p. 284. Insert after Note 10.]

A federal district court said no in *In re National Security Letter*, C 11-02173 SI, 2013 WL 1095417 (N.D. Cal. Mar. 14, 2013), reasoning that the Second Circuit's creative reconstruction of the statute with the help of the executive branch crossed the line between adjudicating and legislating.

> . . . As an initial matter, the Court finds that it is not within its power to "conform" the NSL nondisclosure provisions, as did the Second Circuit. The statutory provisions at issue — as written, adopted and amended by Congress in the face of a constitutional challenge — are not susceptible to narrowing or conforming constructions to save their constitutionality. . . . [T]he narrow defects in the statutes under review in those cases [in which the courts did so "conform" the statute under challenge] bear little resemblance to the multiple constitutional inadequacies identified by the Court in the NSL nondisclosure provisions. . . .
>
> . . . [Alternatively,] the government asserts that this Court should rely on the "canon of constitutional avoidance." Here, however, the Court cannot ignore express language in the statute in order to come up with "reasonable interpretations" that would be constitutional.
>
> The government also relies on a line of cases where courts accepted limiting constructions offered by the government to avoid striking down content-neutral time, place and manner restrictions on speech. Again, those cases are inapposite to the situation here, where Congress has drafted a very

specific statute aimed at preventing speech on a particular subject, and redrafted amendments to it to address identified constitutional deficiencies. In light of the language actually and intentionally used by Congress in amending the statute after it was initially struck down as unconstitutional by two different district courts in the Second Circuit, this Court finds there is no "reasonable construction" that can avoid the constitutional infirmities that have been identified.

The Court also finds that the unconstitutional nondisclosure provisions are not severable. . . .

Id. at *14-*15.

[NSL p. 680, CTL p. 293. Replace *United States v. Arnold* with the following opinion.]

United States v. Cotterman

United States Court of Appeals for the Ninth Circuit, Mar. 8, 2013
709 F.3d 952 (en banc)

McKEOWN, Circuit Judge: Every day more than a million people cross American borders, from the physical borders with Mexico and Canada to functional borders at airports such as Los Angeles (LAX), Honolulu (HNL), New York (JFK, LGA), and Chicago (ORD, MDW). As denizens of a digital world, they carry with them laptop computers, iPhones, iPads, iPods, Kindles, Nooks, Surfaces, tablets, Blackberries, cell phones, digital cameras, and more. These devices often contain private and sensitive information ranging from personal, financial, and medical data to corporate trade secrets. And, in the case of Howard Cotterman, child pornography. . . .

This watershed case implicates both the scope of the narrow border search exception to the Fourth Amendment's warrant requirement and privacy rights in commonly used electronic devices. The question we confront "is what limits there are upon this power of technology to shrink the realm of guaranteed privacy." *Kyllo v. United States*, 533 U.S. 27, 34 (2001). More specifically, we consider the reasonableness of a computer search that began as a cursory review at the border but transformed into a forensic examination of Cotterman's hard drive. . . .

I. Factual Background and Procedural History

[Cotterman and his wife were crossing the border on their way home to the United States from a vacation in Mexico. During the primary border inspection, a watch list returned a hit, indicating that Cotterman was a sex offender who had been previously convicted on two counts of use of a minor in sexual conduct, two counts of lewd and lascivious conduct upon a child, and three counts of child molestation. This hit raised a question for border agents whether Cotterman was potentially involved in child sex tourism. He was therefore subjected to a secondary inspection of his car which retrieved two laptop computers and three digital cameras. A border agent inspected the electronic devices and found what appeared to be family and other personal photos, along with several password-protected files.

The agents allowed the Cottermans to leave the border but retained the Cottermans' laptops and a digital camera. An agent then took the laptops and cameras 170 miles to an ICE office in Tucson, Arizona, for further forensic examination. Opening the password-protected files, a computer expert found hundreds of images of child pornography.

A grand jury indicted Cotterman for a host of offenses related to child pornography. Cotterman moved to suppress the evidence gathered from his laptop and the fruits of that evidence. The lower court granted the motion, and the government appealed.] . . .

III. The Border Search

The broad contours of the scope of searches at our international borders are rooted in "the long-standing right of the sovereign to protect itself by stopping and examining persons and property crossing into this country." [*United States v. Ramsey*, 431 U.S. 606 (1977),] at 616. Thus, border searches form "a narrow exception to the Fourth Amendment prohibition against warrantless searches without probable cause." *United States v. Seljan*, 547 F.3d 993, 999 (9th Cir. 2008) (en banc) (internal quotation marks and citation omitted). Because "[t]he Government's interest in preventing the entry of unwanted persons and effects is at its zenith at the international border," *United States v. Flores-Montano,* 541 U.S. 149, 152 (2004), border searches are generally deemed "reasonable simply by virtue of the fact that they occur at the border." *Ramsey,* 431 U.S. at 616.

This does not mean, however, that at the border "anything goes."

Seljan, 547 F.3d at 1000. Even at the border, individual privacy rights are not abandoned but "[b]alanced against the sovereign's interests." *United States v. Montoya de Hernandez,* 473 U.S. 531, 539 (1985). That balance "is qualitatively different . . . than in the interior" and is "struck much more favorably to the Government." *Id.* at 538, 540. Nonetheless, the touchstone of the Fourth Amendment analysis remains reasonableness. The reasonableness of a search or seizure depends on the totality of the circumstances, including the scope and duration of the deprivation.

In view of these principles, the legitimacy of the initial search of Cotterman's electronic devices at the border is not in doubt. . . . But the search here transformed into something far different. The difficult question we confront is the reasonableness, without a warrant, of the forensic examination that comprehensively analyzed the hard drive of the computer.

A. The Forensic Examination Was Not an Extended Border Search

Cotterman urges us to treat the examination as an extended border search that requires particularized suspicion. Although the semantic moniker "extended border search" may at first blush seem applicable here, our jurisprudence does not support such a claim. We have "define[d] an extended border search as any search away from the border where entry is not apparent, but where the dual requirements of reasonable certainty of a recent border crossing and reasonable suspicion of criminal activity are satisfied." *United States v. Guzman-Padilla,* 573 F.3d 865, 878-79 (9th Cir. 2009) (internal quotation marks and citations omitted). The key feature of an extended border search is that an individual can be assumed to have cleared the border and thus regained an expectation of privacy in accompanying belongings.

Cotterman's case is different. Cotterman was stopped and searched at the border. Although he was allowed to depart the border inspection station after the initial search, some of his belongings, including his laptop, were not. The follow-on forensic examination was not an "extended border search." A border search of a computer is not transformed into an extended border search simply because the device is transported and examined beyond the border.

To be sure, our case law has not always articulated the "extended border search" doctrine with optimal clarity. But the confusion has come in distinguishing between facts describing a functional border search and those describing an extended border search, not in defining the standard for a search at the border. The "functional equivalent" doctrine effectively extends the border search doctrine to all ports of entry, including airports. A routine customs search at the "functional equivalent" of the border is "analyzed as a border search" and requires neither probable cause nor reasonable suspicion. This case involves a search initiated at the actual border and does not encounter any of the difficulties surrounding identification of a "functional" border. As to the extended border search doctrine, we believe it is best confined to cases in which, after an apparent border crossing or functional entry, an attenuation in the time or the location of conducting a search reflects that the subject has regained an expectation of privacy. . . .

B. Forensic Examination at the Border Requires Reasonable Suspicion

It is the comprehensive and intrusive nature of a forensic examination — not the location of the examination — that is the key factor triggering the requirement of reasonable suspicion here. The search would have been every bit as intrusive had Agent Owen traveled to the border with his forensic equipment. Indeed, Agent Owen had a laptop with forensic software that he could have used to conduct an examination at the port of entry itself, although he testified it would have been a more time-consuming effort. To carry out the examination of Cotterman's laptop, Agent Owen used computer forensic software to copy the hard drive and then analyze it in its entirety, including data that ostensibly had been deleted. This painstaking analysis is akin to reading a diary line by line looking for mention of criminal activity — plus looking at everything the writer may have erased.

Notwithstanding a traveler's diminished expectation of privacy at the border, the search is still measured against the Fourth Amendment's reasonableness requirement, which considers the nature and scope of the search. Significantly, the Supreme Court has recognized that the "dignity and privacy interests of the person being searched" at the border will on occasion demand "some level of suspicion in the case of highly intrusive searches of the person." *Flores-Montano,* 541 U.S. at 152. Likewise, the Court has explained that "some searches of property are so destructive," "particularly offensive," or overly intrusive in the manner in which they are carried out as to require particularized suspicion. . . .

We are now presented with a case directly implicating substantial personal privacy interests. The private information individuals store on digital devices — their personal "papers" in the words of the Constitution — in stark contrast to the generic and impersonal contents of a gas tank. We rest our analysis on the reasonableness of this search, paying particular heed to the nature of the electronic devices and the attendant expectation of privacy.

The amount of private information carried by international travelers was traditionally circumscribed by the size of the traveler's luggage or automobile. That is no longer the case. Electronic devices are capable of storing warehouses full of information. The average 400-gigabyte laptop hard drive can store over 200 million pages — the equivalent of five floors of a typical academic library. Even a car full of packed suitcases with sensitive documents cannot hold a candle to the sheer, and ever-increasing, capacity of digital storage.

The nature of the contents of electronic devices differs from that of luggage as well. Laptop computers, iPads and the like are simultaneously offices and personal diaries. They contain the most intimate details of our lives: financial records, confidential business documents, medical records and private emails. This type of material implicates the Fourth Amendment's specific guarantee of the people's right to be secure in their "papers." U.S. Const. amend. IV. The express listing of papers "reflects the Founders' deep concern with safeguarding the privacy of thoughts and ideas — what we might call freedom of conscience — from invasion by the government." *Seljan,* 547 F.3d at 1014 (Kozinski, C.J., dissenting). These records are expected to be kept private and this expectation is "one that society is prepared to recognize as 'reasonable.' " *Katz v. United States,* 389 U.S. 347, 361 (Harlan, J., concurring).

Electronic devices often retain sensitive and confidential information far beyond the perceived point of erasure, notably in the form of browsing histories and records of deleted files. This quality makes it impractical, if not impossible, for individuals to make meaningful decisions regarding what digital content to expose to the scrutiny that accompanies international travel. A person's digital life ought not be hijacked simply by crossing a border. When packing traditional luggage, one is accustomed to deciding what papers to take and what to leave behind. When carrying a laptop, tablet or other device, however, removing files unnecessary to an impending trip is an impractical solution given the volume and often intermingled nature of the files. It is also a time-consuming task that may not even effectively erase the files.

The present case illustrates this unique aspect of electronic data. Agents found incriminating files in the unallocated space of Cotterman's laptop, the space where the computer stores files that the user ostensibly deleted and maintains other "deleted" files retrieved from web sites the user has visited. Notwithstanding the attempted erasure of material or the transient nature of a visit to a web site, computer forensic examination was able to restore the files. It is as if a search of a person's suitcase could reveal not only what the bag contained on the current trip, but everything it had ever carried.

With the ubiquity of cloud computing, the government's reach into private data becomes even more problematic. In the "cloud," a user's data, including the same kind of highly sensitive data one would have in "papers" at home, is held on remote servers rather than on the device itself. The digital device is a conduit to retrieving information from the cloud, akin to the key to a safe deposit box. Notably, although the virtual "safe deposit box" does not itself cross the border, it may appear as a seamless part of the digital device when presented at the border. With access to the cloud through forensic examination, a traveler's cache is just a click away from the government.

As Justice Scalia wrote, "It would be foolish to contend that the degree of privacy secured to citizens by the Fourth Amendment has been entirely unaffected by the advance of technology." *Kyllo,* 533 U.S. at 33-34. Technology has the dual and conflicting capability to decrease privacy and augment the expectation of privacy. While the thermal imaging device in *Kyllo* threatened to expose the hour at which "the lady of the house" took her daily "sauna and bath," *id.* at 38, digital devices allow us to carry the very papers we once stored at home. . . .

This is not to say that simply because electronic devices house sensitive, private information they are off limits at the border. The relevant inquiry, as always, is one of reasonableness. But that reasonableness determination must account for differences in property. Unlike searches involving a reassembled gas tank, or small hole in the bed of a pickup truck, which have minimal or no impact beyond the search itself — and little implication for an individual's dignity and privacy interests — the exposure of confidential and personal information has permanence. It cannot be undone. Accordingly, the uniquely sensitive nature of data on electronic devices carries with it a significant expectation of privacy and thus renders an exhaustive exploratory search more intrusive than with other forms of property.

After their initial search at the border, customs agents made copies of the hard drives and performed forensic evaluations of the computers that took days to turn up contraband. It was essentially a computer strip search. An exhaustive forensic search of a copied laptop hard drive intrudes upon privacy and dignity interests to a far greater degree than a cursory search at the border. It is little comfort to assume that the government — for now — does not have the time or resources to seize and search the millions of devices that accompany the millions of travelers who cross our borders. It is the potential unfettered dragnet effect that is troublesome. . . .

International travelers certainly expect that their property will be searched at the border. What they do not expect is that, absent some particularized suspicion, agents will mine every last piece of data on their devices or deprive them of their most personal property for days (or perhaps weeks or even months, depending on how long the search takes). Such a thorough and detailed search of the most intimate details of one's life is a substantial intrusion upon personal privacy and dignity. We therefore hold that the forensic examination of Cotterman's computer required a showing of reasonable suspicion, a modest requirement in light of the Fourth Amendment.

IV. Reasonable Suspicion

Reasonable suspicion is defined as "a particularized and objective basis for suspecting the particular person stopped of criminal activity." *United States v. Cortez,* 449 U.S. 411, 417-18 (1981). This assessment is to be made in light of "the totality of the circumstances." *Id.* at 417. "[E]ven when factors considered in isolation from each other are susceptible to an innocent explanation, they may collectively amount to a reasonable suspicion." *United States v. Berber-Tinoco,* 510 F.3d 1083, 1087 (9th Cir. 2007). We review reasonable suspicion determinations de novo, reviewing findings of historical fact for clear error and giving "due weight to inferences drawn from those facts by resident judges and local law enforcement officers." *Ornelas v. United States,* 517 U.S. 690, 699 (1996).

In the district court and in supplemental briefing, the government argued that the border agents had reasonable suspicion to conduct the initial search and the forensic examination of Cotterman's computer. We agree. . . .

[The court cited Cotterman's prior record, his travel patterns, and Mexico's reputation for sex tourism as factors in calculating such suspicion.]

To these factors, the government adds another — the existence of password-protected files on Cotterman's computer. We are reluctant to place much weight on this factor because it is commonplace for business travelers, casual computer users, students and others to password protect their files. Law enforcement "cannot rely solely on factors that would apply to many law-abiding citizens," *Berber-Tinoco,* 510 F.3d at 1087, and password protection is ubiquitous. National standards require that users of mobile electronic devices password protect their files. Computer users are routinely advised — and in some cases, required by employers — to protect their files when traveling overseas.

Although password protection of files, in isolation, will not give rise to reasonable suspicion, where, as here, there are other indicia of criminal activity, password protection of files may be considered in the totality of the circumstances. To contribute to reasonable suspicion, encryption or password protection of files must have some relationship to the suspected criminal activity. Here, making illegal files difficult to access makes perfect sense for a suspected holder of child pornography. When combined with the other circumstances, the fact that Officer Alvarado encountered at least one password protected file on Cotterman's computer contributed to the basis for reasonable suspicion to conduct a forensic examination.

The existence of the password-protected files is also relevant to assessing the reasonableness of the scope and duration of the search of Cotterman's computer. The search was necessarily protracted because of the password protection that Cotterman employed. . . .

. . . [W]e conclude that the examination of Cotterman's electronic devices was supported by reasonable suspicion and that the scope and manner of the search were reasonable under the Fourth Amendment. Cotterman's motion to suppress therefore was erroneously granted.

Reversed.

CALLAHAN, Circuit Judge, concurring in part, dissenting in part, and concurring in the judgment, with whom CLIFTON, Circuit Judge, joins, and with whom M. SMITH, Circuit Judge, joins as to all but Part II.A: Whether it is drugs, bombs, or child pornography, we charge our government with finding and excluding any and all illegal and unwanted articles and people before they cross our international borders. Accomplishing that Herculean task requires that the government be mostly free from the Fourth Amendment's usual restraints on searches of people and their property. Today the majority ignores that reality by erecting a new rule requiring reasonable suspicion for any thorough search of electronic devices entering the United States. This rule flouts more than a century of Supreme Court precedent, is unworkable and unnecessary, and will severely hamstring the government's ability to protect our borders.

I therefore dissent from Part III of the majority's opinion. I concur in Parts I, II, and IV, and in particular the majority's conclusion in Part IV that the government had reasonable suspicion to conduct the forensic examination of Howard Cotterman's electronic devices. I therefore also concur in the judgment. . . .

II.

. . . Under the border search doctrine, suspicionless border searches are *per se* reasonable. However, the Supreme Court has identified three situations in which they might not be *per se* reasonable, *i.e.,* at least reasonable suspicion is required: (1) "highly intrusive searches of the person;" (2) destructive searches of property; and (3) searches conducted in a "particularly offensive" manner.

Although its opinion is not entirely clear, the majority appears to rely on the first and third exceptions to hold that the search at issue in this case required reasonable suspicion. (There is no claim that the government damaged or destroyed Cotterman's property.) But the exception for "highly intrusive searches of the person," cannot apply here; "papers," even private ones in electronic format, are not a "person." That leaves the exception for searches conducted in a "particularly offensive" manner. The majority relies primarily on the notion that electronic devices are special to conclude that reasonable suspicion was required. The majority is mistaken. . . .

B.

The majority's opinion turns primarily on the notion that electronic devices deserve special consideration because they are ubiquitous and can store vast quantities of personal information. That idea is fallacious and has no place in the border search context. . . .

. . . The fact that electronic devices are capable of storing a lot of personal information does not make an extensive search of them "particularly offensive." We have squarely rejected the idea that the "intrusiveness" of a search depends in whole or in part on the nature of the property being searched. In *United States v. Giberson,* 527 F.3d 882 (9th Cir. 2008), we specifically rebuffed the argument that computers are special for Fourth Amendment purposes by virtue of how much information they store; "neither the quantity of information, nor the form in which it is stored, is legally relevant in the Fourth Amendment context." *Id.* at 888.

. . . If the government may search the contents of a briefcase, car, or mobile home that transits the border, there is no reason it should not also be able to search the contents of a camera, tablet, or laptop that enters the country. All of those things are capable of storing, and often do store, private information. The majority points out that electronic devices can and usually do store much *more* private information than their non-electronic counterparts. But "a port of entry is not a traveler's home," [*United States v. Thirty-Seven (37) Photographs,* 402 U.S. 363 (1971),] at 376, even if a traveler chooses to carry a home's worth of personal information across it. Moreover, a bright-line rule distinguishing electronic from non-electronic devices — of the sort the Supreme Court has made clear has no place in Fourth Amendment jurisprudence — is arbitrary; there is no reason someone carrying a laptop should receive greater privacy protection than someone who chooses (or can only afford) to convey his or her personal information on paper.

In short, today the court erects a new bright-line rule: "forensic examination" of electronic devices "at the border requires reasonable suspicion." The majority never defines "forensic," leaving border agents to wonder exactly what types of searches are off-limits. Even if the majority means to require reasonable suspicion for *any* type of digital forensic border search, no court has ever erected so categorical a rule, based on so general a type of search or category of property, and the Supreme Court has rightly slapped down anything remotely similar. The majority invites — indeed, requires — the Court to do so again.

III. . . .

Apart from being unnecessary, the majority's new limits on the government's border search authority will make it much harder for border agents to do their jobs, for at least two reasons. First, it is common knowledge that border agents at security checkpoints conduct more thorough searches not simply of those persons who arouse suspicion but also of a percentage of travelers on a random basis. Otherwise, a person who appears entirely innocent will have nothing to fear and will not be deterred from carrying something that should not be brought into the country. A checkpoint limited to searches that can be justified by articulable grounds for "reasonable suspicion" is bound to be less effective.

Second, courtesy of the majority's decision, criminals now know they can hide their child pornography or terrorist connections in the recesses of their electronic devices, while border agents, fearing Fourth Amendment or *Bivens* actions, will avoid conducting the searches that could find those illegal articles. The result will be that people and things we wish to keep out of our country will get in — a result hardly in keeping with our "inherent authority to protect, and a paramount interest in protecting," the "territorial integrity" of the United States. The border search doctrine *must* account for the fact that border agents may need time and forensics to bypass "evasive actions" a criminal has taken to hide contraband or other illegal articles from plain view. I would rather leave those difficult decisions "to the discretion of the officers in the field who confront myriad circumstances we can only begin to imagine from the relative safety of our chambers." *United States v. Williams,* 419 F.3d 1029, 1034 (9th Cir.), *cert. denied,* 546 U.S. 1081 (2005). . . .

M. SMITH, Circuit Judge, dissenting, with whom CLIFTON and CALLAHAN, Circuit Judges, join with respect to Part I: I respectfully dissent. Until today, federal courts have consistently upheld suspicionless searches of electronic storage devices at the border. Yet the majority ignores these cases, rewrites long standing Fourth Amendment jurisprudence, and, in narrowing [*United States v. Arnold*, 533 F.3d 1003 (9th Cir. 2008)] creates a circuit split.

While I share some of the majority's concerns about the steady erosion of our personal privacy in this digital age, the majority's decision to create a reasonable suspicion requirement for some property searches at the border so muddies current border search doctrine that border agents will be left to divine on an ad hoc basis whether a property search is sufficiently "comprehensive and intrusive" to require reasonable suspicion, or sufficiently "unintrusive" to come within the traditional border search exception. Requiring border patrol agents to determine that reasonable suspicion exists prior to performing a basic forensic examination of a laptop or other electronic devices discourages such searches, leaving our borders open to electronically savvy terrorists and criminals who may hereafter carry their equipment and data across our borders with little fear of detection. In fact, the majority opinion makes such a legal bouillabaisse out of the previously unambiguous border search doctrine, that I sincerely hope the Supreme Court will grant certiorari, and reverse the holding in this case regarding the level of suspicion necessary to search electronic devices at the border, for the sake of our national security, and the consistency of our national border search law. . . .

I. . . .

C. Expectation of Privacy in Electronic Data at the Border

The majority suggests that travelers at the border have a heightened expectation of privacy in their electronic storage devices, due to the "uniquely sensitive nature of [this] data." There is no question that searches of electronic data are protected by the Fourth Amendment, but we have never found this data to be immune from the border search exception. In fact, these electronic storage devices are hardly a bastion of privacy. When connected to the Internet, they transmit a massive amount of intimate data to the public on an almost constant basis, rendering it unremarkable that they can be searched at the border, where "[t]he government's interest in preventing the entry of unwanted persons and effects is at its zenith." *Flores-Montano,* 541 U.S. at 152.

Indeed, Facebook, for example, now has more than 500 million users, who share more than 25 billion pieces of data each month. Those who opt out of social networking sites are no less susceptible to the ubiquitous Internet cookie, which collects data on users' Internet activities to share or sell with other organizations. Until recently, a federally funded data accumulation system allowed clients to "search tens of billions of data records on individuals and businesses in mere seconds." Considering the steady erosion of our privacy on the Internet, searches of electronic storage devices may be increasingly akin to a well-placed Internet search. Ironically, the majority creates a zone of privacy in electronic devices at the border that is potentially greater than that afforded the Google searches we perform in our own homes, and elsewhere.

The majority muses that "[a] person's digital life ought not be hijacked simply by crossing the border," but it fails to explain why electronic data deserves special protections when we have never extended such protections to the same data in written form. *See Seljan*, 547 F.3d at 1003 ("An envelope containing personal correspondence is not uniquely protected from search at the border."). The documents carried on today's smart phones and laptops are different only in form, but not in substance, from yesterday's papers, carried in briefcases and wallets. The majority contends that electronic devices hold data of a "uniquely sensitive nature" and that, inexplicably, these devices have the "capability to . . . augment the expectation of privacy." *Under the majority's reasoning, the mere process of digitalizing our diaries and work documents somehow increases the "sensitive nature" of the data therein, providing travelers with a greater expectation of privacy in a diary that happens to be produced on an iPad rather than a legal pad.* Such artificial and arbitrary distinctions cannot serve as a reasonable basis for determining privacy rights at the border.

The majority attempts to distinguish electronic devices from papers by the vast amount of data they can hold, noting that "[a] car full of packed suitcases . . . cannot hold a candle to the sheer, and ever-increasing, capacity of digital storage." Yet, "case law does not support a finding that a search which occurs in an otherwise ordinary manner, is 'particularly offensive' simply due to the storage capacity of the object being searched." *Arnold*, 533 F.3d at 1010. The majority contends that it "discuss[es] the typical storage capacity of electronic devices simply to highlight the features that generally distinguish them from traditional baggage." Yet why the majority would bother to distinguish between the storage capacities of electronic devices and traditional luggage is a mystery, unless to support its enhanced protections for electronic devices based on their greater storage capacity.

Mapping our privacy rights by the amount of information we carry with us leads to unreasonable and absurd results. Under the majority's reasoning, a Mini Cooper filled with documents is entitled to less privacy protection at the border than a stretch Rolls-Royce filled with documents; a pickup truck filled with documents is entitled to less protection than an 18 wheeler filled with documents. It appears that those who cannot afford a 64 gigabyte iPad, or the "average" 400 gigabyte hard drive discussed by the majority, will alone be subject to suspicionless searches. The majority's reasoning also protects the rich (who can generally afford more sophisticated devices) to a greater extent than the poor (who are presumably less able to afford those more capable devices.) . . . .

V. Conclusion

Reasonable suspicion has no place in property searches at the border, as the Supreme Court has consistently held. Imposing a reasonable suspicion requirement here forces courts and border patrol agents to engage in just the "sort of decision-making process that the Supreme Court wished to avoid in sanctioning expansive border searches." *Seljan,* 547 F.3d at 1011 (citation omitted) (Callahan, J., concurring). Rather than rewrite the border search exception, as the majority does, I would affirm the district court's application of the extended border search doctrine to Cotterman's case, which appears most appropriate given the extensive lapse in distance and time between the first and the second search. Additionally, I would hold the government to its burden of proof in determining that reasonable suspicion was absent here. Under the doctrine of this case, the majority sweeps in thousands of innocent individuals whose electronic equipment can now be taken away from the border and searched indefinitely, under the border search exception.

I respectfully dissent.

[NSL p. 684, CTL p. 297. Omit Note 4.]

[NSL p. 690, CTL p. 303. Insert after the *Gilmore* decision.]

Ibrahim v. Department of Homeland Security

United States Court of Appeals, Ninth Circuit, Feb. 8, 2012
669 F.3d 983

W. FLETCHER, Circuit Judge: Plaintiff Rahinah Ibrahim is a citizen of Malaysia and mother of four children. She was legally in the United States from 2001 to 2005 as a Ph.D. student at Stanford University. She alleges that the U.S. government has mistakenly placed her on the "No-Fly List" and other terrorist watchlists. On January 2, 2005, she attempted to travel to a Stanford-sponsored conference in Malaysia where she was to present her doctoral research. She was prevented from flying and was detained in a holding cell for two hours at the San Francisco airport. She was allowed to fly to Malaysia the next day, but she was prevented from returning to the United States after the conference. Ibrahim has not been permitted to return to the United States.

Ibrahim brought suit in federal district court seeking, among other things, injunctive relief under the First and Fifth Amendments, with the ultimate aim of having her name removed from the government's watchlists. The district court denied injunctive relief. We reverse and remand for further proceedings.

I. Factual Background

A. Ibrahim's Departure . . .

[Ibrahim was stopped at the airport ticket counter when the airline employee discovered her name on the federal government's No-Fly List. After being detained by the police, she was permitted to go home and told that her name was no longer listed. But when she tried to fly out the next day, she was told that her name was back on the list. She was nonetheless permitted to fly out, but subsequently prevented from boarding a return flight. She filed a "Passenger Identity Verification" request with the TSA to clear her name, but it did not respond for a year.

In the meantime, the Department of State revoked her student visa citing] Ibrahim's "possible ineligibility" under §212(a)(3)(B) of the Immigration & Nationality Act (INA) as the reason for the revocation. That section of the INA provides, among other things, that "[a]ny alien" (1) who "has engaged in terrorist activity"; (2) who "a consular officer, the Attorney General, or the Secretary of Homeland Security knows, or has reasonable ground to believe, is engaged in or is likely to engage after entry in any terrorist activity"; or (3) who "has, under circumstances indicating an intention to cause death or serious bodily harm, incited terrorist activity," is inadmissible to the United States. 8 U.S.C. §1182(a)(3)(B). . . .

B. The Government's Terrorist Watchlists

Since the terrorist attacks of September 11, 2001, the federal government has assembled a vast, multi-agency, counterterrorism bureaucracy that tracks hundreds of thousands of individuals. *See, e.g.,* 6 U.S.C. §§122, 124h, 482, 485; Exec. Order No. 13388, 70 Fed. Reg. 62023 (Oct. 25, 2005). At the heart of this bureaucracy is the Terrorist Screening Center ("TSC"). Established by the Attorney General in 2003 pursuant to a presidential directive, the mission of TSC is "to consolidate the Government's approach to terrorism screening and provide for the appropriate and lawful use of Terrorist Information in screening processes." *See* Homeland Security Presidential Directive/ HSPD-6. Though administered by the FBI, TSC retains personnel from the Departments of State, Homeland Security, and Defense, and other federal agencies.

TSC manages the Terrorist Screening Database ("TSDB"), the federal government's centralized watchlist of known and suspected terrorists. The National Counterterrorism Center nominates known and suspected international terrorists to the TSDB, while the FBI nominates known and suspected domestic terrorists. TSC distributes subsets of the TSDB to other federal agencies to help implement the government's counterterrorism initiatives. TSA uses two subsets of the TSDB — the No-Fly List and the Selectee List — to screen airline passengers. Individuals on the No-Fly List are prohibited from boarding American carriers or any flight having virtually any contact with U.S. territory or airspace. Individuals on the Selectee List are subject to enhanced security screening before boarding an airplane. The State Department uses a subset of the TSDB to screen visa applicants through the Consular Lookout and Support System.

The evidence and procedures used to nominate individuals to the TSDB are kept secret from the general public, as are the names of those in the TSDB. However, thousands of front line law enforcement officers from federal, state, local, territorial, and tribal agencies have access to the TSDB, as do some private sector entities and individuals. As of January 2011, TSC had also agreed to share information with 22 foreign governments.

Since its inception, the TSDB has grown by more than 700%, from about 158,000 records in June 2004 to over 1.1 million records in May 2009. In 2007, these records contained information on approximately 400,000 individuals. As of 2007, the TSDB was increasing at a rate of 20,000 records per month. TSC makes 400 to 1200 changes to the TSDB every day. It is the "world's most comprehensive and widely shared database of terrorist identities."

In theory, only individuals who pose a threat to civil aviation are put on the No-Fly and Selectee Lists, but the Justice Department has criticized TSC for its "weak quality assurance process." In July 2006 — after the events that gave rise to this lawsuit — there were 71,872 records in the No-Fly List. After an internal review, TSC downgraded

22,412 records from the No-Fly List to the Selectee List and deleted entirely an additional 5,086 records. By January 2007, the TSC had cut the No-Fly List by more than half, to 34,230 records. Tens of thousands of travelers have been misidentified because of misspellings and transcription errors in the nomination process, and because of computer algorithms that imperfectly match travelers against the names on the list. TSA maintains a list of approximately 30,000 individuals who are commonly confused with those on the No-Fly and Selectee Lists. One major air carrier reported that it encountered 9,000 erroneous terrorist watchlist matches every day during April 2008.

Nomination and identification errors are so common that TSC organized a redress unit in 2007 to deal with complaints. The redress procedures have been opaque. A 2006 GAO report stated that an individual who submitted a query to TSC's redress unit received an initial response letter that "neither confirms nor denies the existence of any terrorist watch list records relating to the individual." A 2009 internal DHS report stated, "With few exceptions, redress-seekers receive response letters that do not reveal the basis for their travel difficulties, the action the government took to address those difficulties, or other steps that they may take to help themselves in the future."

When Ibrahim filed suit, TSA managed a Passenger Identity Verification program for travelers who believed that they were mistakenly put on the No-Fly or Selectee List. In place of that program, the Department of Homeland Security ("DHS") now manages the Traveler Redress Inquiry Program ("TRIP"). A 2007 Department of Justice audit commended TSC for accurately resolving redress queries, but noted that 45% of the reviewed records contained an error. The 2009 DHS report was less charitable, concluding that the "TRIP website advises travelers that the program can assist them with resolving a range of travel difficulties. Our review of redress results revealed that those claims are overstated. While TRIP offers effective solutions to some traveler issues, it does not address other difficulties effectively, including the most common — watch list misidentifications in aviation security settings."

II. Procedural Background

[Irahim filed suit against DHS, TSA, TSC, the FBI, the Federal Aviation Administration ("FAA"), and individuals associated with these entities (collectively, "the federal defendants"), as well as various state and local entities, asserting a variety of constitutional and state law tort claims. She sought an injunction that would require the government to take her name off its terrorist watch lists, including the No-Fly List, or, in the alternative, to provide procedures under which she could challenge her inclusion on those lists. After proceedings not here relevant, the district court dismissed her claims, accepting the government argument that Ibrahim has no right to assert claims under the First and Fifth Amendments because she is an alien who has voluntarily left the United States. She appealed that dismissal and other rulings omitted here.] . . .

IV. Discussion . . .

B. Constitutional Claims

Claim 13 . . . alleges that the placement of Ibrahim's name on the government's terrorist watchlists violates her right to freedom of association under the First Amendment and her rights to equal protection and due process under the Fifth Amendment.

At this point in the litigation, no court has attempted to determine the merits of Ibrahim's claims under the First and Fifth Amendments. The parties have not briefed whether her placement on a terrorist watchlist violates her rights to freedom of association, equal protection, and due process. The only question before us is whether Ibrahim even has the right to assert such claims.

We begin with the uncontested proposition that if Ibrahim had remained in the United States, she would have been able to assert claims under the First and Fifth Amendments to challenge her placement on the government's terrorist watchlists. It is well established that aliens legally within the United States may challenge the constitutionality of federal and state actions. Even aliens who are in the United States illegally may bring constitutional challenges, *see, e.g., Plyler v. Doe,* 457 U.S. 202, 211–12 (1982); *Wong Wing v. United States,* 163 U.S. 228, 237 (1896), including the ability to challenge the revocation of a visa. The question in this case is whether Ibrahim lost the right she otherwise had because she left the United States.

The Supreme Court has held in a series of cases that the border of the United States is not a clear line that separates aliens who may bring constitutional challenges from those who may not. For example, a resident alien who voluntarily leaves the United States on a brief trip with an intent to return is constitutionally entitled to a due process hearing if the government seeks to exclude her upon return to the United States. *See, e.g., Landon v. Plasencia,* 459 U.S. 21, 34 (1982) (resident alien entitled to constitutional due process hearing in exclusion proceedings upon re-entry after a "few days" abroad); *Rosenberg v. Fleuti,* 374 U.S. 449, 450 (1963) (entry after innocent, casual, and brief excursion abroad did not qualify as "entry" for immigration purposes); *Kwong Hai Chew,* 344 U.S. at 593–95 (resident alien entitled to constitutional due process hearing after exclusion following a five-month voyage abroad). *See also Boumediene v. Bush,* 553 U.S. 723 (2008) (aliens held as enemy combatants outside the *de jure* sovereign territory of the United States may petition for habeas corpus to challenge the constitutionality of their detention); *Al Maqaleh v. Gates,* 605 F.3d 84, 95–96 (D.C. Cir. 2010) (location of alien outside the United States is only a factor in determining the extraterritorial reach of the Constitution); *Nat'l Council of Resistance of Iran v. Dep't of State,* 251 F.3d 192 (D.C. Cir. 2001) (a foreign organization with property in the United States entitled to constitutional due process hearing before Secretary of State may classify it as a "foreign terrorist organization"); *Cardenas v. Smith,* 733 F.2d 909, 915 (D.C. Cir. 1984) (Colombian national outside the United States entitled to assert due process claim against U.S. government based on seizure of her Swiss bank account); *In re Aircrash in Bali, Indonesia on April 22, 1974,* 684 F.2d 1301, 1308 n.6 (9th Cir. 1982) (nonresident aliens suing on same cause of action as citizens have the right to assert takings claim).

In *United States v. Verdugo-Urquidez,* 494 U.S. 259 (1990), the Supreme Court wrote that "aliens receive constitutional protections when they have come within the territory of the United States and developed substantial connections with this country." *Id.* at 271. The Court's statement in *Verdugo-Urquidez* was an elaboration of its earlier language in *Johnson v. Eisentrager,* 339 U.S. 763 (1950), that an alien "is accorded a generous and ascending scale of rights as he increases his identity with our society." *Verdugo-Urquidez,* 494 U.S. at 269 (quoting *Eisentrager,* 339 U.S. at 770) (internal quotations omitted). The Court wrote in *Boumediene* that the right of an alien outside the United States to assert constitutional claims is based on "objective factors and practical concerns" rather than "formalism." 553 U.S. at 764. In determining the constitutional rights of aliens outside the United States, the Court applies a "functional approach" rather than a bright-line rule. *Id.*

A comparison of Ibrahim's case with *Verdugo-Urquidez, Eisentrager*, and *Boumediene* is instructive.

In *Verdugo-Urquidez,* plaintiff had been arrested in Mexico and brought against his will to the Mexico-United States border, where he was turned over to United States authorities and imprisoned in the United States while awaiting trial on narcotics smuggling charges. The Court held that the plaintiff had "no previous *significant voluntary connection* with the United States" and therefore had no right to assert a Fourth Amendment challenge to searches and seizures of his property by United States agents in Mexico. *Verdugo-Urquidez,* 494 U.S. at 271 (emphasis added).

Relying on *Verdugo-Urquidez,* the government insists that Ibrahim left the United States "voluntarily" and that she thereby forfeited any right to assert constitutional claims she might have had if she had remained in the United States. The government mistakes the nature of the *Verdugo-Urquidez* inquiry. Under *Verdugo-Urquidez,* the inquiry is whether the alien has voluntarily established a connection with the United States, not whether the alien has voluntarily left the United States. The circumstances of an alien's departure may cast some light on whether the alien has established, and wishes to maintain, a voluntarily established connection with the United States. But the mere fact that an alien's departure is voluntary tells us very little. In Ibrahim's case, she left the United States to attend a Stanford-sponsored conference to present her academic research, performed in connection with her Ph.D. studies at Stanford, and she expected to return to Stanford after the conference to complete her studies. Ibrahim thus did not intend to sever her established connection to the United States by her voluntary departure, but rather to develop that connection further.

In *Eisentrager,* the plaintiffs were German citizens who had been arrested in China, convicted of violating the laws of war after adversary trials before a U.S. military tribunal in China, and sent to a prison in Germany to serve their sentences. The Supreme Court held that they did not have a right to seek a writ of habeas corpus under our Constitution. The Court summarized:

> [To agree with plaintiffs that they are entitled to seek habeas] we must hold that a prisoner of our military authorities is constitutionally entitled to the writ, even though he (a) is an enemy alien; (b) has never been or resided in the United States; (c) was captured outside of our territory and there held in military custody as a prisoner of war; (d) was tried and convicted by a Military Commission sitting outside the United States; (e) for offenses

> against laws of war committed outside the United States; (f) and is at all times imprisoned outside the United States.

339 U.S. at 777.

Ibrahim's case is unlike that of the plaintiffs in *Eisentrager.* She has not been convicted of, or even charged with, any violation of law. She is a citizen of a country with which we have never been at war. She contends that the placement of her name on the government's terrorist watchlists is a mistake. Her contention is not implausible, given the frequent mistakes the government has made in placing names on these lists. She has established a substantial voluntary connection with the United States through her Ph.D. studies at a distinguished American university, and she wishes to maintain that connection.

In *Boumediene,* the plaintiffs were aliens who had been designated as enemy combatants and who were detained at the United States Naval Station in Guantanamo. Plaintiffs had not been tried or convicted of any crime. They sought federal habeas corpus. The government argued that because plaintiffs were aliens who had committed acts outside the United States and were being detained outside the United States, they were not entitled to seek habeas relief. The Court rejected the government's proposed bright-line rule, calling it a "formal, sovereignty-based test." 553 U.S. at 764. The Court wrote that while the United States does not have *de jure* sovereignty over the Naval Station at Guantanamo Bay, it "maintains *de facto* sovereignty." *Id.* at 755. Applying a "functional approach," *id.* at 764, the Court held that the plaintiffs in *Boumediene,* unlike the plaintiffs in *Eisentrager*, had a right to seek a writ of habeas corpus.

Ibrahim shares an important similarity with the plaintiffs in *Boumediene.* The *Boumediene* plaintiffs and Ibrahim both sought (or seek) the right to assert constitutional claims in a civilian court in order to correct what they contend are mistakes. In *Boumediene,* plaintiffs sought the right to try to establish they were not, in fact, enemy combatants. Ibrahim seeks the right to try to establish that she does not, in fact, deserve to be placed on the government's watchlists.

The government in *Boumediene* proposed a bright-line "formal sovereignty-based test" under which the absence of *de jure* jurisdiction over Guantanamo would have meant that plaintiffs had no right to seek habeas corpus under the Constitution. The Court disagreed, adopting instead a "functional approach" under which the absence of *de jure* jurisdiction was not determinative. *Id.* at 764. The government proposes a similar bright-line "formal sovereignty-based test" in Ibrahim's case. Under the government's proposed test in this case, any alien, no matter how great her voluntary connection with the United States, immediately loses all constitutional rights as soon as she voluntarily leaves the country, regardless of the purpose of her trip, and regardless of the length of her intended stay abroad. The government's proposed test is not the law. The law that we are bound to follow is, instead, the "functional approach" of *Boumediene* and the "significant voluntary connection" test of *Verdugo-Urquidez.*

Under *Boumediene* and *Verdugo-Urquidez,* we hold that Ibrahim has "significant voluntary connection" with the United States. She voluntarily established a connection to the United States during her four years at Stanford University while she pursued her Ph.D. She voluntarily departed from the United States to present the results of her research at a Stanford-sponsored conference. The purpose of her trip was to further, not to sever, her connection to the United States, and she intended her stay abroad to be brief.

We do not hold that tourists, business visitors, and all student visa holders have the same connection to the United States as Ibrahim. Nor do we hold that Congress is without authority to exclude undesirable aliens from the United States and to prescribe terms and conditions for entry and re-entry of aliens. We hold only that Ibrahim has established "significant voluntary connection" with the United States such that she has the right to assert claims under the First and Fifth Amendments. Like the Court in *Boumediene,* we express no opinion on the validity of the underlying constitutional claims. . . .

Conclusion

We hold that Ibrahim has significant voluntary connection to the United States and she may therefore assert claims against the federal defendants for prospective relief under the First and Fifth Amendments. . . .

We REVERSE in part, [and for reasons not relevant here] AFFIRM in part, and VACATE in part. We REMAND for further proceedings consistent with this opinion. Costs to Appellant.

DUFFY, District Judge: I dissent. . . . The majority relies on a number of cases to show that certain aliens located outside the United States can challenge the constitutionality of U.S. laws. One such case is *Kwong Hai Chew v. Colding,* 344 U.S. 590 (1953). . . . [But in *Kwong*,][t]he

Supreme Court recognized that, while Kwong Hai Chew was on the high seas, he was at all times under the jurisdiction of the United States, as evidenced by the American flag on the S.S. Sir John Franklin.

. . . In the instant case, Petitioner resides in Malaysia and, therefore, does not enjoy the right of constitutional challenge.

Slightly more instructive on the issue of whether aliens located outside of the United States can bring constitutional claims is *Boumediene v. Bush,* 553 U.S. 723 (2008). . . . [In that case,] [t]he Supreme Court's decision did not disregard the extraterritoriality of the claims being asserted, but focused instead on the fact that Boumediene and his fellow petitioners held at Guantánamo Bay were in U.S. custody following capture in, and transfer from, various foreign lands. Here, the Petitioner, knowing that she could be forever banned from returning to this country, voluntarily left and returned to her native land, outside of U.S. jurisdiction. No one can believe that she did not know exactly the consequences of the choice she made.

In *Johnson v. Eisentrager,* 339 U.S. 763 (1950), a group of German nationals sought the writ of habeas corpus after being arrested by the United States Army in China, convicted of violating the laws of war by a Military Commission sitting in China, and imprisoned in Germany. . . . [L]ike the petitioners in *Eisentrager,* the Petitioner does not find herself under U.S. jurisdiction, whether *de jure* or *de facto,* as did the petitioners in *Boumediene.*

I must also note a crucial distinction between *Boumediene* and *Eisentrager* on the one hand and the present case on the other. The petitioners in the habeas cases cited above sought to challenge their detention at U.S. hands, whereas the Petitioner is not in our custody and therefore can have no grounds on which to seek similar relief. . . .

The majority distinguishes *Verdugo-Urquidez* by finding that Petitioner "established a substantial voluntary connection with the United States through her studies at a distinguished American university." I cannot come to the same conclusion. If we were to hold today that Petitioner may assert her constitutional claims because she formed a "substantial voluntary connection with the United States" while here on a student visa, then we would be hard pressed not to allow all alien students who studied in the United States and subsequently left the country to bring constitutional claims in our courts.

. . . If this were sufficient to vest constitutional rights in an alien located outside of the United States to bring actions in the United States against the government, there would be a significant number of aliens in the world just waiting to get into court. For example, a visitor to this country who overstays his visa, makes a livelihood in this country for a substantial amount of time, and chooses voluntary departure when caught as an illegal alien, could fit within the class of people who would have such rights. He would have been in the country for a "substantial time" and would have friends and contacts in this country — as would most illegal aliens. As such, he would most likely have the desire and intention to return to this country.

As this example shows, the majority holding is too broad, while the government's bright line argument based on extraterritoriality is too narrow and hidebound for use in the modern world.

In the case at bar, however, there is no need to set forth a definitive test because the simple answer is that Petitioner has not shown a "substantial voluntary connection" with the United States, which is the measurement the majority believes the precedent would require. The Petitioner does not suggest that she ever worked in or paid taxes to the United States or indeed did anything (except study at a university) to indicate that she ever made a conscious decision to live in this country or to accept any of the responsibilities of a permanent resident. She merely came to acquire the education available and thereby improve her position in her own native country. Obviously, the Petitioner is quite content in having advanced from assistant professor at the University Putra Malaysia prior to obtaining her doctorate to associate professor and Deputy Dean of that university now. At all times that she was in the United States, her main objective was to personally benefit from this country. Any contribution the Petitioner made to the United States was incidental to this objective. That, to my mind, is totally insufficient to constitute a substantial voluntary connection. . . .

[NSL p. 810, CTL p. 424. Insert after *Rasul v. Myers*.]

Al-Zahrani v. Rodriguez

United States Court of Appeals, District of Columbia Circuit, Feb. 21, 2012
669 F.3d 315

[Relatives of two non-citizens who died while detained as "enemy combatants" at Guantánamo Bay brought suit seeking damages arising from the alleged mistreatment and eventual death of the detainees. In its earlier decision in *Rasul v. Myers*, 563 F.3d 527 (D.C. Cir. 2009) (per curiam) (*Rasul II*), the Court of Appeals held that Guantánamo detainees could not pursue damages claims for constitutional violations against federal officials because (1) no clearly established law existed with respect to the detainees' constitutional rights (and so the defendants were entitled to qualified immunity), and, in any event, (2) "special factors" counseled hesitation with respect to recognizing a *Bivens* remedy for Guantánamo detainees. In another earlier decision, *Ali v. Rumsfeld*, 649 F.3d 762 (D.C. Cir. 2011), the Court of Appeals likewise concluded that Guantánamo detainees could not pursue claims under the Alien Tort Statute, 28 U.S.C. §1350. The district court relied on these decisions in dismissing the plaintiffs' claims. In the following opinion, the Court of Appeals affirmed, albeit for different — and broader — reasons.]

SENTELLE, Chief Judge: . . .

Background

. . . Beginning in January of 2002, Yasser Al-Zahrani, Jr., a citizen of Saudi Arabia, and Salah Ali Abdullah Ahmed Al-Salami, Jr., a citizen of Yemen, were detained at the United States military base at Guantanamo Bay, Cuba, as "enemy combatants." In 2004, under the then-current procedure of the United States military, [CSRTs] reviewed the detention of the two and confirmed the earlier determination that both detainees were enemy combatants. On June 10 of 2006, both men, along with a third detainee, died. Although the cause of death is the subject of dispute in the current litigation, a Naval Criminal Investigative Service report concluded that the deaths were the result of suicide by hanging.

On January 7, 2009, the plaintiffs, as fathers of the two named decedents, filed an action against the United States, twenty-four named, current, or former officials of the United States, and one hundred unnamed "John Doe" officials of the United States, seeking money damages relating to the deaths of the two detainees and alleging that the defendants had subjected the decedents to torture, arbitrary detention, and ultimately, wrongful death. The defendants moved for the dismissal of plaintiffs' by-then amended complaint. The district court dismissed the complaint pursuant to Rule 12(b)(6) of the Federal Rules of Civil Procedure for failure to state a claim upon which relief could be granted.

For the reasons more fully set forth below, we affirm the judgment of dismissal, although we further hold that the dismissal is for a lack of jurisdiction rather than the failure to state a claim for relief.

Analysis

. . . Because a federal court without jurisdiction cannot perform a law-declaring function in a controversy, "the Supreme Court [has] held 'that Article III jurisdiction is always an antecedent question' to be answered prior to any merits inquiry." *Public Citizen v. U.S. District Court for the District of Columbia*, 486 F.3d 1342, 1346 (D.C. Cir. 2007) (quoting *Steel Co. v. Citizens for a Better Env't*, 523 U.S. 83, 101 (1998)). Therefore, rather than proceed to weigh the adequacy of the complaint to state a claim, as did the District Court, we first examine the jurisdiction of the courts to entertain plaintiffs' claims and find that jurisdiction wanting.

In October of 2006, Congress enacted the Military Commissions Act. Section 7 of the MCA included an amendment to the habeas corpus statute. The amended statute reads:

> (1) No court, justice, or judge shall have jurisdiction to hear or consider an application for a writ of habeas corpus filed by or on behalf of an alien detained by the United States who has been determined by the United States to have been properly detained as an enemy combatant or is awaiting such determination.
>
> (2) Except as provided in [section 1005(e)(2) and (e)(3) of the Detainee Treatment Act of 2005], no court, justice, or judge shall have jurisdiction to hear or consider any other action against the United States or its agents relating to any aspect of the detention, transfer, treatment, trial, or conditions of confinement of an alien who is or was detained by the United States and has been determined by the United States to have been properly detained as an enemy combatant or is awaiting such determination.

28 U.S.C. §2241(e)(1) and (2).

The present litigation rather plainly constitutes an action other than habeas corpus brought against the United States and its agents relating to "aspect[s] of the detention . . . treatment . . . [and] conditions of confinement of an alien" as described in the MCA. Therefore, as the District Court noted, this action is excluded from the jurisdiction of this court by the "plain language" of an Act of Congress. This ends the litigation and requires that we affirm the dismissal of the action.

. . . It is true that the Supreme Court, in its review of our decision in

Boumediene, found §7 of the MCA to be constitutionally defective. *Boumediene v. Bush*, 553 U.S. 723, 787-92 (2008). However, the *Boumediene* appeal involved a decision applying the first subsection of §7 governing and barring the hearing of applications for writs of habeas corpus filed by detained aliens. . . . Subsection 2 of the MCA, which governs and bars the present litigation, has no effect on habeas jurisdiction. The Suspension Clause is not relevant and does not affect the constitutionality of the statute as applied in "treatment" cases [such as this one]. . . .

Appellants argue that §2241(e)(2)'s jurisdictional bar is unconstitutional because it fails to provide a proper remedy for violations of their constitutional rights. But the only remedy they seek is money damages, and, as the government rightly argues, such remedies are not constitutionally required. The Supreme Court has made this eminently clear in its jurisprudence finding certain of such claims barred by common law or statutory immunities, and applying its "special factors" analysis in preclusion of *Bivens* claims. Further, the Court applies that analysis to preclude *Bivens* claims even in cases such as the present one, where damages are the sole remedy by which the rights of plaintiffs and their decedents might be vindicated. For example, in *United States v. Stanley*, the Court refused to create a *Bivens* cause of action for a military serviceman who had been secretly administered doses of LSD; in doing so, the Court noted that it was "irrelevant to [the analysis] whether the laws currently on the books afford Stanley . . . an 'adequate' federal remedy for his injuries." 483 U.S. 669, 683 (1987). As we have recently said, "Not every violation of a right yields a remedy, even when the right is constitutional." *Kiyemba v. Obama*, 555 F.3d 1022, 1027 (D.C. Cir. 2009), *reinstated as amended by Kiyemba v. Obama*, 605 F.3d 1046 (D.C. Cir. 2010) [(per curiam)]. In light of this, we see no basis on which to invalidate Congress's decision to foreclose such claims as plaintiffs'.

Conclusion

. . . [W]e hold that 28 U.S.C. §2241(e)(2) deprives this court of jurisdiction over appellants' claims. We further hold that the Supreme Court did not declare §2241(e)(2) unconstitutional in *Boumediene* and the provision retains vitality to bar those claims. We therefore conclude that the decision of the District Court dismissing the claims should be affirmed, although for a lack of jurisdiction under Rule 12(b)(1) rather than for failure to state a claim under Rule 12(b)(6).

[NSL p. 810, CTL p. 424. Insert after Note 2.]

3. *Jurisdiction-Stripping and Bivens Claims*. *Al-Zahrani* holds that Congress validly took away federal jurisdiction over *Bivens* suits for damages by former Guantánamo detainees because, unlike the habeas remedy at issue in *Boumediene v. Bush*, 553 U.S. 723 (2008), "such remedies are not constitutionally required." Although the Supreme Court has never identified a case in which the Constitution *does* require a damages remedy for a violation of a specific constitutional provision, it has never expressly forsworn such a possibility, either. Indeed, it has repeatedly alluded to the "'serious constitutional question' that would arise if a federal statute were construed to deny any judicial forum for a colorable constitutional claim," *Webster v. Doe*, 486 U.S. 592, 603 (1988), as the D.C. Circuit construes the MCA in *Al-Zahrani*. Given that, should the D.C. Circuit have done more to explain why the MCA validly divested the courts of jurisdiction? More fundamentally, why didn't *Al-Zahrani* simply rely on *Rasul*?

[NSL p. 887; CTL p. 501. Insert after Note 6.]

In re Guantanamo Bay Detainee Continued Access to Counsel

United States District Court, District of Columbia, Sept. 6, 2012
892 F. Supp. 2d 8

[One of the more difficult issues to arise in the post-*Boumediene* Guantánamo habeas litigation concerns what to do once a detainee's case is over — whether because the detainee lost his habeas petition on the merits, declined to pursue further proceedings, or otherwise. In the summer of 2012, the Department of Justice began seeking to require counsel for detainees whose cases had been dismissed to sign a new "Memorandum of Understanding" (MOU), one of the provisions of which would have left entirely to the discretion of the executive branch the terms and conditions under which counsel could continue to meet — or otherwise communicate — with their clients. Several of the lawyers promptly objected, arguing that the government was violating protective orders issued by the D.C. district court that govern the mechanics of the Guantánamo litigation. In the decision that follows, Chief Judge Lamberth ruled in favor of the detainees' counsel — but he also may have gone farther.]

ROYCE C. LAMBERTH, Chief Judge:

I. INTRODUCTION

. . . [T]his case is about whether the Executive or the Court is charged with protecting habeas petitioners' right to access their counsel. Petitioners contend that the terms and conditions of this Court's 2008 Protective Order ("Protective Order" or "P.O.") govern their access to counsel regardless of whether they are currently petitioning for habeas relief. The Government argues that once a detainee's habeas petition is terminated, the Court's Protective Order expires and the Executive has the prerogative of assuring counsel-access. . . . [F]or the reasons below, the Court finds that the Protective Order governs access to counsel issues for Guantanamo detainees who have a right to petition for habeas corpus relief, whether or not such a petition has been dismissed or denied.

II. BACKGROUND . . .

B. Legal Background

[After summarizing the long history of the Guantánamo habeas litigation in the Supreme Court, Chief Judge Lamberth began by reiterating the district court and Supreme Court's conclusions that the detainees were entitled to the assistance of counsel in bringing their habeas petitions.] . . .

These rulings raised significant questions about counsels' access to detainees and classified information. The Court first began to address this problem in *Al Odah* [*v. United States*, 346 F. Supp. 2d 1 (D.D.C. 2004)], where Judge Kollar-Kotelly found that the Court had power "to fashion procedures by analogy to existing procedures, in aid of the Court's jurisdiction and in order to develop a factual record as necessary for the Court to make a decision on the merits of" detainee habeas claims. 346 F. Supp. 2d at 6; *see also Harris v. Nelson*, 394 U.S. 286, 299 (1969). Using this power, she proposed a framework for detainee counsel-access. *Al Odah*, 346 F. Supp. 2d at 13-15. The Government subsequently moved for a Protective Order "to prevent the unauthorized disclosure or dissemination of classified national security information." *In re Guantanamo Detainee Cases*, 344 F. Supp. 2d 174, 175 (D.D.C. 2004). . . . In November 2004 [Judge Joyce Hens Green] issued an "Amended Protective Order and Procedures for Counsel Access to Detainees," which set guidelines and procedures for counsel-access to both detainees and classified information. . . .

III. THE GOVERNMENT'S PROPOSED MEMORANDUM OF UNDERSTANDING (MOU)

Despite the fact that the Government never opposed the Protective Order or brought any violations of the Protective Order to the Court's attention, at some point during the Spring of 2012 the Government felt it necessary to promulgate its own procedures for counsel-access at Guantanamo, which it styled as a "Memorandum of Understanding" (MOU). The MOU is meant to replace the Protective Order for those detainees whose cases have been dismissed or whose petitions have been denied on the merits. The Government repeatedly avers that its proposed MOU provides "essentially the same" counsel-access provisions as the Protective Order. "The lady doth protest too much, methinks." William Shakespeare, *Hamlet*, Act III, Scene II. Far from providing "essentially the same" provisions, the MOU, in truth, significantly modifies the Protective Order.

For example, the Protective Order assumes that counsel for detainees have a "need to know," which allows them to view classified information in their own and related Guantanamo cases. P.O. at ¶ I.D.28. Counsel for detainees are also specifically allowed to discuss with each other relevant information, including classified information, "to the extent necessary for the effective representation of their clients." *Id.* And, the Protective Order assures that counsel have continuing access to certain classified information, including their own work-product. *Id.* at ¶¶ I.D.23, 25.

The MOU, on the other hand, strips counsel of their "need to know" designations, and explicitly denies counsel access to all classified documents or information which counsel had "previously obtained or created" in pursuit of a detainee's habeas petition. MOU [12-1] at ¶8(b).

Counsel can obtain access to their own classified work-product only if they can justify their need for such information to the Government. MOU [12-1] at ¶8(b). "Need to know" determinations for this and other classified information would be made by the Department of Defense Office of General Counsel (DoD OGC), in consultation with the pertinent classification authorities within DoD and other agencies. *Id.* However, there is no assurance that such determinations will be made in a timely manner. As this Court is keenly aware from experience, the inter-agency process of classification review can stretch on for months. It is very likely that this provision would result in result in lengthy, needless and possibly oppressive delays. It would also require counsel to divulge some analysis and strategy to their adversary merely to obtain their past work-product. Further, the MOU countermands the Protective Order and specifically denies counsel for detainees the privilege of sharing information amongst themselves in the pursuit of representing their clients unless specifically authorized to do so by "the appropriate government personnel." *Compare* Protective Order at ¶ I.D.28 *with* MOU [12-1] at ¶8(a)(10). The MOU does not define who such personnel would be.

While this Court is empowered to enforce the Protective Order, all "disputes regarding the applicability, interpretation, enforcement, compliance with or violations of" the MOU are given to the "final and unreviewable discretion of the Commander, Commander, Joint Task Force-Guantanamo Bay" (JTF-GTMO). MOU [12-1] at ¶8(f). The MOU further gives the JTF-GTMO Commander complete "authority and discretion" over counsels' access to classified information and to detainees, including in-person visits and written communications. *Id.* at ¶6. Apparently, the MOU also gives the Government authority to unilaterally modify its terms. Resp. Opp. [12] at 11, n.3 ("Although not stated in the MOU itself, the Government has advised petitioners' counsel that . . . it anticipates limiting the number of attorneys who may have continued access to a detainee under the MOU to two. Similarly, the Government also anticipates limiting the number of translators for each detainee to one."). Importantly, the MOU is only applicable to attorneys who have represented detainees under the Protective Order; there are no provisions allowing for attorney substitutions or for new counsel. *See* MOU [12-1] at ¶3.

Unlike the Protective Order, which repeatedly states that the Government may not unreasonably withhold approval of matters within its discretion, the MOU places no such reasonableness requirement on the Commander of JTF-GTMO. Because the MOU does not come into effect until countersigned by the Commander at JTF-GTMO, the Commander could presumably refuse to sign the MOU, leaving a detainee in the lurch without access to counsel. *Id.* at ¶11. The MOU also states that both the "operational needs and logistical constraints" at Guantanamo as well as the "requirements for ongoing military commissions, periodic review boards, and habeas litigation" will be prioritized over counsel-access. *Id.* at 8(c). This provision is particularly troubling as it places a detainee's access to counsel, and thus the detainee's constitutional right to access the courts, in a subordinate position to whatever the military commander of Guantanamo sees as a logistical constraint.

IV. STANDARD OF REVIEW . . .

The long history of the Great Writ . . . firmly establishes that it is the high duty of the Court, not the Executive, to "call the jailer to account" in habeas proceedings, *Boumediene* [*v. Bush*, 553 U.S. 723 (2008),] at 745-46 (internal citations omitted), and to ensure that access to the courts is "adequate, effective, and meaningful." *Bounds v. Smith*, 430 U.S. 817, 822 (1977). Practically, this means "that the privilege of habeas corpus entitles the prisoner to a *meaningful opportunity to demonstrate* that he is being held pursuant to 'the erroneous application or interpretation' of relevant law." *Boumediene*, 553 U.S. at 779 (quoting *INS v. St. Cyr*, 533 U.S. 289, 302 (2001)) (emphasis added).

In the context of Guantanamo Bay habeas litigation, "access to the Court means nothing without access to counsel." *Al-Joudi v. Bush*, 406 F. Supp. 2d 13, 22 (D.D.C. 2005). They are inseparable concepts and must run together.

To say that Petitioners' ability to investigate the circumstances surrounding their capture and detention is "seriously impaired" is an understatement. The circumstances of their confinement render their ability to investigate nonexistent. Furthermore, it is simply impossible to expect Petitioners to grapple with the complexities of a foreign legal system and present their claims to this Court without legal representation. Petitioners face an obvious language barrier, have no access to a law library, and almost certainly lack a working knowledge of the American legal system. Finally, this Court's ability to give Petitioners' claims the "careful consideration and plenary processing" which is their due would be stymied were Petitioners to proceed unrepresented by counsel. *Al Odah*, 346 F. Supp. 2d at 9. This reasoning holds true whether petitioners are seeking to file a habeas petition or are actively litigating one.

V. ANALYSIS

The Government maintains that in the absence of an "active or impending" habeas case, or where it is "speculative" that a detainee will bring a renewed petition, "the primary responsibility for . . . respecting rights of counsel access the detainee may have[ ] should fall in the first instance to the [E]xecutive branch." Resp. Opp. [12] at 2–3; Hr'g Trans. at 6–7, 15. The Government further argues that this Court has no power to address the counsel-access question unless and until petitioners demonstrate that the counsel-access voluntarily provided by the Government's MOU "has impeded their ability to present new habeas petitions to the Court." Resp. Opp. [12] at 15.[11] The Government's reasoning is substantially flawed and confuses the roles of the jailer and the judiciary in our constitutional separation-of-powers scheme. The Court is simply not obliged to give the Executive the opportunity to create its own counsel-access provisions before stepping in and fashioning such procedures. To do so would be to allow the Government to transgress on the Court's duty to safeguard individual liberty by "calling the jailer to account." *Boumediene*, 553 U.S. at 745–46.

As an initial matter, the Court is somewhat nonplussed as to why the counsel-access issue is being re-litigated at all. This Court faced a very similar issue in *Al Odah*. The Government there allowed Guantanamo detainees to meet with counsel under Government issued "Procedures for Counsel Access to Detainees at Guantanamo Bay, Cuba." 346 F. Supp. 2d at 5. Judge Kollar-Kotelly, in a well-reasoned opinion, flatly rejected the Government's proposed procedures. *Id*. at 9-14. She held that "the Government . . . [was] not entitled to unilaterally impose procedures that abrogate the attorney-client relationship" and that

---

11. The Government later avers that petitioners have no freestanding right to counsel, and that in the domestic context, the Sixth Amendment right to counsel does not attach until the commencement of adversarial proceedings. But this case is not about detainees' right to counsel. The Government has conceded that petitioners here have a right to counsel. This case concerns the rules under which detainees, who are already represented by counsel, can continue to meet with their counsel absent a habeas petition currently before the Court.

petitioners' "access to attorneys [was] not a matter of Government discretion." *Id.* at 5, 10.

The Protective Order has been in place for nearly four years and there is no record that its provisions have threatened classified information or caused any harm to the military's operation of the Guantanamo Bay Naval Base. The Government itself argues that the MOU and the Protective Order provide essentially the same protections. In the first instance, this raises the question of why the Government felt it necessary to promulgate the MOU at all. The old maxim "if it ain't broke, don't fix it" would seem to caution against altering a counsel-access regime that has proven safe, efficient, and eminently workable. Indeed, the Government's [lawyers] had no answer when the Court posed this question in oral arguments. The best that they could muster was to argue that the Protective Order simply left a vacuum of procedural rules in the absence of an "active or impending" habeas petition. Of course, when it comes to power, the Government, as much as nature, abhors a vacuum.

A. The Judiciary, and not the Executive, is Charged with Ensuring Access to the Courts.

Regardless, the Government's position here, while not unreasonable, is untenable. The Government's argument presumes that petitioners who are not actively litigating habeas petitions do not have the same need to access their counsel as detainees who are currently litigating. The Government presented no case law to substantiate this two tiered regime or to support this assumption, and the Court finds none. Instead, the Government argues that the courts have been leery of involving themselves in the operation of jails, and that it would inappropriate for the Court to involve itself, at this point, with the Executive's determination of what procedures appropriately provide counsel-access to detainees.

The Court cannot disagree that in the prison context access to counsel is merely a "means for ensuring a reasonably adequate opportunity to present claimed violations of fundamental constitutional rights to the court." *Lewis v. Casey*, 518 U.S. 343, 351 (1996) (internal quotation marks omitted). The Court likewise agrees that in the prison context, the political branches of Government are responsible for running their own facilities and "manag[ing] prisons in such fashion that official interference with the presentation of claims will not occur." *Id.*

at 349. But it does not follow that the judiciary has secondary responsibility for ensuring prisoners have adequate access to the courts.

At the outset, the Government's reason simply falls flat because, as the Government itself notes, "the detention facility [at Guantanamo Bay] . . . is not a corrections facility." Resp. Lt'r [28] at 2, Aug. 21, 2012. If it were, under Navy Regulations, detainees would have unconditional access to their attorneys. Dep't of Navy Corrections Manual, Art. 1640–80, Sec. 3 ¶2.c (Mar. 29, 2011), *available at* http:// www. public. navy. mil/ bupers- npc/ reference/ instructions/ BUPERSInstructions/ Documents/1640.22.pdf ("Under no condition shall any prisoner be prevented from consulting or corresponding with counsel or the authorized representative of counsel . . . .").

But even in the prison context, the Supreme Court has zealously guarded against policies that threaten prisoners' ability to effectively challenge their detention. It has held, in no uncertain words, that the "state and its officers may not abridge or impair a prisoner's right to apply to a federal court for a writ of habeas corpus." *Ex parte Hull*, 312 U.S. 546, 549 (1941). Such abridgment need not be conspicuous or direct. . . .

While the Executive may have the responsibility for regulating its facilities, the Court is charged with ensuring that prisoners are "provided with the tools . . . to challenge the conditions of their confinement." *Casey*, 518 U.S. at 355. This is especially true in the context of Guantanamo: "The gravity of the separation-of-powers issues raised by these cases and the fact that these detainees have been denied meaningful access to a judicial forum for a period of years render these cases exceptional." *Boumediene*, 553 U.S. at 772. . . . The Court does not see how these petitioners, who speak no English, have no legal training, and who cannot be expected to remain up to date with new legal and political developments can have the requisite tools to bring habeas petitions without access to counsel.

B. The Government's MOU Transgresses the Judiciary's Duty to Ensure Detainees Have Access to the Courts by Giving the Military Unreviewable Discretion over Counsel-Access Questions.

The MOU not only threatens separation-of-powers principles by usurping the judiciary's duty to ensure access to the courts, it also takes from the courts the power to adjudicate controversies relating to the MOU. The MOU gives the military commander of Guantanamo "final and unreviewable discretion" over "disputes regarding the applicability, interpretation, enforcement, compliance with or violations of" the MOU. MOU [12-1] at ¶8.f. Such controversies will necessarily implicate detainees' access to the courts. . . . Far from merely putting in place rules governing how it will run its own facilities and protect classified information, the Government wants to place itself as the sole arbiter of when a habeas petitioner is "seeking" to challenge his own detention and when a habeas case is "impending," and thus when a detainee can have access to counsel. But "access to the Court means nothing without access to counsel." *Al-Joudi*, 406 F. Supp. 2d at 22. Thus, the MOU actually gives the Government final, unreviewable power to delay, hinder, or prevent access to the courts. . . .

C. The Government Lacked Authority to Issue the MOU.

It is clear that the Government had no legal authority to unilaterally impose a new counsel-access regime, let alone one that would render detainees' access to counsel illusory. Because it is emphatically the duty of the Courts to assure access to habeas relief, *Harris*, 394 U.S. at 292, and because "petitioners' access to attorneys is not a matter of Government discretion," *Al Odah*, 346 F. Supp. 2d at 10, the Government's MOU is null ab initio. If the Court here were to allow the Executive to substitute its MOU for the Protective Order, regardless of whether it provides "essentially the same" counsel-access provisions or not, the Court would be abdicating its great responsibility to guarantee that its doors remain open to these detainees. *Cf. United States v. Stevens*, 559 U.S. 460 ("We would not uphold an unconstitutional statute merely because the Government promised to use it responsibly."). If the separation-of-powers means anything, it is that this country is not one ruled by Executive fiat. Such blanket, unreviewable power over counsel-access by the Executive does not comport with our constitutional system of government. Therefore, it is the opinion of this Court that the Protective Order continues to govern detainee-counsel access for the purpose of bringing habeas petitions so long as detainees can bring habeas petitions before the Court. . . .

[In the remainder of Part V, Chief Judge Lamberth explained why his analysis was consistent with the court's "equitable" powers vis-a-vis habeas, and why the history and language of the Protective Order also supported such a result.]

VI. SUFFICIENT EVIDENCE EXISTS FOR THE COURT TO ISSUE A PERMANENT INJUNCTION IF IT SO DESIRED

[In this Part, Chief Judge Lamberth offered detailed analysis of why, notwithstanding the high bar imposed by the Supreme Court's *Casey* decision, the detainees could be entitled to a permanent injunction barring enforcement of the MOU if they sought such relief.]

VII. CONCLUSION

The Court has an obligation to assure that those seeking to challenge their Executive detention by petitioning for habeas relief have adequate, effective and meaningful access to the courts. In the case of Guantanamo detainees, access to the courts means nothing without access to counsel. And it is undisputed that petitioners here have a continuing right to seek habeas relief. It follows that petitioners have an ongoing right to access the courts and, necessarily, to consult with counsel. Therefore, the Government's attempt to supersede the Court's authority is an illegitimate exercise of Executive power. The Court, whose duty it is to secure an individual's liberty from unauthorized and illegal Executive confinement, cannot now tell a prisoner that he must beg leave of the Executive's grace before the Court will involve itself. This very notion offends separation-of-powers principles and our constitutional scheme.

For the foregoing reasons, the Court finds that the Protective Order continues to govern access to counsel for all petitioners in the above captioned case. . . .

NOTES AND QUESTIONS

1. *Access to Counsel Before and After Boumediene.* Chief Judge Lamberth makes much out of Judge Kollar-Kotelly's decision in *Al Odah*, which first recognized the Guantánamo detainees' right of access to counsel. But that decision was grounded in the federal habeas statute, which the Supreme Court had just held to apply to Guantánamo in the *Rasul* case. Does Chief Judge Lamberth identify the *source* of the right of access to counsel in his opinion? If so, where?

Toward the end of his opinion, Chief Judge Lamberth writes that "it is undisputed that petitioners here have a continuing right to seek habeas relief. It follows that petitioners have an ongoing right to access the courts and, necessarily, to consult with counsel." *Does* it follow? Put another way, is *Continued Access* a narrow holding, merely reaffirming that the judge-made protective orders in the Guantánamo cases continue to apply to the detainees even after their cases have been terminated? Or, as this language suggests, is it a broad — and potentially momentous — holding that the Constitution's Suspension Clause (the source of the right to seek habeas relief) might also *itself* confer a right of access to counsel in at least some cases, as part of the "meaningful opportunity" to challenge detention that *Boumediene* held it to require? Wouldn't such a holding have significant consequences far beyond the specific issue in the *Continued Access* case — indeed, far beyond Guantánamo?

2. *The Continued Access Decision and the Future of Guantánamo.* Critics of Chief Judge Lamberth's opinion have seized upon the argument that continuing access to counsel for detainees whose cases have been dismissed is futile, whether because *Boumediene* only requires one bite at the judicial-review apple, or because, on the merits, a Guantánamo detainee who has already lost his habeas petition is doomed to fail should he try again, based upon res judicata and other considerations. *See, e.g.*, Andrew Kent, *Do Boumediene Rights Expire?*, 161 U. Penn. L. Rev. PENNumbra 20 (2012).

On the former point, should the Guantánamo cases follow "ordinary" rules of habeas litigation, including the well-established principle that res judicata does not apply, *see, e.g.*, *Sanders v. United States*, 373 U.S. 1, 8 (1963), meaning that there is no inherent bar on second-or-successive habeas petitions challenging executive detention? Indeed, under *Boumediene*, might executive detention cases present even *stronger* arguments against res judicata, because, unlike detention in the post-conviction context, the length of executive detention is not usually fixed *ab initio,* and the same source of detention authority may, in fact, vary as time goes on? *See, e.g.*, Stephen I. Vladeck, *Access to Counsel, Res Judicata, and the Future of Habeas at Guantanamo*, 161 U. Penn. L. Rev. PENNumbra 78 (2012). On the latter point, the decision in *Continued Access* helps to provide a fascinating lens into the potential future of the Guantánamo habeas litigation. *Will* there come a point when detainees whose detention has already been upheld will nevertheless be able to argue that the government's authority to hold them under the 2001 Authorization for Use of Military Force (AUMF) has expired? Could such an argument be advanced if and when the remaining U.S. ground troops in Afghanistan are removed? If and when the AUMF is repealed? Does either of these possibilities help to explain why Chief Judge Lamberth was at such pains to preserve these detainees' right to continue to have access to counsel — and, therefore, to the courts?

[NSL5 p. 892, CTL2 p. 506. Insert at end of chapter.]

National Defense Authorization Act for Fiscal Year 2012

Pub. L. No. 112–81, 125 Stat. 1298, 1562-1564 (2011)

§1021. Affirmation of Authority of the Armed Forces of the United States to Detain Covered Persons Pursuant to the Authorization for Use of Military Force.

(a) In General. — Congress affirms that the authority of the President to use all necessary and appropriate force pursuant to the Authorization for Use of Military Force (Public Law 107–40; 50 U.S.C. 1541 note) includes the authority for the Armed Forces of the United States to detain covered persons (as defined in subsection (b)) pending disposition under the law of war.

(b) Covered Persons. — A covered person under this section is any person as follows:

(1) A person who planned, authorized, committed, or aided the terrorist attacks that occurred on September 11, 2001, or harbored those responsible for those attacks.

(2) A person who was a part of or substantially supported al-Qaeda, the Taliban, or associated forces that are engaged in hostilities against the United States or its coalition partners, including any person who has committed a belligerent act or has directly supported such hostilities in aid of such enemy forces.

(c) Disposition under Law of War. — The disposition of a person under the law of war as described in subsection (a) may include the following:

(1) Detention under the law of war without trial until the end of the hostilities authorized by the Authorization for Use of Military Force.

(2) Trial under chapter 47A of title 10, United States Code (as amended by the Military Commissions Act of 2009).

(3) Transfer for trial by an alternative court or competent tribunal having lawful jurisdiction.

(4) Transfer to the custody or control of the person's country of origin, any other foreign country, or any other foreign entity.

(d) Construction. — Nothing in this section is intended to limit or expand the authority of the President or the scope of the Authorization for Use of Military Force.

(e) Authorities. — Nothing in this section shall be construed to affect existing law or authorities relating to the detention of United States citizens, lawful resident aliens of the United States, or any other persons who are captured or arrested in the United States. . . .

§1022. Military Custody for Foreign Al-qaeda Terrorists.

(a) Custody Pending Disposition under Law of War. —

(1) In General. — Except as provided in paragraph (4), the Armed Forces of the United States shall hold a person described in paragraph (2) who is captured in the course of hostilities authorized by the Authorization for Use of Military Force (Public Law 107–40) in military custody pending disposition under the law of war.

(2) Covered Persons. — The requirement in paragraph (1) shall apply to any person whose detention is authorized under section 1021 who is determined —

(A) to be a member of, or part of, al-Qaeda or an associated force that acts in coordination with or pursuant to the direction of al-Qaeda; and

(B) to have participated in the course of planning or carrying out an attack or attempted attack against the United States or its coalition partners.

(3) Disposition under Law of War. — For purposes of this subsection, the disposition of a person under the law of war has the meaning given in section 1021(c) . . . .

(4) Waiver for National Security. — The President may waive the requirement of paragraph (1) if the President submits to Congress a certification in writing that such a waiver is in the national security interests of the United States.

(b) Applicability to United States Citizens and Lawful Resident Aliens. —

(1) United States Citizens. — The requirement to detain a person in military custody under this section does not extend to citizens of the United States.

(2) Lawful Resident Aliens. — The requirement to detain a person in military custody under this section does not extend to a lawful resident alien of the United States on the basis of conduct taking place within the United States, except to the extent permitted by the Constitution of the United States.

(c) Implementation Procedures. — . . .

(2) . . .

(B) . . . [T]he requirement for military custody under subsection (a)(1) does not require the interruption of ongoing surveillance or intelligence gathering with regard to persons not already in the custody or control of the United States.

(C) . . . [A] determination under subsection (a)(2) is not required to be implemented until after the conclusion of an interrogation which is ongoing at the time the determination is made and does not require the interruption of any such ongoing interrogation. . . .

(d) Authorities. — Nothing in this section shall be construed to affect the existing criminal enforcement and national security authorities of the Federal Bureau of Investigation or any other domestic law enforcement agency with regard to a covered person, regardless whether such covered person is held in military custody. . . .

Statement by the President on H.R. 1540

Dec. 31, 2011

Today I have signed into law H.R. 1540, the "National Defense Authorization Act for Fiscal Year 2012." . . .

. . . I have signed this bill despite having serious reservations with certain provisions that regulate the detention, interrogation, and prosecution of suspected terrorists. . . .

Section 1021 affirms the executive branch's authority to detain persons covered by the 2001 Authorization for Use of Military Force (AUMF) (Public Law 107-40; 50 U.S.C. 1541 note). This section breaks no new ground and is unnecessary. The authority it describes was included in the 2001 AUMF, as recognized by the Supreme Court and confirmed through lower court decisions since then. . . . I want to clarify that my Administration will not authorize the indefinite military detention without trial of American citizens. . . .

Section 1022 seeks to require military custody for a narrow category of non-citizen detainees who are "captured in the course of hostilities authorized by the Authorization for Use of Military Force." This section is ill-conceived and will do nothing to improve the security of the United States. The executive branch already has the authority to detain in military custody those members of al-Qa'ida who are captured in the course of hostilities authorized by the AUMF, and as Commander in Chief I have directed the military to do so where appropriate. I reject any approach that would mandate military custody where law enforcement provides the best method of incapacitating a terrorist threat. While section 1022 is unnecessary and has the potential to create uncertainty, I have signed the bill because I believe that this section can be interpreted and applied in a manner that avoids undue harm to our current operations. . . .

. . . [U]nder no circumstances will my Administration accept or adhere to a rigid across-the-board requirement for military detention. . . .

Barack Obama

Presidential Policy Directive/PPD-14 — Requirements of the National Defense Authorization Act

Feb. 28, 2012

SUBJECT: Procedures Implementing Section 1022 of the National Defense Authorization Act for Fiscal Year (FY) 2012 . . .

A rigid, inflexible requirement to place suspected terrorists into military custody would undermine the national security interests of the United States, compromising our ability to collect intelligence and to incapacitate dangerous individuals. This Directive specifies policies and procedures designed to ensure that section 1022 of the NDAA is implemented in a manner that is consistent with the national security and foreign policy interests of the United States. . . .

II. WAIVERS TO PROTECT NATIONAL SECURITY INTERESTS . . .

B. Protection of U.S. National Security Interests. In accordance with section 1022(a)(4) of the NDAA, and consistent with section 1022(c)(2), which provides the executive branch with broad discretion to design implementing procedures to ensure that the requirements of section 1022 do not interfere with various authorities necessary to disrupt or respond to terrorism threats, and to ensure that counterterrorism professionals have clear guidance and appropriate tools at their disposal to accomplish their mission effectively, I hereby waive the requirements of section 1022(a)(1), regardless of whether an individual has yet been determined to be a Covered Person, and certify that it is in the national security interests of the United States to do so, when:

> placing a foreign country's nationals or residents in U.S. military custody will impede counterterrorism cooperation, including but not limited to sharing intelligence or providing other cooperation or assistance to the United States in investigations or prosecutions of suspected terrorists;
>
> a foreign government indicates that it will not extradite or consent to the transfer of individuals to the United States if such individuals may be placed in military custody;
>
> an individual is a lawful permanent resident of the United States who is arrested inside the United States or is arrested by a Federal agency on the basis of conduct taking place in the United States, to the extent the individual is subject to the requirement of section 1022(a)(1);
>
> an individual has been arrested by a Federal agency in the United States on charges other than terrorism offenses (unless such individual is subsequently charged with one or more terrorism offenses and held in Federal custody in connection with those offenses);
>
> an individual has been arrested by State or local law enforcement, pursuant to State or local authority, and is transferred to Federal custody;
>
> transferring an individual to U.S. military custody could interfere with efforts to secure an individual's cooperation or confession; or
>
> transferring an individual to U.S. military custody could interfere with efforts to conduct joint trials with co-defendants who are ineligible for U.S. military custody or as to whom a determination has already been made to proceed with a prosecution in a Federal or State court.

C. Authority to Issue Additional Categorical National Security Waivers. The Attorney General, in consultation with other senior national security officials, shall have authority to waive the requirements of section 1022(a)(1) of the NDAA in the national security interests of the United States for categories of conduct or categories of individuals consistent with section 1022(a)(4).

D. Authority to Issue Individual National Security Waivers. The Attorney General, in consultation with other senior national security officials, shall have the authority to waive the requirements of section 1022(a)(1) of the NDAA in the national security interests of the United States on an individual, case-by-case basis, consistent with section 1022(a)(4). A decision to issue such a waiver shall take into account factors such as: the legal and evidentiary strength of any criminal charges that may be brought against the individual; the likely punishment if convicted; the impact on intelligence collection of maintaining the individual in law enforcement custody; the legal and investigative risks posed by a transfer to U.S. military custody; the effect any transfer to U.S. military custody would likely have on cooperation by the individual in custody; the effect any transfer to U.S. military custody would likely have on cooperation by foreign governments in a particular investigation or related investigations; the risk associated with litigation concerning the legal authority to detain the individual pursuant to the 2001 AUMF, as informed by the laws of war; and the need to preserve a long-term disposition of the individual that adequately mitigates the threat the individual poses and protects the national security interests of the United States. A waiver is also appropriate if the Attorney General determines, in consultation with other senior national security officials, that a prosecution of the individual in Federal, State, or a foreign court will best protect the national security interests of the United States. . . .

III. LAW ENFORCEMENT ARRESTS OF INDIVIDUALS BELIEVED TO BE COVERED PERSONS . . .

B. Screening. For each individual in [the custody of the FBI or other federal law enforcement agency], a screening shall commence as soon as practicable after sufficient information is available, in the estimation of the Attorney General, to establish that probable cause exists to believe that the individual is a Covered Person and that the individual is not currently subject to a National Security Waiver. . . .

C. Process for Making Covered Person Determinations. . . .

No further action shall be required under section 1022(a)(1) of the NDAA or the procedures set out in this Directive if the Attorney General, in coordination with other senior national security officials,

> determines that there is not clear and convincing evidence that such individual is a Covered Person;
>
> determines that such individual is subject to a categorical National Security Waiver specified in section II(B) or issued pursuant to section II(C) of this Directive; or
>
> issues an individual National Security Waiver under section II(D) of this Directive. . . .

F. Effect of Covered Person Determination. A determination that an individual is a Covered Person not subject to a National Security Waiver shall be without prejudice to that individual's appropriate disposition under the law of war in accordance with sections 1021(c) and 1022(a)(3) of the NDAA, the national security and foreign policy interests of the United States, and the interests of justice. . . .

V. NO ABRIDGMENT OF DOMESTIC LAW ENFORCEMENT

. . . After a Covered Person determination is made and implemented, the Department of Justice and the FBI shall retain lead responsibility for coordinating the investigation, including interrogation, while the Covered Person is held in military custody pending disposition under the law of war. . . .

Hedges v. Obama

United States District Court, Southern District of New York, Sept. 12, 2012
890 F. Supp. 2d 424, *order stayed by* 2012 WL 4075626 (2nd Cir. 2012)

KATHERINE B. FORREST, District Judge: . . . Plaintiffs are a group of writers, journalists, and activists whose work regularly requires them to engage in writing, speech, and associational activities protected by the First Amendment. They have testified credibly to having an actual and reasonable fear that their activities will subject them to indefinite military detention pursuant to [§1021(b) of the National Defense Authorization Act for Fiscal Year 2012 ("the NDAA"), Pub. L. No.

112–81, 125 Stat. 1298 (Dec. 31, 2011) (referred to herein as "§1021(b)(2)")].[1]

At [a] March hearing, the Government was unable to provide this Court with any assurance that plaintiffs' activities . . . would not in fact subject plaintiffs to military detention pursuant to §1021(b)(2). Following the March hearing . . . the Government fundamentally changed its position.

. . . [In May], the Government put forth the qualified position that plaintiffs' particular activities, as described at the hearing, if described accurately, if they were independent, and without more, would not subject plaintiffs to military detention under §1021. The Government did not — and does not — generally agree or anywhere argue that activities protected by the First Amendment could not subject an individual to indefinite military detention under §1021(b)(2). The First Amendment of the U.S. Constitution provides for greater protection: it prohibits Congress from passing any law abridging speech and associational

---

[1. Later in the opinion the lead plaintiff is described in part as follows:

> Christopher Hedges has been a foreign correspondent and journalist for more than 20 years. During that time, he has published numerous articles and books on topics such as al-Qaeda, Mohammad Atta, and the Paris bombing plot; he is a Pulitzer Prize winner. . . .
>
> . . . His work has involved interviewing al-Qaeda members who were later detained. He has reported on 17 groups contained on a list of known terrorist organizations prepared by the U.S. Department of State. . . .
>
> Hedges's work has involved investigating, associating with and reporting on al-Qaeda. . . .
>
> Hedges has recently spoken at events in Belgium and France, and could encounter people associated with groups that are "hostile to the U.S. government." *Id.* at 174. . . .
>
> Hedges testified that his oral and written speech as well as associational activities have been chilled by §1021: he does not understand what conduct is covered by §1021(b)(2), but does understand that the penalty of running afoul of it could be indefinite military detention. He anticipated having to change his associational activities at speeches he was giving as a result of §1021. Hedges testified that prior to the passage of §1021, he never feared his activities could subject him to indefinite military detention by the United States.

890 F. Supp. 2d at 432-433.]

rights. To the extent that §1021(b)(2) purports to encompass protected First Amendment activities, it is unconstitutionally overbroad.

A key question throughout these proceedings has been, however, precisely *what* the statute means — *what* and *whose* activities it is meant to cover. That is no small question bandied about amongst lawyers and a judge steeped in arcane questions of constitutional law; it is a question of defining an individual's core liberties. The due process rights guaranteed by the Fifth Amendment require that an individual understand what conduct might subject him or her to criminal or civil penalties. Here, the stakes get no higher: indefinite military detention — potential detention during a war on terrorism that is not expected to end in the foreseeable future, if ever. The Constitution requires specificity — and that specificity is absent from §1021(b)(2).

Understanding the scope of §1021(b)(2) requires defining key terms. At the March hearing, the Government was unable to provide definitions for those terms. The Government had prior notice of precisely which terms were at issue based upon allegations in the complaint, declarations, depositions, the briefing and oral argument. In particular, plaintiffs commenced this lawsuit asserting — and they continue to assert — that the phrases "associated forces," "substantially supported," and "directly supported" all are vague. . . . [T]he Government nevertheless did not provide particular definitions. . . .[2] The Government's terse arguments do not resolve the Court's concerns. The

---

[2. In an earlier opinion in this case the Court quoted the following dialogue from the transcript of oral argument:

> The Court then asked: Give me an example. Tell me what it means to substantially support associated forces.
> Government: I'm not in a position to give specific examples.
> Court: Give me one.
> Government: I'm not in a position to give one specific example.
> The Court then asked: What does "directly supported" mean?
> Government: We have not said anything about that in our brief.
> Court: What do you think it means?
> Government: . . . Your Honor, we had focused so much on the phrase that was challenged by the plaintiffs, "substantial support" that I have not thought through exactly and we have not come to a position on what "direct support" and what that means.

2012 WL 1721124, *13 (S.D.N.Y. May 16, 2012).]

statute's vagueness falls short of what due process requires.

The Government presents a variety of arguments which, if accepted, would allow the Court to avoid answering the constitutional questions raised in this action. As discussed below, however, the Court rejects each.

First, the Government argues that this Court should not permanently enjoin §1021(b)(2) on the basis that plaintiffs lack standing. At the March hearing, plaintiffs testified credibly to their specific past activities and concerns. At that hearing, the Court repeatedly asked the Government whether those particular past activities could subject plaintiffs to indefinite military detention; the Government refused to answer.

Article III of the Constitution, allowing federal courts to entertain only actual cases and controversies, requires that a plaintiff have standing to pursue a claim. Plaintiffs here, then, must show that they have a reasonable fear that their actions could subject them to detention under §1021(b)(2). . . . [Here the court recalls the Government's initial noncommital position regarding plaintiffs' potential liability, described above, as well as its subsequent qualified statement.]

. . . [T]he Court must — and does — take seriously the Government's position at the March hearing. In other words, the Government did not offer a position at the March hearing sufficient to rebut plaintiffs' credible testimony as to their reasonable fear of detention under §1021(b)(2) and thus, its newly espoused position cannot erase what it said previously. Plaintiffs have standing.

Second, the Government implicitly argues that its new position renders this action moot. It does not. The Government has explicitly stated that its position is applicable with respect to only those activities to which the plaintiffs testified at the March hearing. Thus, any protected First Amendment activities in which plaintiffs have engaged since then might subject them to indefinite military detention. The plaintiffs — writers, journalists, activists — testified credibly that they are continuing, and would continue without the fear of detention, these activities. An actual case or controversy remains.

Third, the Government argues that even in the absence of its proffered assurance, plaintiffs cannot have standing since §1021 is simply a reaffirmation of the 2001 Authorization for Use of Military Force, Pub. L. No. 107-40, 115 Stat. 224 (2001) (the "AUMF") — and since plaintiffs were never detained under the AUMF in the ten years since its passage, they cannot have a *reasonable* fear that they will be detained under §1021(b)(2) now. The Court rejects that argument.

The AUMF and §1021 have significant differences, discussed below. Those differences can be traced to the legislative history and case law surrounding the AUMF. Section 1021 appears to be a legislative attempt at an ex post facto "fix": to provide the President (in 2012) with broader detention authority than was provided in the AUMF in 2001 and to try to ratify past detentions which may have occurred under an overly-broad interpretation of the AUMF. That attempt at a "fix" is obscured by language in the new statute (*e.g.*, "reaffirmation") that makes it appear as if this broader detention authority had always been part of the original grant. It had not.

Based on what is known about the history of the executive branch's use of detention authority (via reported cases and statements by the Government), sometime between September 18, 2001 (the date of the AUMF) and December 31, 2011 (the date of the NDAA) — without congressional authorization — the executive branch unilaterally extended its interpretation of its military detention authority to a scope resembling what was passed into law as §1021(b)(2). Detentions have been challenged via habeas petitions. Courts have warned the Government about the limits of congressional authorization for detention authority (with respect to the AUMF) [as in *Hamdi v. Rumsfeld,* 542 U.S. 507 (2004)], and that the "laws of war" — to which the Government has repeatedly referred in its opposition to the Guantanamo habeas petitions as providing a basis for detention — was not and should not be part of domestic law [as in *Al–Bihani v. Obama,* 590 F.3d 866 (D.C. Cir. 2010)].

In March 2009, the Government presented its view of its detention authority under the AUMF — explicitly referring to that view as a "refinement" and limiting its application to then-current Guantanamo detainees. That position bears clear similarities to §1021(b)(2). In contrast to those statements, in this proceeding the Government argues that its interpretation has always been consistent and has always included the various elements now found in §1021(b)(2). Indeed the Government argues that no future administration could interpret §1021(b)(2) or the AUMF differently because the two are so clearly the same. That frankly makes no sense, particularly in light of the Government's inability at the March and August hearings to define certain terms in — or the scope of — §1021(b)(2). Accordingly, the Government cannot point to a lack of detention pursuant to the AUMF as eliminating the reasonable basis for plaintiffs' stated fears regarding

§1021(b)(2).

Fourth, the Government argues that even if plaintiffs have standing, this Court should essentially "stay out of it" — that is, exercise deference to the executive and legislative branches and decline to rule on the statute's constitutionality. In particular, the Government argues that the fact that the statute relates to military detention during a time of war both justifies §1021(b)(2) breadth and requires judicial deference. The Court rejects that argument as well.

The Court is mindful of the extraordinary importance of the Government's efforts to safeguard the country from terrorism. In light of the high stakes of those efforts as well as the executive branch's expertise, courts undoubtedly owe the political branches a great deal of deference in the area of national security. *See Holder v. Humanitarian Law Project*, 130 S. Ct. 2705, 2711 (2010). Moreover, these same considerations counsel particular attention to the Court's obligation to avoid unnecessary constitutional questions in this context. Nevertheless, the Constitution places affirmative limits on the power of the Executive to act, and these limits apply in times of peace as well as times of war. *See, e.g., Ex parte Milligan*, 71 U.S. (4 Wall.) 2, 125–26 (1866). Heedlessly to refuse to hear constitutional challenges to the Executive's conduct in the name of deference would be to abdicate this Court's responsibility to safeguard the rights it has sworn to uphold.

And this Court gives appropriate and due deference to the executive and legislative branches — and understands the limits of its own (and their) role(s). But due deference does not eliminate the judicial obligation to rule on properly presented constitutional questions. Courts must safeguard core constitutional rights. A long line of Supreme Court precedent adheres to that fundamental principle in unequivocal language. Although it is true that there are scattered cases — primarily decided during World War II — in which the Supreme Court sanctioned undue deference to the executive and legislative branches on constitutional questions, those cases are generally now considered an embarrassment (*e.g., Korematsu v. United States,* 323 U.S. 214 (1944) (upholding the internment of Japanese Americans based on wartime security concerns)), or referred to by current members of the Supreme Court (for instance, Justice Scalia) as "wrong" (*e.g., Ex parte Quirin,* 317 U.S. 1 (1942) (allowing for the military detention and execution of an American citizen detained on U.S. soil)). Presented, as this Court is, with unavoidable constitutional questions, it declines to step aside.

The Government also argues that, at most, the Court's role should be limited to a post-detention habeas review. That argument is without merit and, indeed, dangerous. Habeas petitions (which take years to be resolved following initial detention) are reviewed under a "preponderance of the evidence" standard (versus the criminal standard of "beyond a reasonable doubt") by a single judge in a *civil* proceeding, not a jury of twelve citizens in a criminal proceeding which can only return a guilty verdict if unanimous. If only habeas review is available to those detained under §1021(b)(2), even U.S. citizens on U.S. soil, core constitutional rights available in criminal matters would simply be eliminated. No court can accept this proposition and adhere truthfully to its oath.

. . . The Court finds that §1021(b)(2) is facially unconstitutional: it impermissibly impinges on guaranteed First Amendment rights and lacks sufficient definitional structure and protections to meet the requirements of due process. . . .

[The court goes on to provide a detailed analysis of each of the conclusions outlined above, then concludes with a permanent injunction against enforcement of §1021(b)(2) "in any manner, as to any person."]

[NSL p. 944, CTL p. 558. Insert after Note 2.]

Department of Justice, Office of Public Affairs, Statement of Attorney General Eric Holder on Closure of Investigation into the Interrogation of Certain Detainees

Aug. 30, 2012

available at http://www.justice.gov/opa/pr/2012/August/12-ag-1067.html

The Attorney General announced today the closure of the criminal investigations into the death of two individuals while in United States custody at overseas locations. Below is some background on the investigation and the Attorney General's statement.

BACKGROUND ON INVESTIGATION:

On Jan. 2, 2008, Attorney General Michael Mukasey selected Assistant U.S. Attorney (AUSA) John Durham of the District of Connecticut to conduct a criminal investigation into the destruction of interrogation videotapes by the Central Intelligence Agency (CIA).

On Aug. 24, 2009, based on information the Department received pertaining to alleged CIA mistreatment of detainees, Attorney General Eric Holder announced that he had expanded Mr. Durham's mandate to conduct a preliminary review into whether federal laws were violated in connection with the interrogation of specific detainees at overseas locations. Attorney General Holder made clear at that time, that the Department would not prosecute anyone who acted in good faith and within the scope of the legal guidance given by the Office of Legal Counsel regarding the interrogation of detainees. Accordingly, Mr. Durham's review examined primarily whether any unauthorized interrogation techniques were used by CIA interrogators, and if so, whether such techniques could constitute violations of the torture statute or any other applicable statute.

In June of last year, the Attorney General announced that Mr. Durham recommended opening full criminal investigations regarding the death of two individuals while in United States custody at overseas locations, and closing the remaining matters. The Attorney General accepted that recommendation. Today, the Attorney General announced that those two investigations conducted over the past year have now been closed.

ATTORNEY GENERAL STATEMENT:

"AUSA John Durham has now completed his investigations, and the Department has decided not to initiate criminal charges in these matters. In reaching this determination, Mr. Durham considered all potentially applicable substantive criminal statutes as well as the statutes of limitations and jurisdictional provisions that govern prosecutions under those statutes. Mr. Durham and his team reviewed a tremendous volume of information pertaining to the detainees. That review included both information and matters that were not examined during the Department's prior reviews. Based on the fully developed factual record concerning the two deaths, the Department has declined prosecution because the admissible evidence would not be sufficient to obtain and sustain a conviction beyond a reasonable doubt.

"During the course of his preliminary review and subsequent investigations, Mr. Durham examined any possible CIA involvement with the interrogation and detention of 101 detainees who were alleged to have been in United States custody subsequent to the terrorist attacks of September 11, 2001. He determined that a number of the detainees were never in CIA custody. Mr. Durham identified the matters to include within his review by examining various sources including the Office of Professional Responsibility's report regarding the Office of Legal Counsel memoranda related to enhanced interrogation techniques, the 2004 CIA Inspector General's report on enhanced interrogations, additional matters investigated by the CIA Office of Inspector General, the February 2007 International Committee of the Red Cross Report on the Treatment of Fourteen 'High Value Detainees' in CIA Custody, and public source information.

"Mr. Durham and his team of agents and prosecutors have worked tirelessly to conduct extraordinarily thorough and complete preliminary reviews and investigations. I am grateful to his team and to him for their commitment to ensuring that the preliminary review and the subsequent investigations fully examined a broad universe of allegations from multiple sources. I continue to believe that our Nation will be better for it.

"I also appreciate and respect the work of and sacrifices made by the men and women in our intelligence community on behalf of this country. They perform an incredibly important service to our nation, and they often do so under difficult and dangerous circumstances. They deserve our respect and gratitude for the work they do. I asked Mr. Durham to conduct this review based on existing information as well as new information and matters presented to me that I believed warranted a thorough examination of the detainee treatment issue.

"I am confident that Mr. Durham's thorough reviews and determination that the filing of criminal charges would not be appropriate have satisfied that need. Our inquiry was limited to a determination of whether prosecutable offenses were committed and was not intended to, and does not resolve, broader questions regarding the propriety of the examined conduct."

[NSL p. 944, CTL p. 558. Insert at the end of Note 2.]

On December 13, 2012, Senator Dianne Feinstein, chair of the Senate Intelligence Committee, released a statement, excerpted here, concerning the issuance of a classified report, *Study of the Central Intelligence Agency's Detention and Interrogation*, initiated by the committee in March 2009:

The committee's report is more than 6,000 pages long. It is a comprehensive review of the CIA's detention program that includes details of each detainee in CIA custody, the conditions under which they were detained, how they were interrogated, the intelligence they actually provided and the accuracy — or inaccuracy — of CIA descriptions about the program to the White House, Department of Justice, Congress and others. . . .

The report is based on a documentary review of more than 6 million pages of CIA and other records, extensively citing those documents to support its findings. There are more than 35,000 footnotes in the report. I believe it to be one of the most significant oversight efforts in the history of the United States Senate, and by far the most important oversight activity ever conducted by this committee.

. . . I will provide the report to President Obama and key executive branch officials for their review and comment. The report will remain classified and is not being released in whole or in part at this time. The committee will make those decisions after receiving the executive branch comments.

The report uncovers startling details about the CIA detention and interrogation program and raises critical questions about intelligence operations and oversight. . . .

Conducting oversight is sometimes a difficult and unpleasant task for all involved, but I am confident the CIA will emerge a better and more able organization as a result of the committee's work. I also believe this report will settle the debate once and for all over whether our nation should ever employ coercive interrogation techniques such as those detailed in this report.

I strongly believe that the creation of long-term, clandestine "black sites" and the use of so-called "enhanced-interrogation techniques" were terrible mistakes. The majority of the Committee agrees. . . . [*available at* http://www.feinstein.senate.gov/public/index.cfm/2012/12/feinstein-statement-on-cia-detention-interrogation-report.]

[NSL p. 951; CTL p. 565. Insert as new Note 4.]

4. *Contractor Liability After Kiobel.* After the Supreme Court decided *Kiobel v. Royal Dutch Petroleum Co.*, this *Supplement* p. 19, the district court threw out *Al Shimari* on the ground that the Alien Tort Statute does not encompass *any* claims arising outside the territorial United States, even if the defendants were U.S. contractors operating on a U.S. military base. *See Al Shimari v. CACI Int'l, Inc.*, No. 08-cv-827, 2013 WL 3229720 (E.D. Va. June 25, 2013). Is this a faithful application or extension of *Kiobel*? Whether or not it is, is this a more

coherent basis on which to foreclose civil liability for military contractors than the preemption theory endorsed in *Saleh*? Is it possible that there is a *stronger* argument for applying the ATS extraterritorially in these cases, given that state law will usually provide adequate remedies for torts committed within the territorial United States, but might not so provide for overseas abuses?

[NSL p. 951, CTL p. 565. Insert at end of chapter.]

Padilla v. Yoo

United States Court of Appeals, Ninth Circuit, May 2, 2012
678 F.3d 748

FISHER, Circuit Judge: After the September 11, 2001 attacks on the United States, the government detained Jose Padilla, an American citizen, as an enemy combatant. Padilla alleges that he was held incommunicado in military detention, subjected to coercive interrogation techniques and detained under harsh conditions of confinement, all in violation of his constitutional and statutory rights. In this lawsuit, plaintiffs Padilla and his mother, Estela Lebron, seek to hold defendant John Yoo, who was the Deputy Assistant Attorney General in the U.S. Department of Justice's Office of Legal Counsel (OLC) from 2001 to 2003, liable for damages they allege they suffered from these unlawful actions. Under recent Supreme Court law, however, we are compelled to conclude that, regardless of the legality of Padilla's detention and the wisdom of Yoo's judgments, at the time he acted the law was not "sufficiently clear that every reasonable official would have understood that what he [wa]s doing violate[d]" the plaintiffs' rights. We therefore hold that Yoo must be granted qualified immunity, and accordingly reverse the decision of the district court.

As we explain below, we reach this conclusion for two reasons. First, although during Yoo's tenure at OLC the constitutional rights of convicted prisoners and persons subject to ordinary criminal process were, in many respects, clearly established, it was not "beyond debate" at that time that Padilla — who was not a convicted prisoner or criminal defendant, but a suspected terrorist designated an enemy combatant and confined to military detention by order of the President — was entitled to the same constitutional protections as an ordinary convicted prisoner or accused criminal. Second, although it has been clearly established for decades that torture of an American citizen violates the Constitution, and we assume without deciding that Padilla's alleged treatment rose to the level of torture, that such treatment *was* torture was not clearly established in 2001-03.

I. BACKGROUND

A. . . .

[For the background of Padilla's initial arrest, military detention, and subsequent transfer to civilian custody, see NSL pp. 855-857 or CTL pp. 469-471.]

Padilla and his mother, Estela Lebron, filed this civil action against John Yoo, in his individual capacity, on January 4, 2008, two years after Padilla's military detention ended. . . . Padilla and Lebron alleged that Padilla was imprisoned in the military brig without charge and without the ability to defend himself or to challenge his conditions of confinement. They alleged that during Padilla's detention, he suffered gross physical and psychological abuse upon the orders of high-ranking government officials as part of a systematic program of abusive interrogation mirroring the alleged abuses committed at Guantanamo Bay, including extreme isolation; interrogation under threat of torture, deportation and even death; prolonged sleep adjustment and sensory deprivation; exposure to extreme temperatures and noxious odors; denial of access to necessary medical and psychiatric care; substantial interference with his ability to practice his religion; and incommunicado detention for almost two years, without access to family, counsel or the courts. . . .

. . . From 2001 to 2003, Yoo was Deputy Assistant Attorney General at OLC. Padilla and Lebron alleged that Yoo set in motion Padilla's allegedly illegal interrogation and detention, both by formulating unlawful policies for the designation, detention and interrogation of suspected "enemy combatants" and by issuing legal memoranda designed to evade legal restraints on those policies and to immunize those who implemented them. They alleged that, in doing so, Yoo abdicated his ethical duties as a government attorney and abandoned his office's tradition of providing objective legal advice to the President.

The complaint alleged that Yoo publicly acknowledged in his book, *War By Other Means,* that he stepped beyond his role as a lawyer to participate directly in developing policy in the war on terrorism. It alleged that Yoo shaped government policy in his role as a key member of a small, secretive and highly influential group of senior administration officials known as the "War Council," which met regularly "to develop policy in the war on terrorism." It alleged that Yoo acted outside the scope of his employment at OLC by taking instructions directly from White House Counsel Alberto Gonzales and providing Gonzales with verbal and written advice without first consulting Attorney General John Ashcroft. The complaint alleged that, in his role as the de facto head of war-on-terrorism legal issues, Yoo wrote and promulgated a series of memoranda that ultimately led to Padilla's allegedly unlawful treatment . . . .

The complaint alleged that these memoranda advised that there were no legal constraints on the Executive's policies with respect to the detention and interrogation of suspected terrorists. It alleged that the memoranda "did not provide the fair and impartial evaluation of the law required by OLC tradition and the ethical obligations of an attorney to provide the client with an exposition of the law adequate to make an informed decision." Rather, it alleged that Yoo "intentionally used the Memos to evade well-established legal constraints and to justify illegal policy choices that he knew had already been made — sometimes by virtue of his own participation in the War Council."

The complaint also alleged that Yoo personally participated in Padilla's unlawful military detention. Quoting from Yoo's book, it alleged that Yoo "personally 'reviewed the material on Padilla to determine whether he could qualify, legally, as an enemy combatant, and issued an opinion to that effect.'" It alleged that Ashcroft relied on Yoo's opinion in recommending to the President that Padilla be taken into military custody.

The complaint alleged that Padilla's designation as an enemy combatant, military detention, conditions of confinement and program of interrogation violated his rights to procedural and substantive due process, not to be subjected to cruel or unusual punishment or treatment that shocks the conscience, to freely exercise his religion, of access to information, to association with family members and friends, of access to legal counsel, of access to the courts, against compelled self-incrimination and against arbitrary and unconstitutional seizure and military detention. It alleged violations of the First, Fourth, Fifth, Sixth and Eighth Amendments to the United States Constitution, Article III of the Constitution, the Habeas Suspension and Treason Clauses of the Constitution and the Religious Freedom Restoration Act (RFRA), 42 U.S.C. §2000bb. . . .

B.

Yoo moved to dismiss the action for failure to state a claim upon which relief could be granted. He argued that the complaint failed to state a claim for money damages on three grounds. First, he argued that the plaintiffs could not state an action for damages because *Bivens* . . . did not apply. [In *Lebron v. Rumsfeld*, 670 F.3d 540 (4th Cir. 2012), the Fourth Circuit relied on this argument in dismissing Padilla's damages suit against those military and law enforcement officials directly involved in his detention and alleged mistreatment]. Second, Yoo argued that he was entitled to qualified immunity because the complaint failed to allege facts sufficient to establish his personal responsibility for the constitutional and statutory violations alleged in the complaint. Third, Yoo argued that he was entitled to qualified immunity because the complaint failed to allege a violation of clearly established constitutional or statutory rights. . . .

II. DISCUSSION

A.

The outcome of this appeal is governed by the Supreme Court's decision in *Ashcroft v. al-Kidd,* 131 S. Ct. 2074 (2011) [NSL p. 754; CTL p. 368]. . . .

The Court [in *al-Kidd*] began by reaffirming the general principle that "[q]ualified immunity shields federal and state officials from money damages unless a plaintiff pleads facts showing (1) that the official violated a statutory or constitutional right, and (2) that the right was 'clearly established' at the time of the challenged conduct." *Id.* at 2080. Significant here, under the second prong, a "Government official's conduct violates clearly established law when, at the time of the challenged conduct, '[t]he contours of [a] right [are] sufficiently clear' that every 'reasonable official would have understood that what he is doing violates that right.'" *Id.* at 2083. "We do not require a case directly on point, but existing precedent must have placed the statutory or constitutional question beyond debate." *Id.* The Court emphasized that "[q]ualified immunity gives government officials breathing room to make reasonable but mistaken judgments about open legal questions," *id.* at 2085, and admonished us "not to define clearly established law at a high level of generality." *Id.* at 2084. . . .

Here, the complaint alleged that Yoo, as a Justice Department attorney, participated in policy decisions and rendered legal opinions that ultimately authorized federal officials to designate Padilla as an enemy combatant, take him into military custody, hold him incommunicado without access to the courts or counsel and subject him to both coercive interrogation techniques and harsh conditions of confinement, in violation of his constitutional and statutory rights.

Padilla and Lebron acknowledge that at the time Yoo served as Deputy Assistant Attorney General at OLC, there did not exist a "single judicial opinion," holding that a United States citizen held in military detention as an enemy combatant possessed rights against the kind of treatment to which Padilla was subjected. They argue, however, that it was clearly established that Padilla possessed such rights because any reasonable official would have understood during 2001 to 2003 that a citizen detained as an enemy combatant had to be afforded at least the constitutional protections to which convicted prisoners and ordinary criminal suspects were entitled. That argument is foreclosed by *al-Kidd*, which compels us "not to define clearly established law at a high level of generality." . . .

Here, of course, the Supreme Court had not, at the time of Yoo's tenure at OLC, declared that American citizens detained as enemy combatants had to be treated at least as well, or afforded at least the same constitutional and statutory protections, as convicted prisoners. On the contrary, the Supreme Court had suggested in *Ex parte Quirin*, 317 U.S. 1 (1942), the most germane precedent in existence at the time of Yoo's tenure at OLC, that a citizen detained as an unlawful combatant could be afforded *lesser* rights than ordinary prisoners or individuals in ordinary criminal proceedings. . . .

Padilla and Lebron alternatively rely on the Supreme Court's decision in *Hamdi v. Rumsfeld*, 542 U.S. 507 (2004) [NSL p. 831, CTL p. 445], to establish that Padilla's treatment violated clearly established law. . . . When measured against [at least some of the] language in *Hamdi*, Padilla's alleged cruel and degrading treatment appears to have been a violation of his constitutional rights.

Hamdi, however, was not decided until 2004, so it could not have placed Yoo on clear notice of Padilla's constitutional rights in 2001-03 when Yoo was at the Department of Justice. Even after *Hamdi*, moreover, it remains murky whether an enemy combatant detainee may be subjected to conditions of confinement and methods of interrogation that would be unconstitutional if applied in the ordinary prison and criminal settings. Although *Hamdi* recognized that citizens detained as enemy combatants retain constitutional rights to due process, the Court suggested that those rights may not be coextensive with those enjoyed by other kinds of detainees. On the contrary, the Court held that the rights afforded to an enemy combatant detainee "may be tailored" to the circumstances, because "the full protections that accompany challenges to detentions in other settings may prove unworkable and inappropriate in the enemy-combatant setting." *Id.* at 535.

In sum, the plaintiffs did not, through their reliance on either *Hamdi* or cases involving ordinary prison and criminal settings, allege violations of constitutional and statutory rights that were clearly established in 2001-03. During that relevant time frame, the constitutional rights of convicted prisoners and persons subject to *ordinary* criminal process were, in many respects, clearly established. But Padilla was not a convicted prisoner or criminal defendant; he was a suspected terrorist designated an enemy combatant and confined to military detention by order of the President. He was detained as such because, in the opinion of the President — albeit allegedly informed by his subordinates, including Yoo — Padilla presented a grave danger to national security and possessed valuable intelligence information that, if communicated to the United States, could have been helpful to the United States in staving off further terrorist attacks. We express no opinion as to whether those allegations were true, or whether, even if true, they justified the extreme conditions of confinement to which Padilla says he was subjected. In light of Padilla's status as a designated enemy combatant, however, we cannot agree with the plaintiffs that he was just another detainee — or that it would necessarily have been "apparent" to someone in Yoo's position that Padilla was entitled to the same constitutional protections as an ordinary convicted prisoner or accused criminal. Given the unique circumstances and purposes of Padilla's detention, and in light of *Quirin,* an official could have had some reason to believe that Padilla's harsh treatment fell within constitutional bounds. . . .

B.

The absence of a decision defining the constitutional and statutory rights of citizens detained as enemy combatants need not be fatal to the plaintiffs' claims. The Supreme Court has long held that "officials can still be on notice that their conduct violates established law even in novel factual circumstances." *Hope v. Pelzer*, 536 U.S. 730, 741 (2002).

The plaintiffs invoke this principle here. They argue that, even if there is no specific judicial decision holding that the Fifth Amendment's prohibition on government conduct that "shocks the conscience" is violated when the government tortures a United States citizen designated as an enemy combatant, torture of a United States citizen is the kind of egregious constitutional violation for which a decision "directly on point" is not required. We agree with the plaintiffs that the unconstitutionality of torturing a United States citizen was "beyond debate" by 2001.[9] Yoo is entitled to qualified immunity, however, because it was not clearly established in 2001-03 that the treatment to which Padilla says he was subjected amounted to torture.

In 2001-03, there was general agreement that torture meant the intentional infliction of severe pain or suffering, whether physical or mental. The meaning of "severe pain or suffering," however, was less clear in 2001-03. *See, e.g.*, Michael W. Lewis, *A Dark Descent into Reality: Making the Case for an Objective Definition of Torture*, 67 Wash. & Lee L. Rev. 77, 82-83 (2010); Judith Resnik, *Detention, the War on Terror, and the Federal Courts*, 110 Colum. L. Rev. 579, 633-34 (2010); Sanford Levinson, *In Quest of a "Common Conscience": Reflections on the Current Debate About Torture*, 1 J. Nat'l Security L. & Pol'y 231, 231-52 (2005).

In several influential judicial decisions in existence at the time of Yoo's tenure at OLC, for example, courts had declined to define certain severe interrogation techniques as torture:

Ireland v. United Kingdom, 25 Eur. Ct. H.R. (ser. A) (1978), is the European Court of Human Rights' leading decision on torture. The court considered whether five interrogation techniques used by the United Kingdom to interrogate suspected members of the Irish Republican Army violated Article 3 of the European Convention of Human Rights, which prohibits both torture and "inhuman or degrading treatment or punishment." The five techniques at issue were wall standing (i.e., stress positions), hooding, subjection to noise, sleep deprivation and deprivation of food and drink. . . . The court concluded that "[a]lthough the five techniques, as applied in combination, undoubtedly amounted to

---

9. That substantive due process under the Fifth Amendment prohibits the government from engaging in conduct that "shocks the conscience" has long been clearly established. What has not been clearly established is how that standard applies to citizens detained as enemy combatants.

inhuman and degrading treatment," in violation of Article 3, "they did not occasion suffering of the particular intensity and cruelty implied by the word torture as so understood." *Id.* at 80.

In *HCJ 5100/94 Public Committee Against Torture in Israel v. Israel* 53(4) PD 817 [1999] (Isr.), the Israeli Supreme Court considered whether coercive techniques used by Israeli security forces violated international law. The techniques included hooding, violent shaking, painful stress positions, exposure to loud music and sleep deprivation. The court concluded that each of these techniques was illegal, although the court did not address whether they constituted torture rather than cruel, inhuman and degrading treatment, which was also prohibited by international law.

In *Price v. Socialist People's Libyan Arab Jamahiriya*, 294 F.3d 82 (D.C. Cir. 2002), the plaintiffs were two American citizens imprisoned in Libya, allegedly for political reasons. They alleged that they endured deplorable conditions while incarcerated, including urine-soaked mattresses, a cramped cell with substandard plumbing they were forced to share with seven other inmates, a lack of medical care and inadequate food. They also alleged that they were "kicked, clubbed and beaten" by prison guards, and "interrogated and subjected to physical, mental and verbal abuse." The plaintiffs sued Libya under the Foreign Sovereign Immunities Act, alleging torture. The court held that the plaintiffs had failed to adequately allege torture because they did not allege sufficiently *severe* pain or suffering, noting that "[t]he critical issue is the degree of pain and suffering that the alleged torturer intended to, and actually did, inflict upon the victim. The more intense, lasting, or heinous the agony, the more likely it is to be torture." *Id.* at 93. Although the plaintiffs alleged that they suffered "kicking, clubbing, and beatings," there was "no way to determine from the present complaint the severity of plaintiffs' alleged beatings — including their frequency, duration, the parts of the body at which they were aimed, and the weapons used to carry them out." *Id.*

In other decisions in existence at the time of Yoo's OLC tenure, this Circuit found torture, but the treatment at issue was more severe than that to which Padilla was allegedly subjected:

In *Al-Saher v. INS*, 268 F.3d 1143 (9th Cir. 2001), *amended on another ground*, 355 F.3d 1140 (9th Cir. 2004), an immigration case, we concluded that the petitioner was entitled to relief under the Convention Against Torture and Other Cruel, Inhuman or Degrading Treatment or Punishment (CAT) because he had been tortured in Iraq. On one occasion, the petitioner was detained, interrogated and severely beaten for one month. During his interrogations, he was blindfolded and his hands were tied behind his back. On another occasion, he was blindfolded, restrained, beaten and burned with cigarettes over an 8- to 10-day period. Noting that these actions "were specifically intended by officials to inflict severe physical pain" on the petitioner, we held, under CAT, that he suffered torture. *Id.* at 1147-48.

In *Hilao v. Estate of Marcos*, 103 F.3d 789 (9th Cir. 1996), an Alien Tort Statute case, we held that two plaintiffs, Sison and Piopongco, were tortured in the Philippines during the regime of Ferdinand Marcos. Sison had been interrogated by members of the military, who blindfolded and severely beat him while he was handcuffed and fettered; threatened him with electric shock and death; denied him sleep; and imprisoned him for seven months in a suffocatingly hot and unlit cell, measuring 2.5 meters square, during which time he was shackled to his cot, his handcuffs often so tight that the slightest movement made them cut into his flesh. During this period, Sison felt "extreme" and "almost undescribable" pain. After his seven months shackled to his cot, Sison spent more than eight years in detention, approximately five of them in solitary confinement and the rest in near-solitary confinement. In one round of interrogation, lasting six hours, Sison's limbs were shackled to a cot, a towel was placed over his nose and mouth and his interrogators then poured water down his nostrils so that he felt as though he were drowning. The other plaintiff — Piopongco — was arrested, held incommunicado, interrogated, subjected to mock executions and threatened with death.

Here, Padilla alleged that he was subjected to prolonged isolation; deprivation of light; exposure to prolonged periods of light and darkness, including being "periodically subjected to absolute light or darkness for periods in excess of twenty-four hours"; extreme variations in temperature; sleep adjustment; threats of severe physical abuse; death threats; administration of psychotropic drugs; shackling and manacling for hours at a time; use of "stress" positions; noxious fumes that caused pain to eyes and nose; loud noises; withholding of any mattress, pillow, sheet or blanket; forced grooming; suspensions of showers; removal of religious items; constant surveillance; incommunicado detention, including denial of all contact with family and legal counsel for a 21-month period; interference with religious observance; and denial of medical care for "serious and potentially life-threatening ailments, including chest pain and difficulty breathing, as well as for treatment of the chronic, extreme pain caused by being forced to endure stress positions." The complaint also alleged, albeit in conclusory fashion, that Padilla "suffered and continues to suffer severe mental and physical harm as a result of the forty-four months of unlawful military detention and interrogation." It also alleged that Padilla suffered "severe physical pain" and "profound disruption of his senses and personality."

We assume without deciding that Padilla's alleged treatment rose to the level of torture. That it *was* torture was not, however, "beyond debate" in 2001-03. There was at that time considerable debate, both in and out of government, over the definition of torture as applied to specific interrogation techniques. In light of that debate, as well as the judicial decisions discussed above, we cannot say that any reasonable official in 2001-03 would have known that the specific interrogation techniques allegedly employed against Padilla, however appalling, necessarily amounted to torture. Thus, although we hold that the unconstitutionality of torturing an American citizen was beyond debate in 2001-03, it was not clearly established at that time that the treatment Padilla alleges he was subjected to amounted to torture.

C.

For these reasons, we hold that Yoo is entitled to qualified immunity on the plaintiffs' claims.[16] Because we reverse on that basis, we do not address Yoo's alternative arguments that the complaint does not adequately allege his personal responsibility for Padilla's treatment and that a *Bivens* remedy is unavailable.

Our conclusion that Yoo is entitled to qualified immunity does not address the propriety of Yoo's performance of his duties at OLC otherwise. As amici point out, the complaint alleges that Yoo "*intentionally* violated professional standards reflected in OLC practice and *willfully* disregarded the obligations attendant on his office." Amici argue that "[s]uch conduct, if proven, would strike at the very heart of OLC's mission and seriously compromise the ability of the executive to make informed, even lawful, decisions." These allegations have been the subject of an internal Department of Justice investigation of Yoo's compliance with professional standards and are not at issue here.

---

16. We have discretion to decide which of the two prongs of qualified immunity analysis to address first. *See al-Kidd*, 131 S. Ct. at 2080 (citing *Pearson v. Callahan*, 555 U.S. 223, 236 (2009)). Here, we consider only the second prong.

III. CONCLUSION

Yoo is entitled to qualified immunity. The order of the district court denying Yoo's motion to dismiss is therefore reversed in pertinent part.

Reversed.

NOTES AND QUESTIONS

1. *"Clearly Established" Law*. In *Harlow v. Fitzgerald*, 457 U.S. 800 (1982), the Supreme Court articulated the modern standard for qualified immunity. Under *Harlow*, "government officials performing discretionary functions generally are shielded from liability for civil damages insofar as their conduct does not violate clearly established statutory or constitutional rights of which a reasonable person would have known." Thus, damages suits like *Padilla* raise two different questions: the "illegality" question (whether the plaintiff's rights actually *were* violated) and the "liability" question (whether the defendant officer should have known that his conduct violated the plaintiff's "clearly established" rights). Do you see why the plaintiff must prevail on both questions in order to recover, whereas the defendant prevails if either question is resolved in his favor?

2. *Torture vs. CIDT*. Given the *Harlow* standard, what did the Ninth Circuit actually hold in *Padilla*? Did the Court of Appeals decide that Padilla's alleged mistreatment did or did not constitute torture? That it did or did not constitute cruel, inhuman, or degrading treatment (CIDT)? Why does the torture/CIDT distinction seem to matter so much to the Court of Appeals? Was it clear from 2001 to 2003 that torture was prohibited by U.S. law? Was it clear during the same time period that CIDT was unlawful? Was it clear during that time period on which side of the torture/CIDT line Padilla's alleged mistreatment fell? Is it clear today?

3. *The Specificity of the Legal Claim*. In *Padilla*, the court notes the Supreme Court's decision in *Hope v. Pelzer*, 536 U.S. 730 (2002), which rejected the argument that a defendant is entitled to qualified immunity unless the individual right at issue has been clearly established by a prior case squarely on point both legally *and* factually. Instead, *Hope* framed the inquiry as asking whether "in the light of pre-existing law the

unlawfulness [should have been] apparent." 536 U.S. at 739. Given that standard, are you convinced by the *Padilla* court's analysis of prior case law, including the foreign and international decisions discussed earlier? After *Hope*, is the question whether Padilla's alleged mistreatment was as bad as that suffered by the plaintiffs in those cases, or rather whether those cases *should have* established the unlawfulness of the measures that were allegedly authorized against Padilla? Is this a distinction worth a difference?

4. *Footnote 16 and the Order of Battle*. In its decision in *Saucier v. Katz*, 533 U.S. 194 (2001), the Supreme Court mandated an "order of battle" in qualified immunity cases, pursuant to which courts had to first decide the illegality question before turning to the liability question. The justification for such an approach was to ensure that, even in cases in which the unlawfulness of the defendant's conduct was *not* clearly established (where the defendant therefore prevailed on liability), the law *would be* established going forward. Lower-court judges, who were often left to decide constitutional questions that were not necessary to the result, complained bitterly, leading the Supreme Court to abandon the "*Saucier* sequence" in *Pearson v. Callahan*, 555 U.S. 223 (2009). Under *Pearson*, courts *may*, but need not, resolve the illegality question in cases in which the law was not clearly established. In footnote 16, the *Padilla* court cites *Pearson* to explain why it can sidestep whether Padilla's rights were *actually* violated. Do you see why *Padilla* will therefore have virtually no precedential effect? *Should* the Ninth Circuit have decided whether, going forward, Padilla's alleged mistreatment actually *was* a violation of his rights?

5. *National Security Litigation and the Pearson Problem*. Many damages suits against government officers arise out of conduct that can be challenged through other forms of litigation, including suits for prospective relief while the allegedly unlawful conduct is occurring, or as defenses to criminal prosecutions. In those contexts, *Pearson*'s effect on law-formation may not be significant, since judges will have numerous chances to articulate forward-looking principles of constitutional law in similar cases. But the same may not be true in national security litigation, given the far smaller number of putative victims, the uniqueness of many of the claims in such cases, and the government's prosecutorial discretion. Indeed, as the *Padilla* litigation

itself demonstrates, the government will often take affirmative steps to *avoid* a judicial decision on the merits in national security cases. One of us has suggested that "the general rule articulated in *Pearson* will wreak particular havoc in the national security context, potentially freezing (or, at a minimum, substantially slowing) the development of constitutional law with regard to the surveillance, detention, and treatment of terrorism suspects." Stephen I. Vladeck, *The New National Security Canon*, 61 Am. U. L. Rev. 1295, 1328 (2012). If so, and if this is a problem worth a solution, should courts in cases like *Padilla* feel impelled to decide the illegality question even if they are not required to do so? Is there a better solution to this "*Pearson* problem"?

[NSL p. 974, CTL p. 588. Insert after Note 5.]

6. *Remedies from International Courts?* Khaled el-Masri, a German citizen of Lebanese descent, was pulled off a bus at the Macedonian border on New Year's eve 2003 after border guards apparently confused him with an Al Qaeda operative who had a similar name. He was locked in a hotel room in Skopje for 23 days and told that he would be shot if he attempted to leave. He was then taken to the Skopje airport, where he was transferred to a CIA team. CIA operatives stripped al-Masri, then beat, shackled, hooded, and allegedly sodomized him, before flying him to Afghanistan, where he was detained in solitary confinement for more than four months. Once the mistaken identity was confirmed, he was flown to Albania and left on the side of a road.

When el-Masri sought relief in U.S. courts against the CIA for his rendition and mistreatment, his claims were dismissed on state secrets doctrine grounds (*see* NSL pp. 142-158). *El-Masri v. United States*, 479 F.3d 296 (4th Cir. 2007), *cert. den.*, 552 U.S. 947 (2007). However, his claim against the government of Macedonia was vindicated when, in December 2012, the seventeen judges of the European Court of Human Rights ruled unanimously that Macedonia violated Article 5 the European Convention on Human Rights, which prohibits torture and inhuman or degrading treatment. *Case of El-Masri v. The Former Yugoslav Republic of Macedonia*, Grand Chamber, Dec. 13, 2012, *available at* http://www.aclu.org/files/assets/ el_masri_ruling.pdf. The Court awarded el-Masri about $78,000 in damages, finding that his extraordinary rendition was "by its deliberate circumvention of due process . . . anathema to the rule of law and the values protected by the

Convention." *Id.*, para. 239. Macedonian officials should have known, said the Court, that when el-Masri was handed over to U.S. authorities he faced a considerable risk that his Article 5 rights would be violated. The Macedonian government thus failed in its duty to protect el-Masri from such violations, and it actively facilitated his detention in Afghanistan by handing him over to the CIA. Macedonia also violated Article 5 by holding el-Masri for 23 days in the Skopje hotel.

[NSL p. 1032; CTL p. 646. Replace *United States v. Rosen* with the following two cases.]

While *Abu Ali* was a criminal prosecution, the concern about secret evidence carries over to civil cases and immigration proceedings, as the following case shows.

Ibrahim v. Department of Homeland Security (*Ibrahim II*)

United States District Court, Northern District of California, Dec. 20, 2012
2012 WL 6652362

WILLIAM ALSUP, District Judge. . . .

[The background of this case is described *supra*, p. 129 in this *Supplement*.]

1. Secret and *Ex Parte* Communications.

The analysis begins by addressing the request by the government to dismiss this case based on secret evidence the government wishes to show the judge *ex parte* and extra record. It came about as follows:

After the government's second reversal by the court of appeals in this six-year old action, the government again moved to dismiss under Rule 12, again moving on lack-of-standing grounds, even though the standing issue had gone the other way on appeal. While the briefing was in progress, a telephone call came into the court staff saying that a federal agent was on his way from Washington to San Francisco to show the judge confidential records about this case, all to be relied upon by the government in support of its motion to dismiss (but not to be disclosed to the other side). The officer would take back the records after the judge reviewed them and would leave no record behind of what he had shown the judge. Upon hearing of this, the judge suspended this proposed process and called for the briefing that is the subject of this order, namely the extent to which the government may rely on secret *ex parte* communication in connection with its motion to move to dismiss. Pending resolution of that issue, the Court has not reviewed any such *ex parte* communications (and believes they are not even in the courthouse). Nor has it read any of the redacted passages in the briefing (and believes unredacted versions are not even in the courthouse).

Our court of appeals has not spoken directly to our circumstance so this order will review the three most pertinent decisions. In essence, those decisions strongly favor maintenance of our traditional system of fair play in which both sides have notice of the arguments and evidence being used against them. Nonetheless, for good cause, the judge may receive *ex parte* secret communications for deciding ancillary matters, such as discovery privileges, but only in the rarest of circumstances should the judge do so to resolve or to end a case. It is a matter of discretion for the district judge. Now follows an analysis of the three appellate decisions.

In a 1991 appellate decision that our court of appeals was "careful to limit" to the "precise facts of this case," the district judge had reviewed *ex parte* and *in camera* an FBI declaration stating that an FBI agent had been acting within the course and scope of his employment for the United States and then, based thereon, dismissed a civil suit brought by a criminal-investigation target against the agent. This decision is the government's best authority. The plaintiff there challenged the *ex parte/in camera* procedure. The court of appeals was clearly troubled by it, stating:

> While in our judicial system adversary proceedings are the norm and ex parte proceedings the exception, this court has generally recognized the capacity of a district judge to "fashion and guide the procedures to be followed in cases before him." *United States v. Thompson,* 827 F.2d 1254, 1257 (9th Cir. 1987) (finding, in a criminal context, that district court erred in considering government's reasons for utilization of peremptory challenges ex parte). "[D]istrict judges are able to consider matters that may be unique to particular fact situations and tailor procedures to serve the ends of justice. . . ." *Id.* at 1258. We find that the procedure used by the court in the instant case was proper, it adequately balanced the rights of the Government and Meridian. The Government's interest in having FBI documents, which relate to an ongoing investigation, remain confidential

> was clearly satisfied by the court's action; and although Meridian did not have the opportunity to conduct discovery and cross-examine the Government's witnesses, its interests as a litigant are satisfied by the ex parte/in camera decision of an impartial district judge. However, because procedures such as these should be used only in unique situations, we are careful to limit our holding to the precise facts of this case.

Meridian Intern. Logistics, Inc. v. United States, 939 F.2d 740, 745 (9th Cir. 1991). Although there was no reversal per se on the procedural ground, the court of appeals reversed on the merits, holding that the generalized *ex parte* declarations were insufficient to establish that all agent acts had been within the scope of FBI authority.

Meridian is distinguishable for several reasons. First, the dismissal by the district judge was pursuant to a statutory (and public) certification by the Attorney General that the FBI actions involved had all been within the scope and course of FBI employment. . . . The only role of the *ex parte/in camera* declarations was to supply proof to back up the certification as to scope. So, the first point of distinction is the limited role that the declarations played in *Meridian.*

Second, despite its limited role, our court of appeals nonetheless reversed on the merits and held that the declarations were too inadequate and too conclusory to support the scope certification. It remanded for reconsideration and instructed the district judge to "entertain further documentary proof by the parties." *Id.* at 745. This meant that, on remand, both sides would have an opportunity to submit evidence on the scope issue, not just the government.

Third, our court of appeals described the substantive declarations in its public order, stating that they only generally asserted that the agent's investigation had been proper without addressing the specific factual allegation of Meridian's complaint. Put differently, under our system of law, the court felt obliged to explain the basis for its ruling, even if that meant revelation of some of the information in the secret submission.

Fourth, unlike here, the government there at least had the declarations filed in the court record, even if under seal, so that there would be a precise judicial record for appeal. Here, by contrast, the government wishes to whisk away all of its secret evidence and leave no trace behind in our district court records for appellate review. Our court of appeals would have to depend upon an agency bureaucratic process to recreate the same material shown to the district judge.

In short, *Meridian* provides guidance and a word of caution. Our court of appeals limited its holding there "to the precise facts" of that case. Our facts are much different. Here, we have no public statutory certification. We would have no district court record for appellate review. We would have no proceeding where both sides were given a chance to submit documentary proof on the issue, for here no one has a clue what the government's secret evidence purports to address.

In *Gilmore v. Gonzales,* 435 F.3d 1125 (9th Cir. 2006), our court of appeals itself ordered the government to file under seal and *ex parte* materials sufficient to show that a TSA Security Directive was a "final order." This was done on appeal in a suit by someone who refused to give his identification at the airport security check-in and sued to challenge the authority of the TSA to condition the right to travel on showing proper identification. If the TSA Security Directive was a "final order," then the district court lacked subject-matter jurisdiction and only the court of appeals could hear a petition for review. After reviewing the Security Directive *in camera* and *ex parte,* our court of appeals described the directive sufficiently in its ruling to demonstrate that it was indeed a "final order" and then transferred the matter to itself under its own original review jurisdiction. Nothing in this *ex parte* procedure was used to make a ruling on the merits and, indeed, our court of appeals went on to reach the merits in the next passage in the opinion. By contrast, here the government seeks to use *ex parte* communications to defeat plaintiff's case altogether.

Finally, let's turn to a decision of our appellate court most on point. Although Congress later enacted a provision to strip federal courts of subject-matter jurisdiction to review certain immigration proceedings, our court of appeals held — in an action commenced *before* the jurisdiction-stripping enactment — that due process was violated when the government uses secret, classified information to deny resident illegal aliens the privilege of legalization, that is, temporary or permanent resident status. *American-Arab Anti-Discrimination Committee v. Reno,* 70 F.3d 104, 1066-71 (9th Cir. 1995), *vacated on other grounds,* 525 U.S. 471 (1999). This part of the decision by our court of appeals remains good law. Given that in our very case, our court of appeals has now held that Ibrahim, even though voluntarily outside our country, is entitled to assert claims to the same extent as an alien within our borders, it is hard to avoid the *Reno* principle in the instant civil action.

To be sure, there are circumstances where a district judge must and should examine *ex parte* materials *in camera.* When claims of privilege are made in discovery matters to shield material from revelation, we do so to rule on the privilege. But there no one is yet trying to end or to win a case on the merits in secret — rather, the issue is whether the other side has a right to obtain the allegedly privileged evidence. In contrast, where the holder affirmatively seeks to use the evidence to win or to end the case, then, of course, any privilege must be deemed waived and both sides then have access to it, at least under an appropriate protective order. Here the government seeks to affirmatively use allegedly privileged information to dispose of the case entirely without ever revealing to the other side what its secret evidence might be.

Similarly, in the *Rovario* context in criminal cases, we are sometimes called on to hold an *in camera* hearing to examine a confidential informant under oath to determine the extent to which the informant has sufficient evidence helpful to the defense so as to overcome the *Rovario* privilege and require disclosure to the defense of the identity of the witness. *Rovario v. United States,* 353 U.S. 53, 59 (1957). Again, however, in that context, the government is *not* trying to use secret information to convict. It does not wish to use the evidence at all. It is the *other side* that wants to have access to the evidence for potential use in court. And, it might be added, when this is done, the proceeding is reported and the transcript is made part of the record, albeit under seal, for the review by the court of appeals. Before the *in camera* review, moreover, it is the practice of at least this district judge to ask defense counsel to submit a list of questions to be covered by the judge during the *in camera* proceeding.

Similarly, a district judge sometimes reviews potential *Brady* material *in camera* and *ex parte* to rule on whether it must be turned over. Again, in those circumstances, the government does not seek to affirmatively rely on the material. Rather, the question is whether to disclose it for potential use by the other side. These are only examples. There are other *ex parte* circumstances known to the courts but the main point is now evident.

In the exercise of its discretion, here is how the Court concludes such issues should be determined. Where the government seeks to end or win a case entirely based on secret evidence via an *ex parte* communication, it should first submit a precis available to both sides (i) laying out the general purport of the argument and evidence such that the other side will have an opportunity to respond to the general tenor of the proposed submission and (ii) explaining why more detail should not be made available to the other side. Then both sides may address the fairness and need for the *ex parte* procedure and, if it is to be done at all, the parameters for it. The more case dispositive the proposed submission, the more justification should be shown. In sum, only in the rarest of circumstances should a district judge, in his or her discretion, receive *ex parte* argument and evidence in secret from only one side aimed at winning or ending a case over the objection of the other side. Here, the government has not justified its sweeping proposal. It has gone so far as even to redact from its table of authorities some of the reported caselaw on which it relies! This is too hard to swallow.

This order holds that the government has not justified and may not affirmatively seek to dismiss this civil action based upon proposed secret *ex parte* communications with the district judge. If the government seeks to make affirmative use of evidence to end the case, then it must disclose that information — under an appropriate protective order, of course, but nonetheless disclose it. If it does not wish to make such affirmative use, then it may withhold it subject only to the possibility that plaintiff's counsel may eventually seek discovery of it, in which case it may or may not be kept under wraps depending on the strength of the competing discovery consideration at that time and the strength of the privilege asserted.

Therefore, the Court will ignore all of the redacted material in the government briefs on this set of motions and will rule on the same paperwork made available to both sides, which is totally redacted as to the standing issue. The government's latest motion based on lack of standing, being a complete mystery, is **DENIED**. . . .

United States v. Rosen

United States District Court, Eastern District of Virginia, Nov. 1, 2007
520 F. Supp. 2d 786

T.S. ELLIS, III, District Judge. At issue in this Espionage Act prosecution is the government's second motion pursuant to §6(c) of the Classified Information Procedures Act (CIPA), 18 U.S.C. App. 3, to introduce certain summaries, redactions, and substitutions at trial in lieu of certain specific classified information, and to use the "silent witness rule" (SWR) with respect to portions of certain documents and recordings. . . .

I. CIPA Proceedings to Date

Defendants Steven Rosen and Keith Weissman are charged with conspiracy to violate the Espionage Act, in violation of 18 U.S.C. §§793(g) and (e). Rosen is also charged with one count of aiding and abetting alleged co-conspirator Larry Franklin's unauthorized disclosure of national defense information, in violation of 18 U.S.C. §[§]2, 793(d). The Superseding Indictment generally charges that defendants cultivated sources of information within the United States government, obtained or sought to obtain NDI [National Defense Information] from those sources, and disclosed that information to a variety of other individuals not authorized to receive it, including American Israel Public Affairs Committee (AIPAC) staffers, journalists, and foreign government officials. . . .

The government . . . filed a motion, ostensibly pursuant to CIPA §6(c), in which it sought application of the SWR to most of the classified information at issue in the case. The Court struck this motion in its entirety, finding, *inter alia,* that the government's proposed extensive use of the SWR effectively closed the trial to the public and that the government had not adequately justified this trial closure under the applicable standard of *Press-Enterprise Co. v. Superior Court of California,* 464 U.S. 501 (1984). The government has now filed a second CIPA §6(c) motion in which the proposed use of the SWR is significantly reduced, and in which the government also proposes numerous conventional CIPA §6(c) substitutions to be provided to the public and the jury in the same form. The motion has been fully briefed and argued, and is now ripe for resolution.

II. Applicable Law . . .

C. The Silent Witness Rule

In addition to conventional CIPA substitutions, *i.e.* redactions, admissions, and summaries, the government also proposes use of the SWR, a procedure whereby certain evidence designated by the government is made known to the judge, the jury, counsel, and witnesses, but is withheld from the public. Under this procedure, a witness referring to this evidence would not specifically identify or describe it, but would instead refer to it by reference to page and line numbers of a document or transcript, or more commonly by use of codes such as "Person 1," "Country A," etc. The jury, counsel, and the judge would have access to a key alerting them to the meaning of these code designations; the public, however, would not have access to this key.10 Any recordings containing the portions designated for SWR treatment would be played in open court, but would revert to static when the portions designated to be treated under the SWR are reached; thus, the public would not hear these portions. At the same time, however, jurors, counsel, and the judge would listen on headphones to the unredacted recording. This SWR procedure is in sharp contrast to the CIPA procedure, which contemplates that any substitutions, summaries, and redactions will be made available to the public and jury in identical form. . . .

The SWR is a novel evidence presentation technique that has received little judicial attention in the context of the use of classified information in trials. . . . This paucity of judicial precedent on the SWR's use in CIPA cases counsels caution with respect to its use in this context.

The threshold question that must be resolved with respect to the SWR's use in this case is whether it is even permissible to use in the CIPA context. Put differently, the question is whether CIPA provides the exclusive means of dealing with classified information in criminal trials and, even if so, whether the SWR can be said to be authorized by CIPA §6(c) as constituting a species of "summary" or "substitution" under that provision. These are not easily answered questions. Substantial arguments exist on both sides of these questions. Defendants point chiefly to CIPA's comprehensiveness in its prescriptions for the handling of classified information in trial. This comprehensiveness, defendants argue, manifests Congress' intent to forbid the use of any trial presentation techniques not specifically authorized by CIPA, including the SWR. A closely-related statutory construction argument defendants advance relies on the familiar interpretive canon *expressio unius est exclusio alterius,* namely that "[w]hen a statute limits a thing to be done in a particular mode, it [the statute] includes the negative of any other mode." *Diaz v. Va. Hous. Dev. Auth.,* 117 F. Supp. 2d 500, 504 (E.D. Va. 2000). Defendants point further in support of their argument to Rule 26, Fed. R. Crim. P., which in general terms states that trial testimony "must be taken in open court, unless otherwise provided by a statute or by rules adopted under 28 U.S.C. §§2072-2077."

Although not insubstantial, these arguments, in the end, fail to persuade. CIPA, while undeniably detailed in some respects, is neither explicitly nor implicitly exclusive as to the trial treatment of classified information. CIPA provides no answer, for example, to the question whether the classification markings on relevant documents should be removed as inadmissible hearsay as to the issue whether the document's contents are NDI within the meaning of the Espionage Act. Nor does CIPA provide any guidance on whether it might either be appropriate or required to issue a jury instruction limiting the purposes for which the jury might consider a document's classification markings. Similarly, CIPA does not address the question, presented in this case, whether it is appropriate to allow disparate access by experts to certain classified information redacted from a relevant classified trial document. Also not addressed by CIPA is whether witnesses whose identity is classified may appear to testify using a pseudonym, a mask or some other device to conceal the witness's identity. . . .

In sum, CIPA is neither exhaustive nor explicitly exclusive with respect to the presentation of classified testimony or documents at trial. It follows that CIPA cannot be said to exclude the use of the SWR at trial. And, indeed, while no court has squarely addressed this precise question, a few courts have implicitly approved the use of the SWR at trial. Other courts, without using the "SWR" term, have approved the presentation of evidence in one form to the jury and in another form to the public. In doing so, these courts have given effect to Congress' express intent in enacting CIPA that federal district judges "must be relied on to fashion creative and fair solutions to these problems," *i.e.*, the problems raised by use of classified information in trials. S. Rep. 96-823, *reprinted in* 1980 U.S.C.C.A.N. 4294. In short, the SWR is precisely the sort of judicially-created fair solution envisioned by Congress.

Nor is Rule 26 of any aid to defendants' argument. The Rule is general and aspirational and suffers the fate of all general rules: It has wel-established exceptions. Courts in criminal cases have in a variety of circumstances partially closed proceedings to accommodate overriding interests, such as the safety of confidential informants and undercover officers. The SWR is simply another of these exceptions. Of course, the SWR should be used sparingly and only where the standards governing trial closures are met. It may not be used excessively, as was true with the government's first motion pursuant to CIPA §6(c).

Less difficult to answer is the second question posed, namely whether the SWR is merely a species of redaction or substitution authorized by CIPA §6(c). It is not. CIPA §6(c) redactions and substitutions, unlike the SWR, do not effect any closing of the trial to the public. To the contrary, CIPA plainly envisions that substitutions and redactions will be made available in the same form to the public as to the trial participants. This is confirmed not only by the plain meaning of CIPA's text, but also by the absence of any statutory language or legislative history concerning the First Amendment considerations raised by the partial closing of the trial that results from the SWR's use. It is difficult to believe that this important constitutional consequence went unnoticed by CIPA's drafters. It went unnoticed because it was not present; CIPA's redactions and substitutions do not close the trial. The SWR is not part of CIPA. To conclude otherwise impermissibly engrafts on CIPA a judicial gloss of constitutional magnitude never envisioned, discussed, or provided for by CIPA's architects.

Given that the SWR is not part of CIPA and is neither foreclosed by CIPA nor by Rule 26, the question now presented is what standards apply for its application. As explained in [*United States v. Rosen (Rosen VII)*, 487 F. Supp. 2d 703 (E.D. Va. 2007)], use of the SWR constitutes a partial closure of the trial — or, if used extensively, a complete closure of the trial — because it prevents the public from seeing and hearing the complete body of evidence in the case. Of course, the SWR is not *per se* impermissible because it closes the trial, but use of the procedure is permissible only after a searching analysis, both because the rights of the public and defendants to a public trial are constitutionally guaranteed, and also because erroneous deprivation of the right to a public trial is *per se* prejudicial. Specifically, because the SWR effects a partial closure of the trial, the use of the rule must survive scrutiny under *Press-Enterprise*. *Press-Enterprise* requires that before a trial may be closed to the public, the proponent of the closure must demonstrate, and the court must find, (i) that a compelling interest exists to justify the closure, (ii) that the closure is no broader than necessary to protect that interest, and (iii) that no reasonable alternatives exist to closure. Additionally, the court must also make findings concerning these determinations on the record. Importantly, as applied to a trial closure premised on the need to protect classified information, the *Press-Enterprise* inquiry into reasonable alternatives must consider whether a conventional CIPA substitution is feasible in the circumstances.

Although *Press-Enterprise* does not require an explicit finding that a trial closure is fair to defendants, it is appropriate to reject any use of the SWR that is unfair to defendants. This is so for several reasons. First, defendants have a due process right to a fundamentally fair trial. Second,

Press-Enterprise and its progeny are concerned with conventional sealing of proceedings and simply did not foresee or address this novel procedure, which is a "highly artificial" means of presenting evidence that could, in many circumstances, inhibit the ability of witnesses and counsel to communicate with the jury, to the detriment of defendants' ability to present their defense fairly. In other words, conventional sealing of a courtroom under *Press-Enterprise* does not alter the manner in which evidence and argument are presented, but merely restricts who is physically present to hear the evidence and argument. The SWR is different. It has some features of both a trial closure, in that some evidence presented to the jury is kept from the public, and of a CIPA substitution, in that some evidence is discussed in open court only via codes or euphemisms, which, in a limited way, may be viewed as analogous to substitutions allowed by §6(c). Thus, even though the SWR is not a substitution or redaction authorized by CIPA, it is only sensible that both *Press-Enterprise* analysis and a CIPA-like fairness analysis should be undertaken before the SWR's use is authorized. Yet the potential for unfairness from a conventional substitution and from the SWR are different in important ways, a point that merits further elaboration.

Because the SWR, unlike a conventional summary or redaction, permits the jury to view the actual evidence the government seeks to protect from public disclosure, there is no potential for unfairness based on the factfinder's inability to learn relevant, classified facts which have been summarized or redacted out. Yet there is potential for unfairness in the SWR's use; it lies (i) in the awkwardness of presentation and resulting jury confusion, (ii) in witnesses' and counsel's inability to explore fully and argue about the facts protected by the SWR, and (iii) in the prejudice from employing a procedure that suggests to the jury that the information being discussed is a closely-held government secret when the jury itself must decide that very issue. Assessing unfairness of this sort is more difficult than assessing the fairness of a conventional CIPA substitution. Under CIPA §6(c), a court need only consider whether defendants, in making their defense, need to introduce into evidence factual details present in the classified information, but not in the substitution. In other words, §6(c) calls for a focused evidentiary ruling: Are particular facts contained in the classified material, but not in the substitution relevant and significantly exculpatory? In contrast, fairness under the SWR must consider all the mechanics of the SWR's use at trial, including whether the defendants can fairly present evidence, cross-examine, and argue to the jury about the facts protected by the SWR, whether an ordinary juror will be able to follow the evidence and argument if presented by the SWR, and whether the prejudice from the rule's use is curable by an instruction or otherwise. This fairness analysis is no easy task, but it is required.

The SWR's use may entail a second type of potential unfairness to a defendant, namely infringement of a defendant's Sixth Amendment right to a public trial. This right helps ensure that the public sees the evidence and proceedings so that it can make its own assessment about the fairness of the proceedings. This public scrutiny of a trial provides some insurance against an unfair prosecution or proceeding. The public's assessment of the fairness of a trial may be impaired by the use of the SWR if that use distorts the meaning of the underlying evidence. Thus, even if an SWR proposal does not hinder the defense in presenting its case, it may, in certain circumstances not present here, be appropriate to reject or modify an SWR "substitution" or code if the code significantly distorts the meaning of the underlying information. Unlike the effect the SWR may have on a defendant's right to cross-examine, this public trial concern is adequately accommodated by the *Press-Enterprise* test for trial closure, as the analysis for closing a trial under the First Amendment is the same as the analysis required for closing a trial under the Sixth Amendment.

To summarize, because the concerns animating both *Press-Enterprise* and CIPA are present when the SWR is used, it is appropriate to approve use of the SWR only when both tests are satisfied, that is only when the government establishes (i) an overriding reason for closing the trial, (ii) that the closure is no broader, (iii) that no reasonable alternatives exist to closure, and (iv) that the use of the SWR provides defendants with substantially the same ability to make their defense as full public disclosure of the evidence, presented without the use of codes. . . .

This Memorandum Opinion outlines the legal principles governing the disposition of the government's second motion pursuant to CIPA §6(c). A separate classified, sealed order will issue applying the principles elucidated here and setting forth the specific rulings made with respect to the government's second CIPA §6(c) motion.

[NSL p. 1051; CTL p. 665. Insert before Section D.]

C1. The Public Safety Exception to *Miranda*

In the aftermath of the 2013 Boston Marathon bombings a debate was renewed over whether captured terrorism suspects should be detained without trial, tried by civilian court, or tried by military commission. Some argued, as well, that the government should be able to interrogate the suspect without advising him of his rights to counsel and to remain silent under *Miranda v. Arizona*, 384 U.S. 436 (1966). *See, e.g.*, Charlie Savage, *Debate Over Delaying of Miranda Warning*, N.Y. Times, Apr. 20, 2013. Senator Lindsey Graham, among others, urged the Obama administration not to Mirandize Dzokhar Tsarnaev, one of the suspected bombers, and instead to hold him as an enemy combatant in order to interrogate him for intelligence gathering purposes. *See, e.g.*, Wells Bennett, *Senator Graham on Tsarnaev and Miranda*, Lawfare, Apr. 23, 2013, *available at* http://www.lawfareblog.com/2013/04/senator-graham-on-tsarnaev-and-miranda/. But the Supreme Court has already recognized an exception to *Miranda* for interrogations motivated by concern for "public safety," as opposed to ordinary law enforcement. *See New York v. Quarles*, 467 U.S. 649 (1984). As you review the materials that follow, consider how, if at all, the *Quarles* exception illuminates this debate.

U.S. Department of Justice, Federal Bureau of Investigation, Custodial Interrogation for Public Safety and Intelligence-Gathering Purposes of Operational Terrorists Inside the United States[1]

Oct. 21, 2010

Identifying and apprehending suspected terrorists, interrogating them to obtain intelligence about terrorist activities and impending terrorist attacks, and lawfully detaining them so that they do not pose a continuing threat to our communities are critical to protecting the American people. The Department of Justice and the FBI believe that we

---

1. This guidance applies only to arrestees who have not been indicted and who are not known to be represented by an attorney. . . .

can maximize our ability to accomplish these objectives by continuing to adhere to FBI policy regarding the use of *Miranda* warnings for custodial interrogation of operational terrorists[2] who are arrested inside the United States:

1. If applicable, agents should ask any and all questions that are reasonably prompted by an immediate concern for the safety of the public or the arresting agents without advising the arrestee of his *Miranda* rights.[3]

2. After all applicable public safety questions have been exhausted, agents should advise the arrestee of his *Miranda* rights and seek a waiver of those rights before any further interrogation occurs, absent exceptional circumstances described below.

3. There may be exceptional cases in which, although all relevant public safety questions have been asked, agents nonetheless conclude that continued unwarned interrogation is necessary to collect valuable and timely intelligence not related to any immediate threat, and that the government's interest in obtaining this intelligence outweighs the disadvantages of proceeding with

---

2. For these purposes, an operational terrorist is an arrestee who is reasonably believed to be either a high-level member of an international terrorist group; or an operative who has personally conducted or attempted to conduct a terrorist operation that involved risk to life; or an individual knowledgeable about operational details of a pending terrorist operation.

3. The Supreme Court held in *New York v. Quarles*, 467 U.S. 649 (1984), that if law enforcement officials engage in custodial interrogation of an individual that is "reasonable prompted by a concern for the public safety," any statements the individual provides in the course of such interrogation shall not be inadmissible in any criminal proceeding on the basis that the warnings described in *Miranda v. Arizona*, 384 U.S. 436 (1966), were not provided. The court noted that this exception to the *Miranda* rule is a narrow one and that "in each case it will be circumscribed by the [public safety] exigency which justifies it." 467 U.S. at 657.

> unwarned interrogation.[4] . . . Presentment of an arrestee may not be delayed simply to continue the interrogation, unless the defendant has timely waived prompt presentment.

The determination whether particular unwarned questions are justified on public safety grounds must always be made on a case-by-case basis based on all the facts and circumstances. In light of the magnitude and complexity of the threat often posed by terrorist organizations, particularly international terrorist organizations, and the nature of their attacks, the circumstances surrounding an arrest of an operational terrorist may warrant significantly more extensive public safety interrogation without *Miranda* warnings than would be permissible in an ordinary criminal case. Depending on the facts, such interrogation might include, for example, questions about possible impending or coordinated terrorist attacks; the location, nature, and threat posed by weapons that might post an imminent danger to the public; and the identities, locations, and activities or intentions of accomplices who may be plotting additional imminent attacks. . . .

NOTES AND QUESTIONS

1. *Quarles and the Origin of the "Public Safety" Exception.* Although *Quarles* has come to serve as the fountainhead for the "public safety" exception, it was a fairly unexceptional case. There, a rape victim told the police that the perpetrator (who was armed) had just entered a nearby supermarket. When officers arrested the suspect inside the supermarket, they found an empty holster, leading one of the officers

---

4. The Supreme Court has strongly suggested that an arrestee's Fifth Amendment right against self-incrimination is not violated at the time a statement is taken without *Miranda* warnings, but instead may be violated only if and when the government introduces an unwarned statement in a criminal proceeding against the defendant. *See* Chavez v. Martinez, 538 U.S. 760, 769 (2003) (plurality op.); *id.* at 789 (Kennedy, J., concurring in part and dissenting in part); *cf. also id.* at 778-79 (Souter, J., concurring in the judgment); *see also* United States v. Patane, 542 U.S. 630, 641 (2004) (plurality opinion) ("[V]iolations [of the Fifth Amendment right against self-incrimination] occur, if at all, only upon the admission of unwarned statements into evidence at trial."); United States v. Verdugo-Urquidez, 494 U.S. 259, 264 (1990) ("[A] violation [of the Fifth Amendment right against self-incrimination] occurs only at trial.").

to ask the suspect what had happened to the gun. The suspect's answer, which led the officers to where he had hidden the gun, was subsequently suppressed by the trial court on the ground that it obtained in violation of *Miranda*; it was, after all, a statement made in response to an unwarned custodial interrogation. *See New York v. Quarles*, 467 U.S. 649, 651-653 (1984). But the Supreme Court reversed. As then-Justice Rehnquist explained for a 5-4 majority, "Whatever the motivation of individual officers in such a situation, we do not believe that the doctrinal underpinnings of *Miranda* require that it be applied in all its rigor to a situation in which police officers ask questions reasonably prompted by a concern for the public safety." *Id.* at 656.

In other words, where questioning in a custodial interrogation focuses on ongoing concern for public safety, rather than the suspect's specific culpability, statements made by the suspect in response are admissible against him even if they were obtained prior to the administration of the *Miranda* warnings. Otherwise, Rehnquist explained, law enforcement officers would be forced to make a difficult choice — to decide on the spur of the moment and under exigent circumstances

> whether it best serves society for them to ask the necessary questions without the *Miranda* warnings and render whatever probative evidence they uncover inadmissible, or for them to give the warnings in order to preserve the admissibility of evidence they might uncover but possibly damage or destroy their ability to obtain that evidence and neutralize the volatile situation confronting them. [*Id.* at 657-658.]

2. *Justice O'Connor's Objection*. In an unusually strident dissent, Justice O'Connor criticized this reasoning as presenting a false dichotomy grounded in a misunderstanding of *Miranda* — as a bar on interrogations, rather than as an exclusionary rule. (As the FBI guidelines note in footnote 3, the Supreme Court has all but held that *Miranda* is only the latter, and does not bar unwarned interrogations in the abstract.) As she elaborated,

> *Miranda* has never been read to prohibit the police from asking questions to secure the public safety. Rather, the critical question *Miranda* addresses is who shall bear the cost of securing the public safety when such questions are asked and answered: the defendant or the State. *Miranda*, for better or worse, found the resolution of that question implicit in the prohibition against compulsory self-

> incrimination and placed the burden on the State. When police ask custodial questions without administering the required warnings, *Miranda* quite clearly requires that the answers received be presumed compelled and that they be excluded from evidence at trial. [*Quarles*, 467 U.S. at 665 (O'Connor, J., concurring in the judgment in part and dissenting in part).]

Isn't Justice O'Connor correct that *Quarles* would allow law enforcement officers to have their cake and eat it, too? Is that simply a necessary compromise in situations in which there is a serious threat to "public safety"? If so, was *Quarles* (where the threat to public safety consisted of a handgun hidden in a grocery store) an appropriate case *for* the "public safety" exception?

3. *The FBI's "Exceptional Cases" Category.* The FBI guidelines reproduced above are mostly devoted to implementing *Quarles* in practice. But consider the suggestion under point "3" that "[t]here may be exceptional cases in which, although all relevant public safety questions have been asked, agents nonetheless conclude that continued unwarned interrogation is necessary to collect valuable and timely intelligence not related to any immediate threat, and that the government's interest in obtaining this intelligence outweighs the disadvantages of proceeding with unwarned interrogation." Are the guidelines suggesting that such statements may nevertheless be admissible under *Quarles*? Or are they suggesting that there will be cases in which the potential fruits of such statements outweigh the government's need to be able to introduce them against the suspect at trial? If these considerations are already applied by the government, doesn't that undermine Justice Rehnquist's reasoning in *Quarles*, which sought to free the government from such calculus? Or might it suggest, in the alternative, that the FBI has a narrower view of the "public safety" exception than the courts?

4. *The Scope of the "Public Safety" Exception in Terrorism Cases.* How should courts measure the threat to public safety in terrorism cases, where the potential risk to public safety may be far greater than that posed by a single gun hidden in a grocery store, but where it also may be far less imminent and specific? Is there a principled way to define "public safety" in this context? Or was Justice O'Connor correct in *Quarles* when she warned that "[t]he end result will be a finespun new doctrine on public safety exigencies incident to custodial interrogation,

complete with the hair-splitting distinctions that currently plague our Fourth Amendment jurisprudence"? 467 U.S. at 663-664 (O'Connor, J., concurring in the judgment in part and dissenting in part). The following case presents this question rather starkly.

United States v. Abdulmutallab

United States District Court, Eastern District of Michigan, Sept. 16, 2011
2011 WL 4345243

NANCY G. EDMUNDS, District Judge:

[Omar Farouk Abdulmutallab, the "underwear bomber," sustained significant burns while attempting to ignite explosives concealed in his underwear in order to blow up Northwest Flight 253 as it was approaching Detroit, Michigan, on December 25, 2009. He was interrogated by the FBI after his arrest while under treatment at the University of Michigan Hospital, but before advising him of his rights under *Miranda v. Arizona*, 384 U.S. 436 (1966). In the criminal prosecution that followed, Abdulmutallab moved to suppress statements made by him prior to the administration of the *Miranda* warnings. The government replied by arguing that the statements were admissible under the "public safety" exception to *Miranda* articulated in *New York v. Quarles*, 467 U.S. 649 (1984). The district court denied Abdulmutallab's motion to suppress.]

I. Facts — Evidentiary Hearing

On December 25, 2009, when Northwest-Delta Flight 253 landed, U.S. Customs and Border Protection officers met the plane at the gate, having been advised of an incident on board the plane. . . . After assessing the severity of Defendant's burns, U.S. Customs officers transported Defendant to the U of M Hospital for treatment and informed the FBI's Joint Terrorism Task Force of the situation. . . .

Around 3:35 p.m., after he was moved to a room, Defendant was questioned by FBI Special Agent Timothy Waters. Other federal agents were present, including FBI Special Agent Peissig, and U.S. Customs Officer Steigerwald. Before the 3:35 interview began, Special Agent Waters had learned from U.S. Customs and Border Protection Officer Steigerwald that Defendant had admitted that he had detonated an explosive device hidden in his underwear while on Flight 253 and that he was acting on behalf of al-Qaeda. He had also learned from other federal agents that an explosive device similar to the one used by Defendant had been used previously, although not on a plane. He also knew that the explosive device had no mechanical devices associated with it and was thus problematic because it could defeat airport security and, indeed, had done so in this instance. Mindful of Defendant's self-proclaimed association with al-Qaeda and knowing the group's past history of large, coordinated plots and attacks, the agents feared that there could be additional, imminent aircraft attacks in the United States and elsewhere in the world. For these reasons, Agent Waters questioned Defendant for about 50 minutes without first advising him of his *Miranda* rights.

During that interview, . . . Agent Waters asked Defendant where he traveled, when he had traveled, how, and with whom; the details of the explosive device; the details regarding the bomb-maker, including where Defendant had received the bomb; his intentions in attacking Flight 253; and who else might be planning an attack. Every question sought to identify any other potential attackers and to prevent another potential attack. Defendant answered, providing information that helped the agents to determine where to go next and investigate if anyone else might be planning to or was already in the process of carrying a similar device on an aircraft. At the end of the interview, once they received the public safety information, the agents turned their attention to immediately sharing the information with law enforcement and intelligence agencies worldwide.

II. Analysis

A. Voluntariness of Defendant's Statements

[In this part of the opinion, Judge Edmunds concluded that Abdulmutallab's statements were voluntarily given, despite his medical condition at the time of his interrogation.]

B. *Quarles* Exception

Defendant argues that his statements to the federal agents on December 25, 2009 at U of M Hospital should be suppressed because the federal agents failed to first advise him of his *Miranda* rights. The Court disagrees. The circumstances present at the time of Defendant's questioning fall within the public safety exception to *Miranda* recognized in *Quarles*, 467 U.S. at 657. The Sixth Circuit has applied the *Quarles* exception. *See United States v. Talley*, 275 F.3d 560, 564 (6th Cir. 2001) (applying the *Quarles* public safety exception).

The federal courts have extended the logic of *Quarles* to the questioning of terrorism suspects. *See* [*United States v. Khalil*, 214 F.3d 111 (2d Cir. 2000)], at 121. In *Khalil*, the district court determined that the *Quarles* exception to *Miranda* applied when, after a raid on the defendant's apartment where he was injured, officers questioned the defendant at the hospital "about the construction and stability of the bombs" discovered in his apartment and included within the *Quarles* exception the defendant's response to the officer's inquiry "whether he had intended to kill himself in detonating the bombs." *Id.* On appeal, the defendant challenged the district court's "ruling only insofar as the court failed to suppress" his response to the question about his intent to kill himself, arguing that "that question was unrelated to the matter of public safety." *Id.* The Second Circuit resolved the issue as follows:

> We are inclined to disagree, given that [the defendant]'s vision as to whether or not he would survive his attempt to detonate the bomb had the potential for shedding light on the bomb's stability. In any event, even if we were to take a different view as to the relevance of that question, we would conclude that the admission of [the defendant's] response at trial was, at worst, harmless error.

Id. See also In re Terrorist Bombings of U.S. Embassies in E. Africa, 552 F.3d 177, 203 n.19, 204 (2d Cir. 2008) (assuming *Quarles* would apply to exigent circumstances in a terrorism case).

In light of the testimony provided at the evidentiary hearing, the logic of *Quarles* extends to the questioning of Defendant, a terrorism suspect at the time of his December 25, 2009 questioning. The agents' questions were intended to shed light on the obvious public safety concerns in this case and were "necessary to secure . . . the safety of the public[.]" *Quarles*, 467 U.S. at 659. Defendant was asked where he traveled, when he had traveled, how, and with whom; the details of the explosive device; the details regarding the bomb-maker, including where Defendant had received the bomb; his intentions in attacking Flight 253; who else might be planning an attack; whether he associated with, lived with, or attended the same mosque with others who had a similar mind-set as Defendant about jihad, martyrdom, support for al-Qaeda, and a desire to attack the United States by using a similar explosive device on a plane, and what these individuals looked like — all in an attempt to discover whether Defendant had information about others who could be on planes or about to board planes with explosive devices similar to the one Defendant used because, based upon his training, experience, and knowledge of earlier al-Qaeda attacks, this was not a solo incident and the potential for a multi-prong attack existed even if Defendant was unaware of any specific additional planned attack.

Special Agent Waters reiterated that, before he interviewed Defendant, he was aware that Defendant claimed to be acting on behalf of al-Qaeda. The agents were also well aware that on September 11, 2001, al-Qaeda operatives hijacked four airplanes in an attack on the United States that killed almost 3,000 people. Mindful of Defendant's self-proclaimed association with al-Qaeda and knowing the group's past history of large, coordinated plots and attacks, the agents logically feared that there could be additional, imminent aircraft attacks in the United States and elsewhere in the world. . . .

The circumstances present at the time of Defendant's questioning fall within the public safety exception to *Miranda* recognized in *Quarles*. Accordingly, the fact that he was questioned by federal agents at U of M Hospital on December 25, 2009 before receiving *Miranda* warnings does not warrant suppression of his challenged statements. Doing so here was fully justified. . . .

NOTES AND QUESTIONS

1. *Easy Cases and the Public Safety Exception*. In one sense, *Abdulmutallab* is a remarkably easy case for the public safety exception, given that he was arrested while attempting to commit an act of terrorism — and one which could potentially have been part of a larger series of coordinated, imminent attacks. But don't the unique facts of his case also make invocation of the exception especially *unnecessary*, since the government is hardly lacking for physical and other testimonial evidence to use against him at trial? Indeed, isn't the public safety exception only really at issue in cases in which the defendant's statements are a critical part of the government's case-in-chief?

2. *Terrorism Prosecutions and the Public Safety Exception*. How useful a precedent is *Abdulmutallab* for other terrorism cases? On one hand, Judge Edmunds heartily endorses the view that concerns about

related terrorist attacks will generally justify application of the exception. On the other hand, *Abdulmutallab* is atypical insofar as the defendant is being prosecuted for an act of terrorism *after* it was attempted. Most terrorism prosecutions are focused instead on inchoate liability — where no actual act of terrorism has yet taken place. In such cases, where any threat to public safety arises from an impending plot in which the suspect is allegedly involved, won't preserving "public safety" and establishing the suspect's culpability necessarily merge? If so, doesn't *Abdulmutallab* suggest that the government will have wide latitude in interrogating such suspects free from the dictates of *Miranda*, in a manner that won't be true for other classes of crimes (where the distinction between public safety and culpability will remain more evident)?

3. *The Other Shoe: Presentment*. Even *Abdulmutallab* only upholds 50 minutes of "public safety" questioning, suggesting, at least implicitly, that the temporal scope of the *Quarles* exception is quite limited. If it is not, then the other relevant consideration is "presentment" — the requirement that arrestees be brought before a neutral magistrate "without unnecessary delay," Fed. R. Crim. P. 5(a)(1)(A), at which point a suspect will be advised of his rights to counsel and to remain silent, if he has not been already. As a result, under *McNabb v. United States*, 318 U. S. 332 (1943), and *Mallory v. United States*, 354 U. S. 449 (1957), an arrestee's confession is inadmissible if it is given after an unreasonable delay in presentment. *See Corley v. United States*, 556 U.S. 303 (2009). And under *County of Riverside v. McLaughlin*, 500 U.S. 44 (1991), the Fourth Amendment itself requires presentment in all cases within 48 hours. Taken together, these cases would suggest that, at the absolute maximum, the government would be entitled to no more than 48 hours of "public safety" questioning of a suspect before he would have to be apprised of his *Miranda* rights. Is there any argument that the presentment requirement might itself have a "public safety" exception? Would such an exception ever be necessary?

4. *Does Quarles Apply Once a Suspect Invokes? Quarles* clearly allows law enforcement officers to begin to question a suspect without advising him of his *Miranda* rights. But what if, without being so warned, a suspect nevertheless invokes his right to remain silent and/or consult with an attorney? Of course, the government could continue to question a suspect even after he has invoked his rights; *Miranda*, after

all, is only an exclusionary rule. But would *Quarles* apply in such a case to allow for the admission of statements made in response to such post-invocation questioning? What little case law there is on this question suggests that the answer is "no." *See Williams v. Jacquez*, No. S-05-0058, 2011 WL 703616, at *14 (E.D. Cal. Feb. 18, 2011) ("The rationale for the *Quarles* exception does not justify continuing a broad ranging interview after the suspect invokes her right to silence."). But if *Quarles* means what it says, why should it matter whether or not the suspect has invoked his rights?

5. *How Quarles Fits into the Terrorism Disposition Debate.* Return to the debate described at the beginning of these materials. Doesn't *Quarles* strongly support those who favor trying most (if not all) terrorism suspects in civilian courts (who might otherwise object to *Quarles*), insofar as it allows the government both to interrogate terrorism suspects about ongoing threats to public safety without advising them of their *Miranda* rights *and* to use anything the suspects say in response against them at trial? On the flip side, for those who support military detention and/or trial by military commission for new terrorism suspects, and who might otherwise be more sympathetic to *Quarles*, doesn't it militate *against* such arguments insofar as it demonstrates the ability of the civilian courts adequately to accommodate the government's interests in terrorism cases? *See generally* Joanna Wright, Note, *Mirandizing Terrorists?: An Empirical Analysis of the Public Safety Exception*, 111 Colum. L. Rev. 1296 (2011). Ultimately, does *Quarles*' utility in this area — and in preserving the government's flexibility in terrorism cases — help to explain why, despite its controversial nature, its overruling has never been sought?

[NSL p. 1104; CTL p. 718. Insert after Note 6.]

Hamdan v. United States (*Hamdan II*)

United States Court of Appeals, District of Columbia Circuit, Oct. 16, 2012
696 F.3d 1238

[After Congress enacted the 2006 MCA, the government again sought to try Hamdan, the petitioner in *Hamdan v. Rumsfeld*, 548 U.S. 557 (2006) (NSL p. 1075; CTL p. 689), before a military commission.

Hamdan was charged with the two offenses discussed in Notes 2 and 3 above, conspiracy to commit war crimes and "providing material support to terrorism." In August 2008, the commission convicted Hamdan on the material support charges but acquitted on conspiracy, sentencing him to 66 months' imprisonment, including time served. Hamdan was then repatriated to Yemen in late 2008 (and released shortly thereafter), while an appeal of his conviction remained pending. Following a long and unexplained delay, the intermediate appellate court created by the MCA, the Court of Military Commission Review, unanimously upheld his conviction, holding that "providing material support to terrorism" was a recognized violation of the international laws of war. *See United States v. Hamdan*, 801 F. Supp. 2d 1247 (Ct. Mil. Comm'n Rev. 2011) (en banc). Hamdan appealed that decision to the D.C. Circuit, the first Article III court ever to hear a direct post-conviction appeal from a U.S. military commission.]

KAVANAUGH, Circuit Judge: . . .

II

[After recounting the facts, Judge Kavanaugh held that Hamdan's appeal was not moot. While Hamdan had been released from custody, the government could not rebut the doctrinal presumption that collateral consequences attached to Hamdan's conviction.]

III . . .

. . . Even assuming arguendo that Congress had authority under its various Article I war powers to establish material support for terrorism as a war crime in the Military Commissions Act of 2006,[6] we conclude

---

6. Judge Kavanaugh alone concurs in this footnote. . . . Judge Kavanaugh would conclude that Congress has authority under Article I, §8 to establish material support for terrorism as a war crime that, when committed by an alien, may be tried by military commission. Although material support for terrorism is not yet an international-law war crime, Congress's war powers under Article I are not defined or constrained by international law. The Declare War Clause and the other Article I war powers clauses do not refer to international law, unlike the Define and Punish Clause. Moreover, Congress has long prohibited war crimes beyond those specified by international law. *See* 10 U.S.C. §904 (aiding the enemy); *id.* §906 (spying). The U.S. Constitution does not give the

that the Act did not authorize *retroactive* prosecution for conduct that was committed before the Act's enactment and was not prohibited by U.S. law at the time the conduct occurred. Here, Hamdan's conduct occurred from 1996 to 2001 — before enactment of the Military Commissions Act. And as we will explain, the federal statute in effect at the time of Hamdan's conduct — 10 U.S.C. §821 — did *not* authorize prosecution for material support for terrorism.

A

As is clear from the text of the Military Commissions Act of 2006, Congress was quite concerned about the ex post facto implications of retroactively prosecuting someone under the Act for conduct committed before its enactment. Congress tried to deal with any ex post facto problem by declaring in the text of the statute that "[t]he provisions of this subchapter codify offenses that have traditionally been triable by military commissions. This chapter does not establish new crimes that did not exist before its enactment, but rather codifies those crimes for trial by military commission." The Act continued: "Because the provisions of this subchapter (including provisions that incorporate definitions in other provisions of law) are declarative of existing law, they do not preclude trial for crimes that occurred before the date of the enactment of this chapter." [*See* 10 U.S.C. §950p(d).]

As Congress well understood when it appended this unusual statement to the statute, the U.S. Constitution bars Congress from enacting punitive ex post facto laws. *See* U.S. Const. art. I, §9, cl. 3 ("No Bill of Attainder or ex post facto Law shall be passed."). The Ex Post Facto Clause . . . prevents Congress and the Executive from retroactively applying a federal criminal statute to conduct committed before the statute was enacted.

As Congress itself recognized in the statutory text, retroactive prosecution by military commission could similarly raise serious constitutional issues, at the very least. As stated in the statutory text,

---

international community — either directly, or indirectly through the vehicle of international law — a judicially enforceable veto over Congress's exercise of its war powers. Put simply, the United States may be a leader in the international community, not just a follower, when Congress authorizes war against a terrorist organization or makes crimes such as material support for terrorism war crimes triable by military commission. . . .

however, Congress believed that the Act codified no new crimes and thus posed no ex post facto problem. As we explain below, Congress's premise was incorrect. The statute does codify some new war crimes, including material support for terrorism. The question for ex post facto purposes is this: If Congress had known that the Act was codifying some new crimes, would Congress have wanted the new crimes to be enforced retroactively? To begin with, the statutory text reveals a tight causal link between (i) Congress's belief that the statute codified only crimes under pre-existing law and (ii) Congress's statement that the statute could therefore apply to conduct before enactment. That causal link suggests that Congress would *not* have wanted *new* crimes to be applied retroactively. The Executive Branch agrees with that interpretation of the statute, stating: "Congress incorporated ex post facto principles into the terms of the MCA itself." Brief for the United States at 66. At a minimum, we know that the statutory text does not contemplate or address the possibility of retroactively applying new crimes, leaving us with at least something of an ambiguity. And courts interpret ambiguous statutes to avoid serious questions of unconstitutionality. To avoid the prospect of an Ex Post Facto Clause violation here, we interpret the Military Commissions Act of 2006 so that it does not authorize *retroactive* prosecution for conduct committed before enactment of that Act unless the conduct was already prohibited under existing U.S. law as a war crime triable by military commission. In this case, therefore, Hamdan's conviction stands or falls on whether his conduct was prohibited by the pre-existing statute, 10 U.S.C. §821, at the time he committed the conduct.[7]

B

Before enactment of the Military Commissions Act in 2006, U.S. military commissions could prosecute war crimes under 10 U.S.C. §821 for violations of the "law of war." The Government suggests that at the time of Hamdan's conduct from 1996 to 2001, material support for terrorism violated the "law of war" referenced in 10 U.S.C. §821. It is true that in the text of the Military Commissions Act of 2006, Congress

---

7. To be clear, we do not here decide whether or how the Ex Post Facto Clause might apply to this case. As we interpret the statute, that ultimate constitutional question need not be decided.

declared its belief that material support for terrorism was a pre-existing crime under the law of war and thus under 10 U.S.C. §821. But exercising our independent review, as we must when considering the ex post facto implications of a new law, we conclude otherwise. Material support for terrorism was not a war crime under the law of war referenced in 10 U.S.C. §821 at the time of Hamdan's conduct.

Analysis of this issue begins by determining what body of law is encompassed by the term "law of war" in 10 U.S.C. §821. The Supreme Court's precedents tell us: The "law of war" referenced in 10 U.S.C. §821 is the international law of war.[8] [citing *Hamdan*; *Hamdi v. Rumsfeld*, 542 U.S. 507 (2004) (NSL p. 831, CTL p. 445); and *Ex parte Quirin*, 317 U.S. 1 (1942) (NSL p. 823, CTL p. 437), along with other secondary sources.]

We turn, then, to the question whether material support for terrorism is an international-law war crime.

It is true that international law establishes at least some forms of *terrorism,* including the intentional targeting of civilian populations, as war crimes. *See, e.g.,* Rome Statute of the International Criminal Court art. 8(2)(b), July 17, 1998, 2187 U.N.T.S. 90; Geneva Convention Relative to the Protection of Civilian Persons in Time of War (Geneva IV), art. 33, Aug. 12, 1949, 6 U.S.T. 3516, 75 U.N.T.S. 287.

But the issue here is whether *material support for terrorism* is an international-law war crime. The answer is no. International law leaves it to individual nations to proscribe material support for terrorism under their domestic laws if they so choose. There is no international-law proscription of material support for terrorism.

---

8. It has been suggested that courts should not use international law as a free-floating tool to alter how the courts would otherwise interpret a domestic U.S. statute *when the statute does not incorporate or refer to international law. See Al-Bihani v. Obama*, 619 F.3d 1, 5-8 (D.C. Cir. 2010) (Brown, J., concurring in denial of rehearing en banc); *id.* at 9-23 (Kavanaugh, J., concurring in denial of rehearing en banc). [NSL pp. 200, 877; CTL p. 491.] But that interpretive issue is not implicated in this case. As Congress has often done, and as explained in an *Al-Bihani* concurrence, Congress here *explicitly* referred to international law and explicitly incorporated international norms into domestic U.S. law in 10 U.S.C. §821 by means of the express cross-reference to the "law of war." *See id.* at 10, 13-15 (Kavanaugh, J., concurring in denial of rehearing en banc) (explaining that distinction). [Judge Ginsburg did not join this footnote. — Eds.]

To begin with, there are no relevant international *treaties* that make material support for terrorism a recognized international-law war crime. Neither the Hague Convention nor the Geneva Conventions — the sources that are "the major treaties on the law of war" — acknowledge material support for terrorism as a war crime.

Nor does customary international law otherwise make material support for terrorism a war crime. Customary international law is a kind of common law; it is the body of international legal principles said to reflect the consistent and settled practice of nations. It is often difficult to determine what constitutes customary international law, who defines customary international law, and how firmly established a norm has to be to qualify as a customary international law norm. *Cf. Sosa v. Alvarez-Machain*, 542 U.S. 692 (2004) [NSL p. 189].[10]

But here, the content of customary international law is quite evident. Material support for terrorism was not a recognized violation of the international law of war as of 2001 (or even today, for that matter). As we have noted, the Geneva Conventions and the Hague Convention do not prohibit material support for terrorism. The 1998 Rome Statute of the International Criminal Court, which catalogues an extensive list of

---

10. Although customary international law, including the customary international law of war, contains some well-defined prohibitions at the core, the contours of customary international law are imprecise. That imprecision provides good reason for Congress and the Executive, when they want to outlaw violations of perceived international-law norms, to enact statutes outlawing specific conduct, rather than simply prohibiting violation of something as vague as "international law" or "the law of nations" or the "law of war." Congress has done so in many recent statutes, including the Military Commissions Act of 2006.

At the same time, the imprecision of customary international law calls for significant caution by U.S. courts before permitting civil or criminal liability premised on violation of such a vague prohibition. A general prohibition against violations of "international law" or the "law of nations" or the "law of war" may fail in certain cases to provide the fair notice that is a foundation of the rule of law in the United States. Therefore, as the Supreme Court required in an analogous context in *Sosa*, and as the plurality suggested in *Hamdan*, imposing liability on the basis of a violation of "international law" or the "law of nations" or the "law of war" generally must be based on norms firmly grounded in international law. *See Sosa*, 542 U.S. at 724-38; *Hamdan*, 548 U.S. at 602-03 & n.34, 605 (plurality). In this case, the asserted norm has no grounding in international law, much less firm grounding.

international war crimes, makes no mention of material support for terrorism. Nor does the Statute of the International Tribunal for the Former Yugoslavia, the Statute of the International Tribunal for Rwanda, or the Statute of the Special Court for Sierra Leone. Nor have any international tribunals exercising common-law-type power determined that material support for terrorism is an international-law war crime.

Commentators on international law have similarly explained that material support for terrorism is not an international-law war crime. Nor is the offense of material support for terrorism listed in the JAG handbook on the law of war.

In short, neither the major conventions on the law of war nor prominent modern international tribunals nor leading international-law experts have identified material support for terrorism as a war crime. Perhaps most telling, before this case, no person has ever been tried by an international-law war crimes tribunal for material support for terrorism.

Not surprisingly, therefore, even the U.S. Government concedes in this case that material support for terrorism is not a recognized international-law war crime. . . .

To be sure, there is a strong argument that aiding and abetting a recognized international-law war crime such as terrorism is itself an international-law war crime. And there are other similar war crimes. But Hamdan was not charged with aiding and abetting terrorism or some other similar war crime. He was charged with material support for terrorism. And as the Government acknowledges, aiding and abetting terrorism prohibits different conduct, imposes different mens rea requirements, and entails different causation standards than material support for terrorism. If the Government wanted to charge Hamdan with aiding and abetting terrorism or some other war crime that was sufficiently rooted in the international law of war (and thus covered by 10 U.S.C. §821) at the time of Hamdan's conduct, it should have done so.

The Government latches on to a few isolated precedents from the Civil War era to prop up its assertion that material support for terrorism was a pre-existing war crime as of 2001 for purposes of 10 U.S.C. §821. . . . [T]hose cases fail to support the Government's argument. . . . The Government contends that those Civil War precedents illuminate what it calls the "U.S. common law of war" — not the international law of war. But the statutory constraint here imposed by 10 U.S.C. §821 is the international law of war. As the Government told the Supreme Court in

Quirin, "This 'common law of war' is a centuries-old body of largely unwritten rules and principles of *international* law which governs the behavior of both soldiers and civilians during time of war." Brief for the United States at 29, in *Quirin*, 317 U.S. 1 (emphasis added) (citation omitted). To be sure, U.S. precedents may inform the content of international law. But those Civil War precedents fail to establish material support for terrorism as a war crime under the international law of war as of 1996 to 2001. And even the Government admits that material support for terrorism was not an international-law war crime as of 1996 to 2001.

In short, material support for terrorism was not an international-law war crime under 10 U.S.C. §821 at the time Hamdan engaged in the relevant conduct.

* * *

Because we read the Military Commissions Act not to sanction retroactive punishment for new crimes, and because material support for terrorism was not a pre-existing war crime under 10 U.S.C. §821, Hamdan's conviction for material support for terrorism cannot stand. We reverse the decision of the Court of Military Commission Review and direct that Hamdan's conviction for material support for terrorism be vacated.

So ordered.

[Concuring opinion of GINSBURG, Senior Circuit Judge, omitted.]

NOTES AND QUESTIONS

1. *Mootness and Military Commission Appeals*. In his separate concurrence, Judge Ginsburg agreed that Hamdan's appeal was not moot, but "only because precedent so dictates." In particular, Judge Ginsburg argued that none of the collateral consequences that ordinarily attach to criminal convictions are applicable in Hamdan's case. With regard to the immigration consequences of Hamdan's conviction, Judge Ginsburg concluded that Hamdan would be subject to mandatory exclusion should he ever try to enter the United States based solely on the circumstances surrounding his capture. And Judge Ginsburg further decried the "preposterously hypothetical prospect" that Hamdan might one day be subjected to another U.S. trial at which his prior conviction might affect his sentence. If Judge Ginsburg is correct that there are fewer (if any) collateral consequences justifying appeals from military

commission convictions by released defendants, what is the solution?

Although the Supreme Court has regularly recognized the right of military defendants to challenge their amenability to military jurisdiction through a pre-trial habeas petition, Hamdan's attempt to do so was denied in light of the MCA. *See Hamdan v. Gates*, 565 F. Supp. 2d 130 (D.D.C. 2008). Taken together, wouldn't these results create a Catch-22 for military commission defendants facing the prospect of relatively short sentences?

2. *Constitutional Law, or Constitutional Avoidance?* Although the majority opinion in *Hamdan II* turns on the conclusion that Hamdan may not be prosecuted for conduct that was only retroactively defined as a violation of the laws of war, this analysis was based on the language of the MCA, rather than the Constitution's Ex Post Facto Clause — as footnote 7 emphasizes. Is it a fair reading of the MCA to conclude, as Judge Kavanaugh does, that Congress did not *intend* to impose retroactive liability in the MCA, especially given that all of the detainees currently held at Guantanamo were captured *before* the MCA was enacted? Put another way, based on Judge Kavanaugh's analysis, who *could* be charged with "providing material support to terrorism" under the MCA? And if Congress *did* intend to apply the MCA's new offenses to pre-2006 conduct, why do you suppose it nevertheless included the anti-retroactivity language in §950p(d) on which the court relied? Ultimately, although *Hamdan II* does not hold that the MCA violated the Ex Post Facto Clause, *does* it establish the proposition that Congress may not subject an individual to trial by military commission for any offense that a commission could not try at the time of the underlying conduct? Does it at least establish that such a statute would raise serious constitutional questions?

3. *What Pre-2006 Offenses Are Triable?* The core holding of *Hamdan II* is that U.S. military commissions lack jurisdiction over pre-MCA conduct that was not recognized as a violation of the international laws of war at the time it was committed. As for the trickier question of whether particular conduct *was* so recognized, footnote 10 cites *Sosa v. Alvarez Machain* and Justice Stevens' plurality opinion in *Hamdan I* in holding that "liability on the basis of a violation of 'international law' or the 'law of nations' or the 'law of war' generally must be based on norms firmly grounded in international law." In the process, Judge Kavanaugh's opinion both (1) formally adopted the plurality's reasoning

in *Hamdan I* as to the scope of offenses that military commissions may try under 10 U.S.C. § 821; and (2) suggested that the same exceptionally high bar that applies to the recognition of human rights claims grounded in customary international law under the Alien Tort Statute, 28 U.S.C. §1350, should also apply to the government's ability to prosecute enemy combatants for violations of the laws of war. Is it plausible, though, to conclude that the Congress that enacted §821 intended to so tightly circumscribe the authority of military commissions? Put another way, would the offenses tried (under the same statutory authorization) in *Quirin* have met this burden? *Cf. Hamdan*, 548 U.S. at 690–691 (Thomas, J., dissenting).

4. *Footnote 6 and the Article III Problem.* Neither Chief Judge Sentelle nor Judge Ginsburg joined footnote 6 of Judge Kavanaugh's opinion, which would have held that Congress *may* subject to trial by military commissions *future* offenses not recognized as violations of the international laws of war, because "Congress's war powers under Article I are not defined or constrained by international law. The Declare War Clause and the other Article I war powers clauses do not refer to international law, unlike the Define and Punish Clause." Although this statement is clearly correct, *do* any of Congress's other Article I war powers confer the authority to define criminal offenses — especially offenses committed by individuals who are not U.S. service members? Even if so, does it necessarily follow, as Judge Kavanaugh appears to assume, that such offenses can be tried by military — as opposed to civilian — courts? Recall that the Supreme Court in *Quirin* distinguished *Ex parte Milligan*, 71 U.S. (4 Wall.) 2 (1866) (NSL p. 767, CTL p. 381), by holding that the Constitution's jury clauses do not apply to "offenses committed by enemy belligerents against the law of war." 317 U.S. at 41. Would that exception apply to a *prospective* military commission prosecution under the MCA for "providing material support to terrorism"?

5. *Military Commissions After Hamdan II.* Because the military commission acquitted Hamdan on the conspiracy charge, the D.C. Circuit held only that "providing material support to terrorism" was not a violation of the international laws of war at the time of Hamdan's conduct. But doesn't its analysis, coupled with Justice Stevens' conclusion for the plurality in *Hamdan I*, compel the same result for conspiracy charges based on pre-2006 conduct? *See* Steve Vladeck,

Conspiracy and Military Commissions After Hamdan II, Lawfare, Oct. 17, 2012, http://www.lawfareblog.com/2012/10/conspiracy-and-military-commissions-after-hamdan-ii/. Without the ability to charge current detainees with conspiracy or material support (i.e., crimes based on more attenuated involvement in specific hostilities against the United States), what cases can the U.S. government still pursue in military commissions?

6. *The En Banc Proceedings in Al-Bahlul.* On January 25, 2013, and at the government's urging, a three-judge panel of the D.C. Circuit answered the first question raised in Note 5 in the affirmative — holding that "conspiracy" may not be tried by military commissions under the MCA, at least where the relevant conduct pre-dates the MCA's enactment. *See Al Bahlul v. United States*, No. 11-1324, 2013 WL 297726 (D.C. Cir. Jan. 25, 2013) (per curiam). The government then filed a petition to rehear *that* decision (and not *Hamdan II*) en banc, presumably on the ground that the conspiracy charge in *Al Bahlul* presents a stronger case for the government than the material support charge in *Hamdan II*. On April 23, 2013, the D.C. Circuit granted that petition, and the case is scheduled to be argued en banc on September 30, 2013. For a suggestion that the D.C. Circuit may have granted rehearing in *Al Bahlul* not to overturn *Hamdan II*, but rather to strengthen it, see Wells Bennett & Benjamin Wittes, *Breaking News:D.C. Circuit Grants En Banc Rehearing in Al-Bahlul*, Lawfare, http://www.lawfareblog.com/2013/04/ breaking-news-d-c-circuit-grants-en-banc-rehearing-granted-in-al-bahlul/.

[NSL p. 1113, CTL p. 727. Insert at end of chapter.]

Eric Holder, Attorney General, Remarks at Northwestern University School of Law

Mar. 5, 2012,
available at
http://www.justice.gov/iso/opa/ag/speeches/2012/ag-speech-1203051.html

. . .

It's important to note that the reformed [military] commissions draw from the same fundamental protections of a fair trial that underlie our civilian courts. They provide a presumption of innocence and require proof of guilt beyond a reasonable doubt. They afford the accused the right to counsel — as well as the right to present evidence and cross-examine witnesses. They prohibit the use of statements obtained through torture or cruel, inhuman, or degrading treatment. And they secure the right to appeal to Article III judges — all the way to the United States Supreme Court. In addition, like our federal civilian courts, reformed commissions allow for the protection of sensitive sources and methods of intelligence gathering, and for the safety and security of participants.

A key difference is that, in military commissions, evidentiary rules reflect the realities of the battlefield and of conducting investigations in a war zone. For example, statements may be admissible even in the absence of Miranda warnings, because we cannot expect military personnel to administer warnings to an enemy captured in battle. But instead, a military judge must make other findings — for instance, that the statement is reliable and that it was made voluntarily.

I have faith in the framework and promise of our military commissions, which is why I've sent several cases to the reformed commissions for prosecution. There is, quite simply, no inherent contradiction between using military commissions in appropriate cases while still prosecuting other terrorists in civilian courts. Without question, there are differences between these systems that must be — and will continue to be — weighed carefully. Such decisions about how to prosecute suspected terrorists are core Executive Branch functions. In each case, prosecutors and counterterrorism professionals across the government conduct an intensive review of case-specific facts designed to determine which avenue of prosecution to pursue.

Several practical considerations affect the choice of forum.

First of all, the commissions only have jurisdiction to prosecute individuals who are a part of al Qaeda, have engaged in hostilities against the United States or its coalition partners, or who have purposefully and materially supported such hostilities. This means that there may be members of certain terrorist groups who fall outside the jurisdiction of military commissions because, for example, they lack ties to al Qaeda and their conduct does not otherwise make them subject to prosecution in this forum. Additionally, by statute, military commissions cannot be used to try U.S. citizens.

Second, our civilian courts cover a much broader set of offenses than the military commissions, which can only prosecute specified offenses, including violations of the laws of war and other offenses traditionally triable by military commission. This means federal prosecutors have a wider range of tools that can be used to incapacitate suspected terrorists. Those charges, and the sentences they carry upon successful conviction, can provide important incentives to reach plea agreements and convince defendants to cooperate with federal authorities.

Third, there is the issue of international cooperation. A number of countries have indicated that they will not cooperate with the United States in certain counterterrorism efforts — for instance, in providing evidence or extraditing suspects — if we intend to use that cooperation in pursuit of a military commission prosecution. Although the use of military commissions in the United States can be traced back to the early days of our nation, in their present form they are less familiar to the international community than our time-tested criminal justice system and Article III courts. However, it is my hope that, with time and experience, the reformed commissions will attain similar respect in the eyes of the world. . . .

And we will continue to reject the false idea that we must choose between federal courts and military commissions, instead of using them both. If we were to fail to use all necessary and available tools at our disposal, we would undoubtedly fail in our fundamental duty to protect the Nation and its people. That is simply not an outcome we can accept. . . .

[NSL p. 1240. Insert as new Note 4a.]

4a. *Public Access to the Bradley Manning Court Martial.* The Guantánamo military commissions have yet to resolve on the merits the First Amendment questions raised in Note 4, holding in the context of the 9/11 trial that such claims have not yet become ripe. *See, e.g., ACLU v. United States*, No. 13-003 (Ct. Mil. Comm'n Rev. Mar. 27, 2013) (per curiam). But the Court of Appeals for the Armed Forces (CAAF) — the highest court in the military justice system — was confronted with an analogous challenge arising out of the Bradley Manning court martial. A coalition of journalists, advocacy organizations, and media enterprises sought a writ of mandamus to challenge the trial judge's presumptive closure of various of the pre-trial proceedings in Manning's case. In a 3-2 decision, CAAF held that it lacked jurisdiction to provide such relief, reasoning that military (as opposed to civilian) courts have no power to entertain such applications for "civil" relief from third parties. *See Ctr. for Const'l Rights v. United States*, 72 M.J. 126 (C.A.A.F. 2013). For harsh criticism of this reasoning, see Steve Vladeck, *CAAF Rejects*

Jurisdiction Over Bradley Manning Court-Martial Public Access Claims, Lawfare, Apr. 17, 2013, *available at* http://www.lawfareblog.com/2013/04/caaf-rejects-jurisdiction-over-bradley-manning-court-martial-public-access-claims/. Shortcomings aside, at least one of the judges on the Court of Military Commission Review has endorsed a variation of this reasoning. *See ACLU*, slip op. at 2–5 (Silliman, J., concurring).

If the military commissions follow CAAF's lead and hold that they lack the power to entertain First Amendment challenges to closed proceedings, does that suggest that the right of public access identified by the Supreme Court in *Richmond Newspapers* and its progeny is one with no meaningful remedy in the military justice system? Could *civilian* courts entertain collateral pre-trial challenges to the closed nature of military proceedings? Would we want them to? *See, e.g., Ctr. for Const'l Rights*, 72 M.J. at 132 (Baker, C.J., dissenting) (describing the "untenable consequences" for military courts of such reliance upon collateral and interlocutory civilian judicial oversight); *cf. Ctr. for Const'l Rights v. Lind*, No. 13-1504, 2013 WL 3167910 (D. Md. June 19, 2013) (expressing reservations about enjoining ongoing court-martial proceedings).